THE TRUTH ABOUT LIES

THE
TRUTH
ABOUT
LIES

The Illusion *of* Honesty *and* The Evolution *of* Deceit

AJA RADEN

ST. MARTIN'S PRESS ☁ NEW YORK

First published in the United States by St. Martin's Press,
an imprint of St. Martin's Publishing Group

www.stmartins.com

Book design by Richard Oriolo

Library of Congress Cataloging-in-Publication Data

Names: Raden, Aja, author.
Title: The truth about lies : the illusion of honesty and the evolution of deceit /
    Aja Raden.
Description: First edition. | New York, NY : St. Martin's Press, [2021] | Includes
    bibliographical references and index.
Identifiers: LCCN 2020053690 | ISBN 9781250272027 (hardcover) | ISBN
    9781250272034 (ebook)
Subjects: LCSH: Deception. | Truthfulness and falsehood.
Classification: LCC BF637.D42 R34 2021 | DDC 177/.3—dc23
LC record available at https://lccn.loc.gov/2020053690

Our books may be purchased in bulk for promotional, educational, or business use.
Please contact your local bookseller or the Macmillan Corporate and Premium
Sales Department at 1-800-221-7945, extension 5442, or by email at
MacmillanSpecialMarkets@macmillan.com.

First Edition: 2021

10 9 8 7 6 5 4 3 2 1

This book is dedicated to everyone who's ever lied to me.

If nothing else, you made me smarter.

CONTENTS

CONTENTS

Everything has to be taken on trust; truth is only that what is taken to be true. It's the currency of living. There may be nothing behind it, but it doesn't make any difference so long as it is honoured.

—TOM STOPPARD

THE TRUTH ABOUT LIES

INTRODUCTION

The Currency of Living

You shall know the truth, and the truth shall make you mad.
—ALDOUS HUXLEY

Why do you believe what you believe?

You've been lied to. Probably a lot. Maybe you knew, maybe you didn't. Maybe you found out later. The thing is, when we realize we've been deceived, we're always stunned. We can't believe we were taken in: What was I thinking? How could I have believed that?

We always wonder why we believed the lie. But have you ever wondered why you believe the *truth*? People tell you the truth all the time, and you believe them; and if, at some later point, you're confronted with evidence that the story you believed *was indeed true*, you never wonder why you believed it in the first place.

But maybe you should have.

Facts are just that which continue to exist, whether or not you believe them. But there's nothing special about a fact. A fact doesn't sound different from a falsehood. The truth isn't written in italics. So why do we believe we can tell the difference?

The Truth About Lies is a book about famous swindles that endeavors to give a telescopic vision of society through the phenomena and mechanics of belief: why we lie, why we believe, and how, if at all, the acts differ.

In just the same way that there are only a handful of actual original stories in the collective human consciousness upon which all other stories are only variations, so too are there only so many unique, primal lies. From those few original lies, all the others are derived, endlessly iterated, and polished for new audiences. As the American economist John Kenneth Galbraith wrote in his book *The Age of Uncertainty,* "The man who is admired for the ingenuity of his larceny is almost always rediscovering some earlier form of fraud." Ultimately, as original as the lie may seem in the moment, there are only so many ways to deceive. *The Truth About Lies* looks at nine basic cons from several angles, among those: the swindlers who worked them, the lies they told, and the people who were taken in.

Each chapter tells the outrageous story of a classic con and illustrates the mechanism by which it works, using both contemporary and historical examples. From the story of a fake Martian invasion that started a very real riot, *twice,* to the modern madness of Twitter; from a Wild West diamond scam so vast it made fools (and in some cases criminals) of the well-heeled investors of 1872 (including Charles Tiffany) to the tale of that same bait-and-switch scam dressed up in a new investment opportunity called mortgage-backed securities, which nearly toppled the world banking system in 2008.

This book examines the Pyramid Schemes you've heard of, the ones you haven't, and the ones we've all bought into without even realizing.

More important, each chapter examines mechanisms of belief and the persistent—and maybe fundamental—role that too-good-to-be-true and faith-based deals have played in human history. Is the twisted tale of selling Snake Oil, which started the craze for so-called patent medicines and led to America's first Victorian opioid crisis and the subsequent crackdown by the newly formed FDA, really about gullibility, or does the strange science of placebos tell us more about the biology of belief than we realize?

Organized in three parts: Lies We Tell Each Other, Lies We Tell Ourselves, and Lies We All Agree to Believe, *The Truth About Lies* examines the relationship of truth to lie, belief to faith, and deception to propaganda using neurological, historical, sociological, and psychological insights and examples. It will propose that some of our most cherished institutions are essentially massive versions of those self-same, very old cons and also complicate the vision we have of both the habitual liar and the classic "sucker."

My first book, *Stoned,* was ostensibly a book about jewelry, but at its heart *Stoned* sought to answer a single question: Why do people value what they value? The more I thought about it, the more I began to see something else in those stories. I realized that nearly every story in *Stoned,* whether about a scandal surrounding a stolen necklace, an island bought with glass beads, or the invention of the diamond engagement ring, *had a lie right at its center.* That revelation, in combination with the conclusions I had come to in *Stoned*, led me directly to *The Truth About Lies* and to its core question: Why do people believe what they believe?

Ask yourself: What are you sure of? We can start simple; let's just talk about basic facts. How many facts are you *certain* you know? Quite a few of them, probably. You know your ABCs, you know state capitals, you know water molecules are composed of two hydrogen atoms bonded to one oxygen atom.

You know that the earth is round, right?

Are you sure? How did you come by this certainty? Surely you didn't do the calculations yourself. The odds are, if you tried to right now, you wouldn't be able to, because you don't even know exactly *which* geometric calculations were used, thousands of years ago, to determine that fact in the first place. And even if you did know what they were, your math skills probably aren't that strong. My point is not to convince you that the earth is flat—of course it's not. My point is to show you how many truths you accept without ever considering why you believe them to be true. I don't want you to question whether or not the earth is round; I just want you to realize that *you never really did*.

We blindly trust certain facts: things we're taught, things we can observe or reason. And once we "know" these things, we never really question them again. But often we also believe things to be fact simply because we're presented with them. Neurologists refer to this tendency as an honesty bias. It's how we know almost everything that we know: *someone else told us*. Or someone showed us, or we read it in a book. And though honesty bias may sound too stupid to be true,*

---

*Though, if I know any one thing for certain, it's that *nothing* is too stupid to be true.

in a strange, roundabout way, it's what makes us all—as a group—so formidably intelligent.

Without this tendency to trust, to assume, to simply *believe,* every human on earth would be born starting from scratch, unable to benefit from the knowledge of the collective. This bias toward simple belief in the truth of what we are told or shown has allowed humans to build higher, see farther and through shared collective intelligence, become the dominant species on Earth. And yet this vital ability, this necessity to stand on the shoulders of giants and accept secondhand information as truth, is also the very flaw that allows us to be deceived.

Duplicity and credulity are not opposites; they're just two sides of the same very old coin, and can't be spent separately. Could it be that at the ancient and tattered heart of humanity, what drives civilization is the capacity in each of us for both deception and belief—and that without this complex duality, there would also be no progress, no social cohesion, no trust, and no ability to collaborate?

Is it possible, perhaps, that you *must* believe certain lies in order to believe anything at all?

Perception, Persuasion, and the Evolution of Deceit

Natural selection is anything but random.

—RICHARD DAWKINS

One should always play fairly when one has the winning cards.

—OSCAR WILDE

WE TEND TO ASSUME THAT DELIBERATELY TELLING LIES IS some sort of pernicious aberration unique to liars—perhaps the result of a mental defect or, more likely, some sort of moral failing. It is not. We all lie, all the time—including you.

Before you dismiss this thought, consider: human deception and evasion are no different than the animal equivalent of camouflage, spots, and stripes. Charm is our very own version of frilly fins and peacock feathers. Whether it's a stick insect adapted to cheat by hiding among twigs or a pretty pink orchid mantis lying in wait to devour the next gullible hummingbird looking for a little nectar, the effort to deceive, from camouflage to creative bullshit, is an evolutionary arms race as old as organic life.

Humans are not the only species that lies—far from it, in fact; any living species that can communicate, verbally or nonverbally, has absolutely figured it out. Take, for example, the *Cryptostylis* orchid, adapted to both look and smell like the alluring backside of the aptly named orchid-dupe wasp—giving a whole new meaning to honey trap. Or the snake-mimic hawkmoth caterpillar, sporting a pattern resembling the face of a snake to mislead and frighten away any bird that might otherwise see a tasty meal.

Trickery is fundamental to interaction, and the instinct to sometimes subvert or misrepresent objective reality to suit our own needs is fundamental to communication.

In the evolution of deceit, language only came about quite recently, billions of years after more basic and more effective tools of the con. Yet there's some debate that humans may have developed language *specifically* to manipulate each other in new and cleverer ways. It's just the latest innovation in a billion-year-old chess game. As Robert Trivers, professor of anthropology and biological sciences at Rutgers University, put it: "our most prized possession—language—not only strengthens our ability to lie but greatly extends its range."[1]

Consider: when you lie with your scent, your pattern, or your petals you can only lie about *what* you are, and you can only lie about the here and now. Lie with words, and you can lie about anything, anyone, anywhere; you can rewrite facts past, present, and future.

Human speech allows deceptions to transcend space and time.

Learning to lie is one of the earliest developmental milestones children have to hit to be considered functional. Because once we know there *is* truth, the next stage of normal development is to attempt to hide, misrepresent, or swap out that truth. Lying is one of our fundamental building blocks. It's a big part of not just who but *what* we are. When it comes to humans, dishonesty is a feature, not a bug.

These first three chapters explore mechanisms of deceit—how we lie and how lying works—through the lens of three of the world's oldest and most basic cons: the Big Lie, the Shell Game, and the Bait and Switch.

The first, the Big Lie, exploits people's theory of mind through their intrinsic capacity for disbelief simply by employing a lie so big that to disbelieve it would threaten our collective sense of objective reality. If that's too bold—and big-lying is a con for the very bold—you can also manipulate another's *physical* perception; as the Shell Game exploits hardwired flaws in our perceptual cognition. Last, because it's natural to believe our own eyes (even as the Shell Game teaches us we should not), a Bait and Switch allows real evidence to misrepresent fact, leaving the mark to believe whatever you want them to believe.

Deception is an evolutionary tool no different from any other. Whether you're the liar or the dupe, you are acting on instincts, cognitive processes, and abilities billions of years in the making. As we examine these three most basic cons, we will explore not only the nuts and bolts of deception, or how a lie actually works, but also *why* it works, from its evolutionary function and form to what it reveals about our own. Part I, Lies We Tell Each Other, examines the mechanics of lying, the evolution of deceit, and asks the question *How do you tell a lie?*

Now relax; you were quite literally *born* to do this.

THE OLDEST TRICK
IN THE BOOK

Credulity, Duplicity, and
How to Tell a Really Big Lie

The impossible often has a kind of integrity
which the merely improbable lacks.
—DOUGLAS ADAMS

The great mass of people will more easily fall
victims to a big lie than to a small one.
—ADOLF HITLER[1]

THE BIG LIE

As cons go, this one's got training wheels. The Big Lie is accomplished by making an outrageously unbelievable claim with total confidence. It is, very simply, the telling of a great big whopper. Strangely enough, people actually are more likely to believe you if you lie about owning an island than if you lie about owning a boat. And don't worry about the possibility that your mark isn't completely brain-dead—you *want* some healthy skepticism. The Big Lie works in tandem with our belief in truth, rather than in opposition to it: its success is reliant on people's understanding of, and faith in, shared objective reality.

Starting Small

The Big Lie is actually the simplest kind of swindle. All you have to do is tell—and preferably sell—a really outrageously Big Lie. Think: "I own land on Mars and I'm selling time-shares." You don't need to actually have the thing or even evidence that you do; the deception works entirely based on the fact that no reasonable person can believe that another seemingly normal, reasonable person would brazenly lie about something so enormous. As suspicious as the story itself may be, it seems more unbelievable that someone would make a story like that up and expect other people to believe it. But more often than not, *they do believe it.*

The Big Lie's power lies in its audacity.

Humans require a shared idea of reality to function—for instance, if you drop a ball, it will fall down, not up. Time moves forward. Things are mostly what they appear to be (wet, solid, broken, etc.). Liars are bad; crazy people seem crazy. We all believe these things together, and our faith in a universal objective reality is necessary, even if it's not always accurate. In the final analysis it does us far more good than harm, but the fact remains: belief in a shared objective reality can be exploited *just by flagrantly lying.*

We'll talk more in this chapter about what creates this shared template and expectation that we call "reality," how we come by it, and why we need it to function, let alone to believe or disbelieve anything at all. But for now the most important thing to remember is that the tighter we adhere to the very normal and very necessary idea of a shared objective reality, *the more susceptible we actually are to its subversion.*

You Wanna Hear a Really Big Lie?

Gregor MacGregor was the charming, handsome heir to an ancient noble family from Glengyle, Scotland. But like many ancient noble families, the MacGregor family had seen better days. By the time he was born, the MacGregors were making their livings as local tradesmen. And so, like so many other broke aristocrats, MacGregor joined the military, and off he went to seek fortune and glory.

Mostly fortune.

Alas, MacGregor found that there was not enough of either to be had in the Royal Navy, so in 1811 he ditched it and sailed to South America to fight under the command of the legendary Simón Bolívar, El Libertador, in the Venezuelan war of independence against Spain. Bolívar granted MacGregor a commission, ostensibly on the strength of his record in the Royal Navy, or what he *claimed* was his record in the Royal Navy. It was harder to fact check people's resumes in 1811.

MacGregor, though neither a good soldier nor a good leader (he was said to occasionally cut and run, abandoning his men when the odds looked bad), was charming, daring, and flamboyant. He made a name for himself and made his way up through the ranks quite rapidly. So far up the ranks, in fact, that he married Bolívar's daughter. But having no discernible ideology, nor personal loyalty, MacGregor abandoned La Revolucion and moved on to fight in various other skirmishes throughout the region. And by 1820 he'd discovered actual pay-for-play killing when he took a job as a mercenary on an expedition against a Spanish settlement called Portobello, on the Mosquito Coast of Panama.

It was there he claimed to have encountered the pristine paradise of Poyais, an undiscovered country, found and founded by

MacGregor himself, on the Caribbean coast near what is now Nicaragua and Honduras. While Mosquito Coast sounds horribly buggy, it was actually named after the Miskito Amerindians, who dominated the larger region—not the insects. *Mosquito* derives from the Spanish *mosca,* or fly. And so in Spanish *mosquito* means "tiny fly." The fact that the Miskito kingdom was also full of mosquitos is just one of those creepy coincidences that make you question whether or not retro-causality is really that far-fetched.

Seeing the potential in this marvelous, idyllic *new* New World, MacGregor persuaded the local potentate (after getting him blind drunk) to sign over to him 12,500 square miles of territory along what is now Honduras's Black River and to formally acknowledge him as Gregor I, Cazique (prince) of Poyais.[2] Or possibly he named himself Gregor I, Cazique of Poyais. The latter seems slightly more likely, but it's impossible to say, as one man was blackout drunk and the other was a really big liar. Either way, in October 1822, after over a decade of fighting and traveling through the jungles of South America, Gregor MacGregor returned to England from this paradise found. But he didn't come home as mere soldier or even a decorated war hero; MacGregor returned to London as Gregor I, prince of the Caribbean nation of Poyais.[3]

Paradise Found

Upon his return to London in October 1822, MacGregor immediately began a massive media blitz to educate the public about Poyais. He published articles about Poyais in respected journals, describing the land's unspoiled beauty and excessive natural resources. The prose was accompanied by detailed illustrations, which he claimed he'd brought back from the country itself. These pictures showed a land slightly larger than Wales, full of clean, fresh water and fertile soil for cultivation. There were forests full of trees and game and other exotic flora and fauna. The riverbeds were lined with big chunks of gold, and numerous other wonders, including precious gems, all there for the taking.[4]

MacGregor even brought a real-live person back from Poyais, whom he declared an ambassador, as well as a copy of the Poyaisian Constitution and the very land grant and proclamation that made him Cazique of Poyais. He claimed the natives were friendly, that the cities were brimming with culture, and that the land was ripe for development and a Christian colonial ruler—a proposition that was particularly appealing in his native Scotland, as the country had no colonies of its own.

Should anyone require a second source, he pointed them to an entire book published on Poyais, written by one Captain Thomas Strangeways, titled *Sketch of the Mosquito Shore, including the Territory of Poyais.** The captain's account not only confirmed but expanded on MacGregor's description and fantastical claims that Poyais was a land of plenty, brimming with untapped natural resources. Most promising, Strangeways's book described a land of endless summer and triannual harvests, with a tropical climate so warm and inviting that fruit was falling off the trees year-round—and yet remarkably not so hot or wet as to host the sort of biting insects and tropical diseases Europeans had learned to fear.

In addition to the almost unbelievable potential for agriculture,

---

*MacGregor not only published *Sketch of the Mosquito Shore, including the Territory of Poyais,* he also wrote it. Captain Strangeways only ever existed as the most obvious nom de plume ever smirkingly adopted.

prospecting, or just lying on the beach eating tropical fruit, there were urban opportunities as well, for Poyais already had a capital, called Saint Joseph—a small but fully Western city with roads, houses, public buildings, a bank, a civil service, and even an opera house.[5] So if neither farming nor mining (not to mention loitering) was really your thing, there were plenty of other types of work and opportunities for trade that an enterprising colonist could pursue in Poyais. Particularly considering Saint Joseph boasted a deep-water port, perfect for mercantile vessels to come and go, allowing for the development of all sorts of transatlantic commerce.

Fortunes were waiting to be made between the climate, the natural resources, and the abundant available labor in the form of the "Poyers." The Poyers were unreasonably friendly, mythically hardworking natives.[6] They were plentiful enough to build an entire European city, staff the civil service, operate a small military, and do anything else you might need; but at the same time, they were not so plentiful that they took up any space, owned any land, or otherwise got in anyone's way. They were basically Schrödinger's natives. And they were so excited about the idea of white colonists coming to occupy and employ them that they'd supposedly written up a proclamation welcoming them.

Honesty, Authority, and Other Debatable Claims

Does this sound too good to be true? Well, yes, clearly. The whole idea of Poyais being conveniently perfect in every regard and that anyone believed that for a second, sounds stupid as hell—now. But the default setting in humans is to *accept the reality with which they have been presented.*

So much so that a little kink in our thinking called honesty bias constitutes one of the twelve basic cognitive biases that circumscribes our perception of reality. Cognitive biases are systematic errors in cognition that occur in processing and deciphering information we glean from the world around us. They're not mistakes or logical fallacies; they're hardwired limitations in our thought process. Honesty bias is pretty much exactly what it sounds like: a heuristic (a sort of mental shortcut our brains take) in which we accept as true anything we're presented with, in the absence of obvious contradiction. For example, if you ask someone the time and they look at their watch and tell you it's three P.M., you will believe them. You don't reflexively question whether they're lying to you or whether their watch is wrong. Unless, of course, it's too dark out to be three o'clock or you have reason to suspect that the person wants you to be late.

Though cognitive biases tend to skew our judgment badly in some situations, they exist for a reason. Social psychologists believe that cognitive biases aren't there to screw us up but, rather, to help us process information more efficiently. Honesty bias may leave you open to being deceived, but by the numbers, the vast majority of information you're presented with *is true*. Not having to reason that out every millisecond, about every bit of data you encounter, is a valuable neurological ability, a shortcut that allows us to function and learn. Moreover, by compelling us to accept whatever people present us with as true, honesty bias is a huge part of what creates our shared template for reality, which informs our expectations and judgments.

Consider: If I told you that there was a commercial rocket launch this year, taking a shuttle full of paying customers to the moon, would you believe me? You probably would; people believe in the basic reality that they're presented with, and this is ours. Something almost that absurd really does happen in aerospace every year. Just a few years ago a guy launched a red convertible blasting a Bowie album into the void, forever, for no obvious reason at all. Your grandparents wouldn't have believed the story about a commercial passenger shuttle to the moon seventy years ago. Your parents wouldn't have believed it forty years ago. But you and I would. Because most of us have lived our whole lives post–moon landing, post–space stations, post–SpaceX. The space age and its eventual commercialization of space travel is the reality with which we have been presented our whole lives.

So with that in mind: Does Poyais still sound too good to be true?

Yeah, it still does. *But in 1822, so did the rest of the New World.* This was the era of empire building via seized foreign territories, country-sized land claims based on very little, and unimaginable stolen riches. India was real, with its gleaming golden palaces and massive gemstones. The Near East was real, with its vast oceans of sand and ancient stone cities. Australia was real, with its bizarre, exotic flora and fauna. *Why not Poyais?*

A story like the one about the riches and idyllic nature of Poyais, and MacGregor's claim to it, was not completely unbelievable in the 1820s, essentially the heyday of British colonialism. This story, to one degree or another, reflected the reality of the eighteenth and early nineteenth centuries. It was hardly unprecedented to declare a strange, faraway place full of money up for grabs just because someone from Europe went there and tripped over it.

It's a claim that almost seems reasonable in that context.

So when Gregor MacGregor returned to London referring to himself as Highness Gregor I, Cazique of Poyais, and told the world that he was the newly minted prince of a South American paradise they'd never seen or heard of, they mostly just believed him—and they badly wanted to hear about this new country. It didn't hurt that the British had only just lost their North American colonies about forty years earlier and were hungry for more American holdings of their own. Both the royalty and the aristocrats of London accepted all he had to say about Poyais remarkably quickly and easily.[7] And once London's most privileged class had signaled that *they* believed MacGregor's claims, the rest of English society quickly joined them, followed in turn by the commoners of England and Scotland, each stratum of society's trust enhanced by the faith of the one above.

There are a lot of funny quirks in our minds that explain, both neurologically and psychologically, why this sort of cascading failure of basic reason would occur. First and foremost, there's that pesky honesty bias. But another cognitive bias, called authority bias, describes the way in which we tend to trust and are predisposed to believe the people who we see as having *any* kind of authority (including mere social stature) greater than our own. We're wired to believe and trust our "betters," essentially. Authority bias is also a primary factor in why we act in accordance with or follow orders from perceived authority figures—even when we feel like those authority figures might be in the wrong.

The first experiment in authority bias was the Milgram obedience experiment, conducted by Yale University psychology professor Stanley Milgram in 1961.[8] Today it is considered the gold standard in unethical psychological experimentation. In the experiment, which was falsely described to the volunteers as an experiment in "learning and memory," pairs of participants would give and receive tests. In each pair one participant, the "subject," quizzed a second participant, the "learner." Every time the learner got an answer wrong, the subject was ordered to administer increasingly painful and potentially dangerous electric shocks to the learner. They started with 15 volts ("slight shock") and progressed all the way to 450 volts ("danger: severe shock").

The point of the Milgram obedience experiment was not to electrocute volunteers to death; it was to determine if, and for how long, the subjects could be compelled to do as they were bid without any potential reward or risk of punishment for themselves.[9] Would they do it even though they felt that what they were doing was wrong—and kind of sadistic? Would they continue to administer the electric shocks even when the other supposed volunteer wanted them to stop, even when the other person *begged* them to stop, or got scared and decided to alert them to their heart condition, or, after pleading and screaming in pain, fell suddenly, alarmingly silent? Would they continue *just* because the person in charge of the experiment told them to?

Depressingly, the answer is yes.

Most of the participants would indeed, simply because they felt compelled by the perceived authority of the person in charge of the experiment. In fact, 65 percent of them would continue all the way to the end of the experiment, even after their partner had stopped begging for reprieve and had fallen silent. Such is the power of authority bias in human consciousness. It wasn't until after the experiment was over that subjects were told that their partners were not only fine but acting, the electric shocks were never even real.[10]

Stranger still, we defer to the opinions and directives of perceived authority figures even when their authority has *nothing to do with the matter at hand*. For instance, you're more likely to believe a doctor who tells you you're sick than you are a friend who tells you the same. This makes sense: we default to generally trusting and believing people we deem to be authority figures. But what's really interesting is that you'd also be more likely to believe your doctor than your friend if they were to tell you how to program the computer in your car; even if you knew that they knew nothing about it. The same holds true for politicians, professionals, "experts" of any kind—even celebrities. We unconsciously assume that they're better informed than we are, and we are more inclined to take what they say on faith. It's why celebrity product endorsements are so valuable to companies and so lucrative for the celebrities: you're hardwired to trust that a famous actress really does know which fruit juice will prevent aging or that your favorite musician really does have the inside track on which charities are legitimate. We don't believe them because we have any reason to; we believe them because our brain has taken a shortcut.

Like all heuristics, authority bias benefits us—individually and as a cooperative group—we don't need to know everything about our math teacher to trust them when they show us how long division works. But at the same time, it's an open loophole in our thought process that can backfire, as it did here, or be deliberately taken advantage of by bad actors. The fact that the aristocratic classes of England and Scotland fell for His Highness Gregor I's, Cazique of Poyais, Big Lie, and then, like dominoes, everyone else down the social and economic ladder fell for it, too, isn't confusing or absurd; it's predictable, and it's evidence that their brains were all functioning perfectly normally.

Crime Does Pay, Mostly in Cash

Poyais was a land rich in literally everything, except for white Christian colonial overlords—and some start-up cash. So, understandably, MacGregor was looking for investment capital to develop the land and settlers to move there. He started by touring England with a very dramatic and colorful native entourage, all of them immaculately civilized but still charmingly exotic. He spoke about Poyais publicly and privately; he gave interviews and showed exhibits that included all of the samples, pictures, and written materials he'd brought back with him. Finally, when the public could wait no longer, he stopped selling his principality figuratively and began selling it literally. And at that point, all those normally functioning brains went bonkers for Poyais.

In short order, London's lord mayor held a banquet in MacGregor's honor. One patron even set MacGregor and his wife up in a posh country estate. He was already the toast of London society by the time King George IV knighted him, which the king mostly only did to ensure that MacGregor would be motivated to keep Poyais (a very valuable territory) a loyal British colony.

Once he had been made *Sir* Gregor MacGregor by the king, a very legitimate authority figure in his own right, he had no trouble at all securing a loan of £200,000 from the prestigious bank of Sir John Perring & Co. and floating shares in the Poyais venture on the market.[11] That's a big part of how most reasonably Big Lies work—*in parts*: every smaller, previously believed lie lays the groundwork for the next lie to be seen as more credible.

And soon *Sir* Gregor had opened offices for the Poyaisian legation to Britain in London. And then he opened land offices in Edinburgh, Stirling, and Glasgow from which to sell Poyaisian land to eager colonists. He sold estates to both the British and Scottish aristocracy. He also sold the same sort of estates *and* the titles of nobility to accompany them to wealthy commoners looking to move up the social ladder in the New World. He sold vast plantations to the would-be upper class of Poyais and even more modest, hundred-acre farms to average colonists.[12] MacGregor, empowered as the sole potentate of Poyais, also sold social and professional positions in his new world; the wealthier but not quite aristocratic investor could buy anything from a posting as an important government official to a commission in the Poyaisian military. For the enterprising merchant or business investor, he sold monopolies on industries and on various trade goods.

Last but not least, MacGregor *sold money*; that is, he facilitated the exchange of vast amounts of Poyais's official currency* for equal amounts British currency. After all, what good would their British pounds be in the New World, particularly in a country like Poyais that had not only banks and bankers but its own printed, formally recognized legal tender, thanks to MacGregor? If they intended to make a life there, they would need money, and they'd do well to rid themselves of British paper notes that would become worthless as soon as they got there. It was just this thinking that led hundreds of settlers to exchange every penny they had for Poyaisian currency to use in their new home.

MacGregor succeeded in getting seven massive ships' worth of colonists to leave their homes and embark on a journey to the New World, having spent or exchanged everything they had to start a new life in the now famous paradise. In September 1822 and January 1823 the first two ships, the *Honduras Packet* and the *Kennersley Castle*, embarked for Poyais carrying hundreds of passengers as still more ships back in England were filling with people and preparing to set sail, each head on the block worth money.

Over the year and a half leading up to 1823, MacGregor raised far in excess of £200,000 in cash and brought the bond market value of Poyais up to £1.3 million, or about £3.6 billion (or $4.6 billion)

---

*He printed the currency himself in Scotland, as Poyais *was* his country; he claimed to have swindled it from its drunken ruler fair and square.

in today's currency. He personally made hundreds of thousands of pounds, all before the first ship had even dropped anchor.

When the *Honduras Packet* finally did reach land, the colonists had no idea where they were, except that it was definitely not Poyais.

They assumed they had landed in the wrong location, as they found no ready-made cities, no valuable resources, no farmable land, not even edible food. And there were no friendly natives to meet them. There were no unfriendly natives. In fact, there were no signs of *any* other humans at all, because even the climate was a lie; that section of coast was a hot, swampy, mosquito-infested jungle *so uninhabitable* that it remains largely undeveloped to this day.

They did their best to build shelters out of sticks and mud and to find fresh water, but a majority of the stranded settlers died from starvation, exposure, and tropical diseases like yellow fever and malaria on the isolated, dangerous, and basically deserted Mosquito Coast. It wasn't until a small group of survivors—all that was left—was rescued by a passing British ship from a nearby colony in Belize and taken back to London that the disaster was exposed. Gregor MacGregor had not merely oversold Poyais's virtues or exaggerated his ownership or authority in the matter, *he'd actually made up the entire country.*

"Poyais" had never existed at all.

Theory of Mind and Big Lying

It's one thing to make up a girlfriend who lives in Canada. But who makes up *Canada*? You're probably thinking: a crazy person. And that's true—to some degree. At least, *that's what we believe.* So if a person is ostensibly sane, and talks up the existence of a beautiful country no one else has ever visited or heard of, *people are more likely to believe him than not.*

That's a shocking and even kind of scary thought. It sheds light on how easily our own beliefs and preconceived notions about the truth—for example, the notion that only a crazy person would lie about the existence of something as enormous (and demonstrably either true or false) as a whole country—can *themselves* be exploited to deceive.

The Big Lie relies on your disbelief in the possibility that so many of your fundamental assumptions about objective reality could be wrong—far more than it requires your belief in the lie itself. That's why a Big Lie doesn't need to be convincing. In fact, the bigger and more absurd it is—the less believable—the more it reinforces your basic instinct that no one would lie about something so obviously preposterous. But where do we get these beliefs about objective reality, and how do we know that everyone's are the same?

The developing field of social neuroscience emerged about thirty-five years ago with what's known as theory of mind. The term itself was first used by U.S. psychologist David Premack in a now famous experiment carried out on a chimpanzee named Sarah, to try to determine if she possessed self-awareness. The experiment was called the mirror test; Premack's team altered Sarah's appearance by placing a red dot on her forehead. Then they put her in front of a mirror. Instead of assuming she was seeing another chimp with a different appearance and swatting at the imagined intruder, Sarah approached the mirror and instead peered closely at her reflection in the mirror. She reached out her hand to her *own forehead,* not the mirror, and began touching her forehead, attempting to find and wipe away the red dot that didn't belong there. In doing so, she demonstrated that she recognized her own reflection (that she *had* a reflection), understood herself to be an individual, and noticed something out of place.

Suffice it to say, she passed the *Do you know you exist?* test with flying colors.

Since then, however, the term theory of mind has expanded to describe the ability of an individual to take that self-awareness (hey, that's me in the mirror) and sense of objective reality (there's some schmutz on my forehead) and to understand, first, that he or she not only exists as an individual, like Sarah, but also has individual perceptions, thoughts, feelings, and beliefs that cause or can predict reactions to information and, second, that *other people* also have individual perceptions, thoughts, feelings, and beliefs, which similarly create and can predict *their* reactions to information.

Shorthand: theory of mind means the ability to think about what *someone else* might be thinking.

Theory of mind describes the facility to ascribe states of mind or intentions to both oneself and to everyone else. Or as A. M. Leslie defines it in the *International Encyclopedia of the Social and Behavioral Sciences,* "Theory of Mind concerns our ability, not simply to have beliefs as such, but to have beliefs about mental states, including the recursive ability to have beliefs about beliefs."[13] This cognizance that others perceive, think, feel, *and even lie* just as we do lends itself to a sense of objective reality assumed by each individual but tacitly agreed upon by all.

For example, you're in a park and you see a stone wall. Naturally, you assume anyone else in the vicinity can also see the wall. And you make many other assumptions; for instance, that *it is a wall,* that the wall is inanimate, that it's basically solid—you couldn't walk through it—and that it's largely immobile. None of this is remarkable. What *is* remarkable is that you also assume—*you absolutely believe*—that everyone else who sees the wall automatically assumes the same "facts," and accepts these same facts as objectively true.

This active engagement of theory of mind—my thinking about what you see or believe or know about the same wall—is referred to as "mentalizing," a capacity that includes "the critical ability to make inferences about the intentions of other people and their beliefs and to infer whether the emotions or other states signaled by social cues are or are not an accurate reflection of the actual emotional state of the individual"—in other words, to consider whether others might be lying to us.[14]

Theory of mind allows us to think about what another person might think, know, assume, or feel. Additionally, our ability to understand that others think, feel, and have intentions in the same way we ourselves do allows us to attribute a variety of mental and emotional states to other people, and then to use those assumptions to interpret, explain, or predict their responses. Our theory of mind and ability to mentalize also allows us to elicit specific responses from those people and influence their reasoning: to manipulate, *to lie*.

Let's go back to that wall, an instance of our shared objective reality. I know that rocks are hard and solid—and don't generally carry cash. Because I possess a functioning theory of mind, I know that *you know that too*. So, if I stole your wallet and wanted to hide it where I know you wouldn't think to look, inside a false stone in that wall would be a pretty good choice. You might check my pockets, my car, even my bank account—but we both "know" that rocks are solid, so inside of a rock isn't even going to occur to you. You see, it turns out all that's really required to lie is the understanding that other people are thinking in more or less the same way that you are. Once you know that, it's very easy to present others with information that, true or untrue, will elicit the desired response.

Theory of mind, the very thing that allows us to understand that there *is* objective fact—and that others might attempt to subvert it—is *also the very thing that allows us the ability to lie.*

That other people are thinking more or less the same way you are is also why little lies can be so hard to pull off. Remember when I said that it's easier to convince someone that you own an island than a boat? Because we're all sharing a theory of mind, we all *know* that other people lie. It's why we're most on guard when we think someone is trying to sell us something: it pays to be careful. You might think the bigger the potential swindle, the more cautious we'd be, but paradoxically the reverse is true. The Big Lie works not by preying on people's gullibility, but by preying on their *anticipation* of a swindle. Any seemingly sane, normal person with the confidence to assert such a patently unbelievable claim must, we assume, have grounds to back it up. Otherwise, our theory of mind assures us, they would never expect us to believe it. The Big Lie completely subverts our shared sense of objective reality by telling a falsehood so outrageous that it must be true—a falsehood like an entire country, and like the fictitious economy that drove its bond price to the equivalent of $4.6 billion, a falsehood that sent hundreds of settlers in boats out on the open ocean to die.

Natural Born Liars

Once we develop a theory of mind, we begin to recognize and believe in this shared objective reality. Once we believe in it, we immediately look for ways to subvert it—that is, *to deceive.* And I do mean immediately; lying is not only a normal human behavior and a profound adaptive advantage, it's such a fundamental one that we develop and hone it from infancy alongside other basics like walking, talking, and fine-motor skills.

Infants obviously have a far more intense honesty bias than adults. They accept basically everything they're presented with as true—even when they *do* have reason to doubt it. It's how they learn so much more quickly than we do, because cognitive biases exist to help us process almost infinite information more quickly and efficiently, even if it leads to a certain amount of errors. (It's also why their little minds are absolutely *blown* by peek-a-boo.) But in addition to that honesty bias, infants and toddlers also have a fully functioning theory of mind, ready to deceive people.

How do we know that—apart from the fact that they're manipulative little suckers? Actually, that *is* how we know. There's a whole host of important social cognitive skills, including establishing joint attention, intentional communication of any kind, and the ability to imitate specific movements and gestures (like patty-cake or waving back at someone) and facial expressions—all of which belie a functioning theory of mind. And the vast majority of infants have mastered these, at least, by nine months. By eighteen months, most toddlers begin to engage in not just manipulative but deliberately subversive or deceptive behavior: creating distractions, hiding food they don't want to eat, and even imitating their own emotions to elicit a desired, previously observed response (also known as fake crying).

I'm making them sound like tiny sociopaths, but in fact infants are simply accumulating reference points and practicing interactions with people—honing their ability to mentalize—at an incredibly rapid clip. And all the things they're doing are very normal and important—so important, in fact, that if a child hasn't figured out how to blatantly, verbally lie by three or four years old, it's considered a concerning sign of developmental delay.

Based on all these things, researchers have suggested that the ability to understand and predict the behavior of another person (to mentalize) actually has "an innate, biological, and modular basis."[15] In other words: you were born to lie.

And you're not the only one.

Bridge for Sale

In 1925, another purveyor of Big Lies, Count Victor Lustig (probably not his real name, *definitely* not his real title), sold the Eiffel Tower to a scrap-metal dealer. And then he sold it again, a week later, to a different buyer. And then Lustig hightailed it out of Paris, because he did not, in fact, own the Eiffel Tower.[16]

When he got to America, Lustig was in plentiful, if not necessarily good, company: a con man by the name of William McCloundy had sold the Brooklyn Bridge in 1901 and then spent two and a half years in Sing Sing prison for grand larceny—and he'd sold it only once. Decades before him, only a few years after its construction was completed in 1883, another big liar, named Reed C. Waddell, ran the same con, successfully selling the Brooklyn Bridge to unwitting marks for almost twenty years. After Waddell, a pair of brothers named Fred and Charles Gondorf had a go at it and improved on the con, timing beat cops' routes so that they could put out a sign that read BRIDGE FOR SALE and then quickly, if temporarily, take it away again, just as the cops walked back past the bridge. The sign didn't have a price listed, because that changed with each mark. According to an infamous fellow con man, Joseph "Yellow Kid" Weil, "once they sold half the bridge for $250 because the mark didn't have enough cash."[17] The Gondorfs sold the Brooklyn Bridge many times, to many different would-be buyers, for amounts ranging from two or three hundred dollars to one thousand dollars; price dependent upon what they discerned each mark could (and would) pay.

But the year Lustig arrived from Paris, a man named George C. Parker had taken over selling the Brooklyn Bridge. And sell he did. The only thing more unbelievable than how many people *sold* the Brooklyn Bridge is how many people *bought* the Brooklyn Bridge, convinced, among other things, that they'd be able to set up a toll-booth. For about a decade police were constantly taking down obstructions and informing recent buyers that they did not own the throughway.[18] Of all the liars who sold the bridge, Parker might have been the biggest. In fact, Parker, also the infamous seller—if not owner—of the Statue of Liberty, the Metropolitan Museum of Art, and Grant's Tomb, sold the Brooklyn Bridge *so many times* that we have his racket to credit with the famous expression: *"If you believe that, I got a bridge to sell you."*

So what sort of dark arts did men like Waddell, the Gondorfs, Lustig, and Parker use to convince people that they owned, and had the right to sell, these famous monuments? None whatsoever. They just told people that they did—a claim so bold and so outrageous that it must be true—and those people, being basically sane and normal, believed them.

Because who makes up an island? So to speak.

You see, despite the somewhat flexible nature of distinctions between what is true and what is false among humans, and constant disagreement about "The Truth," we all agree that facts are facts.

And that certainty that there are absolutes, and we all perceive and understand and tacitly agree upon them the same way, leaves the door unlocked for deception, because *general belief in truth is absolutely required for lies to work.*

Consider Jefferson Randolph Smith, a fellow hustler working on the opposite side of the country, who set up the first telegraph office out of Skagway, Alaska, in 1898. For the steep price of five dollars, settlers, frontiersmen, and prospectors could send a telegraph message to anyone in the United States. Unsurprisingly, there were lines of customers around the building every day.[19] It was great business and Smith had the market cornered, in no small part because the first telegraph wires didn't actually arrive in Alaska until *two years later.* Smith did *have* telegraph wire, but it only ran from the telegraph desk into the walls of the office, no farther. People lined up and paid five dollars apiece for over a year to send important messages as far away as the wall of Smith's office.[20]

"There are no telegraph wires in Alaska" doesn't seem like a hard piece of information to verify—and, of course, not a single message came in response to the outgoing telegrams, other than those that were requested and prepaid for. So why were people so ready to believe that Smith could send out telegrams, just because he said so?

It's the same odd reason you believe the people you're introduced to when they tell you their name. It's that peculiar neurological quirk: *honesty bias.* We tend, in the absence of evidence, to believe that what we are presented with is true, be it someone's name, a random fact, a complex explanation, even something as obvious as the presence of a physical object before us.

When you walk into a room and see a lamp on a table, naturally you believe there is a lamp on the table. It wouldn't even occur to you that it might be a cleverly disguised bomb or a very large and convincing lamp-shaped piece of candy. It is because of your honesty bias that you don't automatically wonder if that lamp is a hallucination only you can see, any more than you suspect that everyone you meet might be lying about their name. If we didn't lean toward this heuristic, this neurological shortcut, we'd all go insane. While it may be considered one of the twelve basic cognitive biases (and possibly the dumbest one), in the long run, we benefit more from honesty bias—and the shared reality it creates—than we risk in being overly trusting.

Our honesty bias is exploitable but indispensable.

It's also the single adaptation that has allowed humans to develop speech, literacy, history, science, and civilization itself. Margaret Atwood said of storytelling that it's a "very old human skill that gives us an evolutionary advantage. If you can tell young people how you kill an emu, acted out in song or dance, or that Uncle George was eaten by a croc there, don't go there to swim, then those young people don't have to find out by trial and error."[21] And indeed, almost everything you know someone else told you. You don't have to discover, confirm, or even understand every fact or idea you learn because you are, by design, biased to just accept them as true and keep climbing. We don't need to reinvent the wheel with every new encounter; we simply accept that it is, because someone else said so.

That's the very advantage conferred by honesty bias: *collective intelligence.*

Long before there was Google or public libraries or even the written word, we still possessed this peculiar evolutionary advantage: knowledge, wisdom, insight, skill. It doesn't exist in your head or mine but in the collected and accumulated minds of every human, living and dead, who ever was. And to rapidly acquire another's lifetime of experience or problem solving for ourselves, all we need do is ask. And then possess the capacity to believe the answer. This ability, and tendency, to blindly believe what we are presented with to be fact facilitates deception but also knowledge. In a sense, *the inseparable abilities to lie and believe* have played a more important role than opposable thumbs in humans becoming the dominant species on earth.

Selective Reality

Smith's victims believed there were working telegraph wires in Alaska because he said so, and because they had no compelling reason to question it, just as MacGregor's victims believed him. And then they fell victim a second time, not to a con man but to another easily exploitable loophole in our thinking called confirmation bias.

Confirmation bias is a form of unconscious selective perception in which, once you decide something is true, you begin to see evidence to support your belief everywhere you look (like wires running to the wall, other customers waiting in line). You also don't notice or don't remember evidence contrary to your belief (no replies, no wires outside the office walls). Honesty bias with a chaser of confirmation bias creates the conditions in which we can be deceived, over and over, through our own willing participation, in large part because of our need to protect against something called cognitive dissonance. Cognitive dissonance is a state of untenable mental stress. It occurs when you try to hold two conflicting truths (or at least beliefs) in your mind simultaneously. You can't do it. Really. You can't. I mean, some people can, but they're seriously atypical and you probably don't want to know them.

So, what happens when you have to process two conflicting beliefs?

One gets dumped in the idea shredder. And it actually doesn't make a bit of difference which one is more factually accurate: you defend and protect whichever idea you *need to be true* in order not to have been wrong at some point. The psychological and neurological stress experienced during moments of cognitive dissonance are so great, you'll believe anything to protect your preexisting mental paradigm. It's why people refuse to hear proof of things like climate change or see clips of transgressions that they insist didn't happen—in the event that they've already decided they don't believe it.

What Lustig did with the Eiffel Tower, Parker did with the Brooklyn Bridge, and Smith did with his telegraph to nowhere were obviously far less harmful than enticing hundreds of people onto a boat and sending them out to die in a jungle, but they were all still the same basic con that Gregor MacGregor pulled with the nation of Poyais: it's known among con artists as *selling thin air*.[22] The thin-air part is integral to the Big Lie, because by definition a Big Lie is not an exaggeration, misrepresentation, or misdirection about the truth; rather, it rests entirely on the absence of any sort of tangible reality and relies on your combined theory of mind and faith in objective reality to float it enough credit to be believed.

But what Smith and MacGregor did was even more powerful, because the lies they told were ones that other people wanted badly to believe. A too-good-to-be-true business opportunity like Lustig offered was appealing, but not necessarily emotionally compelling in the same way as finally being able to contact faraway loved ones or starting a whole new life in another country. Once they'd stood in line, paid a large sum of money, and sent a telegram, Smith's marks *needed* his lie to be true. As did MacGregor's victims, who could not accept that they'd spent their entire savings, uprooted their lives, journeyed to the other side of the world, and probably lost friends and family, all based on a really Big Lie.

Fantasy Island

The most appalling part of the story of Poyais (and it's all pretty appalling) is how it *ended*—not for the colonists or the investors but for MacGregor—and for the truth in general. When that handful of remaining colonists, impoverished, diseased, and traumatized, finally made it back to London and told their story, you'd think that, if he wasn't already long gone, MacGregor was toast. But you'd be wrong.

People still believed him.

His victims, both his defrauded investors and the few miserable survivors who returned to England, *defended him*: publicly, in writing, in the press. They claimed that it couldn't possibly be MacGregor's fault, employing every excuse on his behalf—from the simple mistake that the ships had left the colonists in the wrong location to the more baroque argument that something "had happened" to Poyais. They became increasingly sure that MacGregor and his vast colony were sabotaged somehow, likely by his other partners or rival agents.[23]

We look around us and wonder constantly how people can cling so tenaciously to their belief in obviously exposed lies. The answer isn't complicated: it's because the lie was so vast, or so meaningful to them, or they simply believed in it *so totally* that they can't be wrong—not about that. The potential cognitive dissonance is simply too destructive to their larger worldview.[24] So they continue to believe the lie. They insist, both to others and to themselves, that the lie is true, because it can't be a lie without threatening other load-bearing beliefs that they rely on, including their belief in their own ability to tell real from make-believe.

Before MacGregor's English victims could reconsider their support, he bolted for Paris, where he ran the exact same Poyais scam in France, but with bigger numbers. This time he secured a £300,000 loan by offering up the imaginary "gold mines of Paulaze" as collateral.[25] You might expect MacGregor to have been grateful for his near escape the first time and to keep a low profile in Paris. Instead, emboldened by his unjust exoneration, he not only did it again, he went *bigger*. Why? Because when we transgress deliberately and are not held to account, we tend to do it again, often on a larger scale. We repeat this behavior because having once tested the waters of other people's perceptions and emerged unscathed, we've learned a most dangerous truth: that *we can*.

It's why Parker sold the Brooklyn Bridge so many times. It's why I've been borrowing my mom's jewelry and then forgetting to tell her (or give it back) for years. It's why you habitually lie about whatever it is that you lie about.

Like all of us, including his victims, Gregor MacGregor possessed a theory of mind and the ability to mentalize, to simulate what others might be thinking. Thus, all that the disaster and his eventual close call in London *really* taught him was that people would absolutely believe him, even with no evidence. And many would still believe him even in the face of concrete evidence that he had lied to them. In fact, the more deeply they had invested in his lie, emotionally or financially, the more fervently and stubbornly they insisted upon believing him.

So why not take Poyais for another spin? As long as everything about the lie was bigger and thus more compellingly unbelievable when he got caught—he'd probably be fine.

MacGregor's second Poyais scam was going really well (for him) and he was almost at the finish line, rounding up and fleecing would-be colonists/murder-victims, when a few random bureaucrats in the French government became suspicious of so many people and so much money headed to a country they had never heard of. Almost as soon as they began to investigate, his story unraveled, and he was thrown in jail and tried for conspiracy and fraud.[26]

Somehow, though, the powers that be—some of them no doubt humiliated investors themselves—felt there was not enough truly persuasive evidence to convict him, and he was allowed to go free. And there he learned another lesson about what other people will and won't (and can't) believe and therefore do: he learned that even if he got caught, most people still probably wouldn't be willing or able to believe with—absolute certainty—that he had done something that obviously evil. Nor would they easily believe that so many seemingly sane, reasonable people could be taken in by such a flagrant and absurd liar.

And so off he went, back to England for a third go.

I Know What You're Thinking

Actually, I don't. But I do know *that* you're thinking, and that fact alone is the greatest evolutionary advantage any of us possess.

Imagine this: a gray fish develops sharp teeth to take a bite out of a brown fish, so the brown fish develops tough scales to block those teeth. Nice. But once that brown fish has protective scaly armor, the gray fish develops powerful hinged jaws to crush him—scales and all. So our brown fish heaves himself up on his fins (now, by definition, feet) to escape onto land. . . . And that's the true—if extremely abridged—story of how fish eventually became reptiles.

Evolution is simply an adaptive arms race, and it goes on and on forever: you develop sight, I develop camouflage, you develop ears, I develop mimicry. You develop a theory of mind, I use it to deceive you. The capacity to lie is ultimately as important to survival as the ability to ward off predators or exploit prey's weaknesses. And just as teeth led to scales, theory of mind begets lying.

The cognitive and behavioral flaws that result in deceit are not flaws at all. No more are the cognitive biases that allow us to be deceived. Both are intrinsic mechanisms of thought and hard-won adaptive advantages in that very arms race. Lying, in various ways, and possessing the ability to believe those lies are necessary.

Theory of mind leads us to assume we're all experiencing the same reality, made up of objectively true facts that we all experience the same way. And that's an advantage in itself; we need a sense of shared reality to function, even if it's only a tacit agreement. The problem with this very necessary (and successful) belief in shared objective reality is that it can be subverted just by breaking the agreement, by flagrantly lying about what is objectively true. This allows for a better adapted individual to exploit that agreed-upon reality, first by being aware of it (honesty bias), then by being aware everyone else is aware and agrees on it (theory of mind), and then finally by making the cognitive leap that one can subvert the whole system by lying. Because of the communally dependent nature of distinctions between what is true and what is false in human society, an outrageous lie, if presented as though true, will be accepted as such.

That's how the Big Lie works. That's why it is the oldest and simplest of cons and why there's no clever or nuanced deception necessary to sell a Big Lie—all that's really required is a mark with a functioning theory of mind and a completely normal belief in shared reality and objective facts: *in the truth.*

In this way, truth and lies are inextricably bound up together.

KEEP YOUR EYE
ON THE BALL

Shell Games, Card Games,
and Mind Games

It's not what you look at that matters, it's what you see.
—HENRY DAVID THOREAU

It costs to be stupid. The stupider you are the more it costs.
—SHERRILL BROWN

THREE-CARD MONTE

Masquerading as a game of chance, Three-Card Monte is the modern incarnation of the world's oldest recorded street hustle: the Shell Game. The current version is a card game played by two people, with three playing cards turned facedown on a flat surface. The center card is a queen. The dealer shows the player the queen and then very quickly and deftly switches the cards' places around while the player watches. Once the dealer stops, the player attempts to guess which position the facedown queen is now holding. By swapping the queen for one of the other two cards before laying it down, sleight of hand is employed by the dealer to ensure that even if you could simultaneously watch all three positions and the movement surrounding them (which you can't) you'd still miss the real trick, and never manage to find the correct card.

You can't win, because the card you're looking for was never even there.

Seeing Things

Yes, facts are facts. But *what are* those facts, again? And how do you discern them?

This particular deception, whether it's performed with cards, cups, shells, or bank accounts, is all about perception—or, rather, *the problem with perception*. Not only can't you believe everything people tell you (or you might end up with a time-share in Poyais), more often than not you can't even believe your own physical senses, much less your memory of them. Seeing may be believing, but it *really* shouldn't be. Your brain doesn't actually have the processing power to deal with all the sensory data available at every second, so, like all gamblers, it cheats. As a result, we often end up seeing what we *expect to see*.

Unlike the Big Lie, and unlike most lies, the Shell Game is a *physical lie*. It exploits basic hardwired flaws in our perceptual cognition to distort and manipulate our perception of reality. This is the basis of magic tricks, optical illusions, and occasionally, foreign policy.

Described as far back as the second century A.D. by Alciphron of Athens, this type of scam was originally run using a bead or pebble hidden beneath one of three overturned cups or shells, lending itself to the disparaging term "Shell Game" to describe any sort of rapid and deliberately confusing transaction that ends with one party getting hustled. This con plays on both your physical perception and your faith in its accuracy: first by priming you to see what your deceiver wants you to see, and then by leading you to believe you can trust what you saw.

And it works on everyone, even con men.

The House Always Wins

One such grifter, and one of the most famous con men in American history, was a street hustler specializing in Three-Card Monte who managed to build a vast criminal empire almost entirely around nothing more than just this sort of sleight of hand. His name was Jefferson Randolph Smith (yeah, the telegraph-wires-to-nowhere guy) and, like a lot of successful con artists, Smith was introduced to the art of the steal when he himself was swindled.

In the mid-1870s, around the age of twelve or thirteen, Smith was working as a Texas cattle puncher, a miserable, backbreaking job, when he was lured into a Shell Game on his way home one night. Needless to say, the operators took him to the cleaners. All evidence to the contrary, he was no fool. At least, not entirely. He realized (too late) that the game was not a game, but rather a manipulation of his perceptions about the seemingly random circumstance, about his fellow "players," and, most of all, about what he thought he saw happen on the table.

He lost six months' wages in just a few minutes but gained a lifelong fascination with sleight of hand.

He left home shortly thereafter, and in little time he had made a fortune and built something of a criminal empire based almost solely on exactly that sort of trick. He ran Shell Games, card games, and other seemingly endless iterations on the same scam all over gold rush country, where he came to be known as "Soapy" Smith, in honor of a version of the Shell Game that a Denver newspaper called "the prize soap racket." He worked with an assortment of accomplices and opened his own gambling hall in Denver, where he was particularly known for fleecing prospectors who, flush after a successful day, felt lucky enough to try a game or two. The Shell Game might have been a small con, but he made it big, eventually winning deeds to plantations and gold claims as far away as Alaska.

Unfortunately for him, he finally pushed his own luck too far, in Skagway in 1898—and surprisingly, not with his fake telegraph wires. Rather, his undoing was brought about by doing what he had been doing for decades—just one time too many. He swindled a miner returning from an exceptional day's prospecting out of $2,500 worth of gold after luring him into a seemingly friendly game of Three-Card Monte.

The miner, feeling rich—and no doubt lucky—was more than happy to play a hand. And he won! Following the usual script, one game became two, when Soapy lost and offered double or nothing for a chance to win his money back. When he lost again two games became three, because who quits when they're winning? Then three became four . . . when suddenly his luck turned and the miner started to lose. And lose and lose and lose. Unable or unwilling to walk away from half his money, and sure he was good at this game a minute ago, he did what everyone does and threw good money after bad. He doubled down one last time and bet the rest of what he had against all he had lost. In a matter of seconds his $2,500 fortune had become Smith's.

The prospector—like everyone who has ever lost money to this particular street hustle—only belatedly realized the game was rigged. But *unlike* most people who fall for this particular con and then feel too foolish to make a fuss, he went to the police. By then the community itself had finally had enough of Soapy Smith's now vast and well-organized crime syndicate. A mob of angry citizens gathered to demand justice—no doubt including at least a few still waiting for replies to the telegrams they'd sent. When Smith encountered them early the next morning, it ended in a shootout and Smith was killed. As his coffin was lowered, one of his men tossed three shells and a pea into his grave, a fitting tribute to the game that both helped make and destroy him.

That game, as simple as it looks, is designed to be unwinnable, so it's no surprise when people lose. The trick is in confusing people's visual perception of physical realities in such a way that they can't see what actually happened and thus can't tell how they've actually been cheated.

For example, in the prize soap racket, Smith stood on a street corner, selling a great pile of bars of soap for a dollar apiece, each in a neat paper wrapper.[1] As he made his sales pitch to the crowd, they watched him wrap *his own cash* around certain bars of soap, then wrap them in paper, just like the others. Some bars, he explained, hid a dollar bill; others contained five, ten, or even twenty; and one or two hid a one-hundred-dollar bill. If you bought one of those, the cash was yours to keep.

Sounds simple, right? Just a matter of luck, really, and how many bars you're willing to buy . . . and on whether you saw what you thought you saw.

The crowd watched him quickly and skillfully shuffle the special bars in among the regular bars, and almost as soon as people began to buy, a lucky customer found cash and waved it around in excitement. People bought more and more, like lotto tickets, trying to find one of the prize bars. As soon as a customer unwrapped a bar and started shouting that they'd found a hundred-dollar bill, Soapy called a halt to the game and auctioned off the remaining bars (including the *one* bar still containing a hundred-dollar bill) to the highest bidders.[2]

Neither the people who bought up the bars one by one nor the high bidder who bought the remaining lot—for far more than a dollar a bar—ever had any chance of finding that second hundred-dollar bill because the truth of the matter is, whatever the crowd *thought* they saw, there was never any money in *any* of the wrappers, let alone a hundred-dollar bill. Smith did wrap the bills that the crowd saw around the soap, in plain sight. But each time he did, he deftly palmed the money as he wrapped the bar of soap in brown paper. Once fully wrapped, all the bars for sale were devoid of cash. The few winners in the crowd were all ringers, only playing along to convince the crowd that there was money in some of the packages and that they had a genuine chance of winning, in the same way Three-Card Monte dealers use associates planted in the crowd to make their card games look winnable.[3]

But it's not a winnable game—not with cards, cups, or in this case soap bars—because you're basing your actions (where'd it go? where'd it land?) on what you saw with your own eyes, when in reality, it was never there at all. Soapy Smith was a violent criminal and an objectively terrible person, but when it came to making you see what he wanted you to *believe you saw*, he ran the racket so well that he's revered to this day by magicians and showmen the world over. The

Magic Castle in Los Angeles still celebrates his birthday every year, and his base of operations in Alaska (the office with no real telegraph lines) has been preserved for tourists.

In fact, there's only one player ever known to have won at Three-Card Monte or a Shell Game: no one special, nor another famous grifter—it was actually one of Soapy Smith's would-be marks. He let Smith talk him into playing, set up the game, and even get as far as distracting him with shills and rapid banter—all par for the course. He let Smith make a dizzying show of switching the shells around. But when the moment came for him to pick one, he instead laid his gun right smack on the table and said that, rather than flipping the correct shell with the pea supposedly under it, he would reveal the winning shell by turning over the two *empty shells* simultaneously. With Soapy's eyes still on the gun, the man flipped over two random shells, showing that there was nothing under either of them. After a moment the man said, threateningly, "I reckon there's no need to turn over the third one."[4]

The way that the man won tells us a lot about how the lie works. The con isn't done with the cards or shells. The con is getting you to play in the first place; flaws in your perceptual cognition do the rest. Accepted wisdom is that the only way to win this game is not to play. But by showing the two empty shells, he forced Smith to either declare him the winner or admit he'd palmed the pea and that there was no game—just a polite mugging.

The Nature of Lying

Humans are hardly the only polite muggers out there. Birds do it, bees do it, viruses and bacteria do it. Microorganisms do it by mimicking cells in our own body to avoid detection. HIV in particular does it by changing the details of its protein coat so frequently it becomes impossible to defend against in any enduring way. Even genes within our own cells engage in deceptive molecular signaling techniques to over-reproduce and outcompete other genes.[5] Ultimately, con artists—despicable though they are—are only doing what all competitive organisms do: exploiting another organism's physical (or in the case of Shell Games, specifically neurological) weakness. Insects lie to flowers, flowers lie to insects, and like us (and pathogens), they most often do it through manipulation of perceptual flaws or the exploitation of another's perceptual shortcutting.

Butterflies are particularly shifty.

Take the blue morpho butterfly; it's the one with the beautiful iridescent sky-blue wings. First lie: that dazzling blue color isn't actually even *there*. It's just an optical illusion, created by blue light selectively reflected off millions of mirror-like, microscopic scales. That vivid blue only exists in your mind—or your eyes, depending on how you see it. The reverse side of their wings has no scales and is a dark, dull brown. But real or reflected, their gaudy wings actually help them to hide in plain sight—just not via camouflage. Rather, they do their best hiding in midair, where they *should be* at their most vulnerable. As they fly, their flapping wings rapidly flash back and forth between visible dark brown and difficult-to-see, reflected sky blue. The effect makes them seem—through a perceptual glitch—to appear and disappear. This strange game of hide-and-seek is called a flashing defense, and it has nothing to do with blending in. Rather, it exploits the inability of many species, particularly birds, to keep their eyes—that is, their brain—fixed on a moving object that doesn't move in a continuous line. The flashing defense makes the blue morpho butterfly seem to rapidly blink in and out of existence as it flies across the sky, making it almost invisible to predators.

Now you see it, now you don't.

Their children are even worse grifters: as larvae they share a symbiotic relationship called mutualism with ants. Mutualism is the name biologists have given to self-serving interactions between species or individual organisms in which both sides benefit, however unintentionally—a sort of formalized win-win. The caterpillar secretes a sugary liquid the ants eat, and the ants protect the tiny caterpillar from small predators. But occasionally a caterpillar will secrete a different liquid, one that mimics the pheromones of the ant's larvae. Because ants trust what they smell the way we trust what we see, they believe this huge thing is one of their tiny larvae and drag it home to the nursery, where they continue to feed and care for the slimy, lying behemoth as if it were one of their own. Because they can't tell that it's not. Meanwhile, emphasis on *mean,* the caterpillar eats the rest of the ant eggs and larvae.

Just like human liars, they're breaking the social contract and they're doing it by exploiting the fact that what one physically perceives is often not what's actually true.

The most common example of successful mutualism is pollination. Bees and flowers coexist in a mutualistic relationship; flowers have nectar and a need to spread their pollen to other flowers, while bees have wings and a need to eat. So, smelling nectar, a bee wriggles its way down the neck of a trumpet flower, getting coated in pollen along the way; drinks the nectar; wriggles back out; and flies away to repeat the process with another flower, exchanging pollen between the two. Neither the bee nor the flower intends to facilitate the survival of the other species, but in fulfilling their own needs, they incidentally fulfill each other's. Mutualism, in one form or another, is crucial to every organism and to the larger biome. So, it would make no sense for either party to subvert the system.

But they do.

Bumblebees have been observed and studied in the act. Rather than waste time and energy attempting to access the nectar—not to mention risk a few ass-in-the-air moments of total exposure to predators—the occasional bumblebee will "cheat." Specifically, they chew a hole through the outside of the flower at its base, allowing the bee to lap up the nectar without ever entering. The flower has been robbed. Then again, the flower also spent a lot of time and energy producing otherwise useless nectar to lure in those marks who would unwittingly spread its pollen.

Nothing exists without objective.

In the same way that trust and trickery function as two mutually necessary halves of one whole, cheating is the flip side of cooperation. They work in tandem, not in opposition. Both cooperation and cheating are dependent on the same basic relationships, perceptual cues, and objectives. The perception of cooperation *is itself a perception,* and therefore one riddled with blind spots, loopholes, and perceptual flaws that can be exploited. One second the butterfly is there; the next, it's vanished. One day the bee is a cooperative pollinator; the next, it's not. By alternating genuine mutualistic behavior with its subversion, organisms that cheat exponentially increase their advantage. And yet cheating is only ever favored in single encounters. Do it all the time and you'll be found out and punished, or at the very least lose your advantage.

The inherent implication is that some cheating is a fundamental component of cooperation.[6] Moreover, *cooperation itself* might be motivated, in part, by the opportunity it affords the cooperator to occasionally cheat. In the same way you can only lie if we all agree upon an objective set of facts, you can only cheat if there is a preexisting expectation of fairness; otherwise, the flower would never let the bee anywhere near it. The ants would stay away from the caterpillars altogether if all they ever did was infiltrate their nests.

As with the Shell Game, the only sure way not to lose would be not to play. But then there'd be no chance of winning, either. From caterpillars to con men—everything living lies. The capacity for deceit—not just in humans, but in all life—is an important asset, honed over millions of generations, and it is an essential part of communication.

Sleight of Mind

But back to the more sophisticated and literal Shell Game. Why *has* everyone for at least the last two thousand years fallen for this simple, obvious scam? The answer, unfortunately, is that we're not that sophisticated. It's tempting to think that we're doing something more complex or meaningful than an insect, but we're not. A blue morpho butterfly engaging its flashing defense is working exactly the same angle as an operator like Soapy Smith, swapping cards or palming folded cash quickly enough to confuse the brain. Everybody falls for sleight of hand because it exploits several intrinsic loopholes in perceptual cognition: the ways in which your brain processes and interprets input from your senses.

In other words, if you have a healthy, normally functioning brain, you literally can't *not* fall for it.

Your brain, specifically your visual cortex—the part of the brain that processes electrical signals from the retina and turns them into images in your mind—functions with a one-tenth-of-a-second delay. What that means in practical terms is that you absolutely cannot believe your eyes, because while your eyes may work, your brain is processing everything your eyes pick up about one-tenth of a second behind what's happening.[7] Your brain just doesn't have the bandwidth to process everything you see, so it fills in most of what's around you with what it *expects* to be around you, almost as though it was just background noise. It's only when something changes radically, a glitch in the matrix, that your brain, still lagging one-tenth of a second behind reality, notices and loops back around to see what's going on.[8]

And the fact that you're living one-tenth of a second in the past isn't your only problem.

There are other exploitable neurological loopholes as well. For example, there's the mirroring effect.[9] Mirroring is the behavior in which one person unconsciously imitates the gesture, posture, or subtle movements of another. Specialized cells in your brain called mirror neurons cause you to mimic the movements, visual cues, and expressions of whomever you're interacting with. This tendency is more or less pronounced, depending on the individual and the extent to which they've developed those neurons, but we all do it, because we all have those mirror neurons. People who are extremely socially awkward are so, in part, because they have a particularly hard time with unconscious mirroring.

Someone smiles, you smile back. Someone looks up suddenly, you look up too. You assume these are conscious choices, but they're not. They are a direct result of functioning mirror neurons creating something known as the Gauchais effect. When employed consciously and deliberately, the Gauchais effect is an incredibly effective way to make people look (or not look) at what you want them to look at, when you want them to look.* As a famous magician put it: "If you are given a choice, you will believe you have acted freely. This is one of the darkest of all psychological secrets."[10]

There's a simple magic trick done with a rubber ball that demonstrates all these tendencies. In the trick, the magician shows you a small rubber ball in the palm of his hand and asks you to watch very closely. As you focus intently on the ball in his hand, he tosses it straight up in the air and catches it as it falls back into his palm. He throws it up again, catches it again, then throws it up for a third or fourth time, at which point the ball vanishes into thin air.

Obviously, the ball didn't just disappear, so what gives?

The way it's played, on the last throw the magician simply never let go of the ball. Though you saw it go up and vanish, really, it never went up at all. What actually happened was the magician *primed* you to see the ball go up in the air every time he released it by moving his hand up before the release, and also by watching the ball rise in the air with his own eyes.[11] You mimic these motions with your own eyes because of the Gauchais effect.

After a few throws your brain begins to take for granted that *the hand goes up, the ball goes up* and *the hand goes down, the ball comes down.* All on its own, your brain decides that this is just not new or important information, and it starts to fill in what you're seeing with what it expects you to see, thereby saving valuable processing power for events you don't already know the outcome of.

It's not until after the last toss that your brain notices something has changed and snaps back to attention—just in time to see the ball *fail* to fall back down. Because your brain had begun to fill in the ball

---

*It's also a pretty effective way to nail a job interview or make a date feel like they really like you.

going up and down for you, as it was expected to, and because your brain is a little slow, you saw the ball go up and only saw it fail to come down when your brain noticed something was wrong a fraction of a second later, leading you to believe that the ball was tossed up in the air and suddenly vanished. But here's the creepy thing—you really *did* see it go up in the air, even though it never left his hand. *Your brain filled in what it expected your eyes were going to see.*

Thus you saw it, and remember seeing it.

So, can you believe your eyes? Absolutely not. Attention is illuminating but equally exclusionary; whatever you are looking at, you've turned the lights off on everything else. And it is extremely limited. Your brain, it turns out, *really* doesn't see much of anything outside the spotlight of your conscious focus, and no matter how closely you're watching, you can't watch everything all the time. Besides, even if you could, your brain is on a cigarette break half the time and just running old clips.

Spotlight, Please

When a magician does this trick (or any other kind of disappearing act or false transfer where a small object seems to vanish or reappear), they first prime your expectations, direct or misdirect your attention, and finally exploit that one-tenth-of-a-second lag in the brain's perception (in this case, of motion) to cause you to see something that isn't there. The phenomenon is called *persistence of vision*—it happens when physical reality moves faster than your neurons can finish firing (which is pretty much always) causing your conscious mind, for a split second, to see a sort of ghost image of what was (or what it believes should have been) there.

A more elaborate demonstration of the same principle is best exemplified by Cups and Balls, a magic trick so old and universal that, just like its less charming brother the Shell Game, it dates back to antiquity, and some version of it is practiced in nearly every country in the world. The trick involves three overturned cups and three identical balls (that you can see; the magician no doubt has more hidden up sleeves and in pockets); one ball sits on top of each overturned cup.

The magician begins by moving each ball under its respective cup, and then lifting the first cup to show that the first ball has disappeared. After setting the first cup back down, next the magician lifts the third cup to show the audience that the missing ball from the first cup has materialized under the third cup, alongside the third ball. After setting the third cup back down over the two balls, they lift the second cup. When they lift the second cup, all three balls have somehow appeared under it, and when they lift it a second time, all three balls are gone. The vanishes and transpositions become faster and more complicated as the magician makes the balls disappear and reappear in increasingly impressive, surprising, and confusing ways.

Though there are three balls, not one, and the point is to *show* them to you, not hide them from you; in the end, it's just a variation on a basic Shell Game. The three balls seem to appear and disappear and move magically from one cup to another because there were actually *more* than the three balls in play the whole time. The magician is practicing elaborate sleight of hand—no different from palming the pea in a Shell Game, just more complex, because it's not adequate to make the ball vanish. It has to reappear somewhere, and there are three of them being manipulated simultaneously. A skilled hand and a significant amount of distraction and misdirection are required, but when done successfully, the effect is, well . . . magical.

Sitting with his partner in a diner in 1975, a young, then unknown magician was practicing Cups and Balls. Because he was in a diner, not a theater, he made do with balled-up paper and overturned water glasses. Because the glasses were clear it was possible to see the "balls" as they were palmed, moved, and replaced. Even just in practice, at a table with his partner, it should have spoiled the illusion. Instead he discovered something remarkable: because our attention can only really focus on one thing at a time and because our perception of reality lags behind reality enough that our brains take constant shortcuts to create a coherent representation of reality, even with clear cups, *the illusion still held.*

Persistence of vision was still in effect, even as the whole trick was laid bare. In fact, it actually made the trick more surprising, confusing, and remarkable, because while his partner was able to see everything happening beneath and behind the clear cups, he *still* saw the balls mysteriously disappearing and reappearing in different places. According to the magician, "The eye could see the moves, but the mind could not comprehend them. Giving the trick away gave nothing away, because you still couldn't grasp it."[12]

Though exposing to the audience how a trick worked won them no fans among professional magicians, the clear glasses reinvented the age-old Cups and Balls. It made the trick better, and the trick made the magician and his partner famous. Very famous. He and his partner would eventually perform that trick, along with many others, under the names Penn and Teller. That unusual approach became the hallmark of their shows; rather than pretending to perform actual feats of magic, they create and deconstruct illusions for the audience in such a way as to expose what Teller refers to as the "everyday fraud of perception."[13]

"Every time you perform a magic trick, you're engaging in experimental psychology," according to Teller. "If the audience asks, 'How the hell did he do that?' then the experiment was successful. I've exploited the efficiencies of your mind."[14] Ultimately, what they revealed to the audience using clear glasses for Cups and Balls wasn't how an old magic trick worked, but rather, how our brains do, and sometimes don't. Our hardwired inability to process information in real time or to deal with perceptual ambiguity results in our brain presenting us with a sort of representative reality—one that we absolutely require to function—but one that often does not accurately represent reality.

Disappearing Acts

If magic tricks are a kind of experimental psychology, then I guess it shouldn't be surprising when experimental psychology occasionally turns into a magic trick, like making a whole person disappear. Which happened about twenty years ago when Daniel Simons and Christopher Chabris conducted a now famous experiment into "a form of invisibility" known as inattentional blindness.[15] It was fairly simple: a group of subjects was shown a video of people playing basketball and given a simple task to perform while they watched; afterward they were asked questions about the video. You've probably seen this video, as it's become a lasting phenomenon, having had stunning ramifications for fields as disparate as criminal justice, psychology, history, and neuroscience.

The video of the basketball game shown to the subjects included, among the other players, three wearing white shirts. The subjects were told to *watch those particular players very closely* and count how many times the white-shirt-wearing players passed the ball. The basketball game proceeds normally throughout the video, but around thirty seconds into the clip, someone wearing a full gorilla costume casually walks onto the court, in the middle of the ongoing game, looks right at the camera, and begins chest thumping. Then simply walks away. The game continues, throughout the odd occurrence, uninterrupted.[16]

When the video ended, the subjects were asked if they had watched it very closely, and if so, what did they see? Some of them saw the correct number of passes; some of them did not. But a majority of the subjects looked right at the gorilla and saw *nothing at all.*

In this case, the problem isn't delayed perceptual cognition—the gorilla was there for a while—the problem is that spotlight created by attention. You recall I said you don't really see what's outside the spotlight? I meant that literally. Your brain is just making most of it up, based on expectation. It wasn't quick; they didn't miss it. They just didn't *expect* to see a gorilla (in fact, they very reasonably expected *not to see a gorilla* in the midst of a basketball game) and so they did not see one. "This form of invisibility," according to Simons, "depends not on the limits of the eye, but on the limits of the mind."[17]

In the same way your brain will show you what it strongly anticipates your eyes are about to see, like that rubber ball going up on the third toss, it can also *not* show you something that it strongly does not anticipate. Just like the rubber-ball trick, but in the reverse. Your visual cortex, it seems, is just as susceptible to confirmation bias and cognitive dissonance as your conscious mind. The subject's brains quite literally could not believe their eyes—so they just filtered the gorilla out of the scene.*

Which kinda makes you wonder what other bizarre things you've photoshopped out of your own field of vision: Ghosts? UFOs? Sea monsters? Probably not . . . but there's just *no way* to know for sure, is

---

*Sort of like "The Dress," another viral Internet sensation (appearing blue and black to some, white and gold to others), that highlighted the chasm between what we're certain we see and what's actually there.

there? While I obviously can't speak to the truly fantastical, I can tell you with certainty what *else* your brain has very frequently refused to see: any *unexpected change,* no matter how big, obvious, or important. As Simons puts it, "We consciously see only a small subset of our visual world, and when our attention is focused on one thing, we fail to notice other, unexpected things around us—including those we might want to see."[18]

The Problem with Perception

In 2010, Daniel Simons decided to take advantage of the fact that the invisible-gorilla video had gone viral and follow up that experiment with another one that doubled down on our refusal to see what's right in front of us.[19] It was essentially the same experiment, the same video, the same task, except this time, according to Simons, because of the viral sensation the first video had caused, "viewers were *expecting* the gorilla to make an appearance. And it did. But the viewers were so focused on watching for the gorilla that they overlooked other unexpected events, such as the curtain in the background changing color."[20]

This subset of inattentional blindness is referred to as change blindness, and it's even more disturbing. Essentially, if something changes—even radically—and you're not expecting it to, your mind often won't acknowledge that it did. And while that idea would be unsettling enough if it only applied to sleight of hand, repetitive background stimuli, or magic tricks, it turns out that it holds true for large and complex events as well.

For example, in another of Simons's experiments into just that— the magnitude and scope of change blindness—he had an experimenter behave as though they were lost, as a pretext to stop random strangers walking down the street and ask for assistance. The experimenter would approach the unwitting subject and, explaining that they were lost, ask for help finding their way. Once the subject was well engaged in giving the experimenter directions, two more members of the team (appearing as rude pedestrians) would walk right between the subject and experimenter, momentarily blocking the subject's view of the man he was just speaking to. In that brief moment, the experimenter quickly and seamlessly swapped physical places with one of the two "pedestrians," walking away with the other as though nothing had happened, leaving the subject in midconversation with a completely different, only vaguely similar-looking, person.

Weird, right? If that happened to you—if you were speaking with a stranger, and a pair of people walked between the two of you, and suddenly the stranger you were speaking to a second before had transformed or been somehow replaced by a totally different person— *you'd notice,* right? You'd be stunned, right? If you're thinking, "Yes, I would," you'd be wrong. Just like all those people who failed to see a gorilla in the middle of a basketball game, the majority of Simons's subjects carried on their conversation with the new partner and never noticed a thing.

Facts remain immutable regardless of your opinion or perception of them. That's precisely what makes them facts. But while facts are objective, how do you determine what those facts *actually are*? If your brain manufactures the vast majority of what you see and hear and feel based not on actual sensory input but, rather, on your individual expectations of what that input should be, then how certain are you of those facts? Are you *sure* you saw that rubber ball? Are you sure you *didn't* see a gorilla?

Do you want to *bet* on it?

Because the fact that magicians, street hustlers, and petty thieves have been successfully running the same con for thousands of years would suggest . . . maybe you shouldn't. The problem with perception is that it's all in our mind. It's not an infallible transmission of facts from the world to our brains; it's not an indelible record of those facts. Perception is just short of an opinion.

If your brain refuses to see a gorilla, then your eyes are sort of irrelevant. And so, frankly, *is the gorilla*. We cobble together our own record of reality from memory, expectation, biases, and inattention. It's no wonder two people can never exactly agree on what they saw—nobody *really* saw anything. They only think they did, because their brain showed them something. At the same time, that's all there is to seeing. What's a brain to do? It's why witness statements are always an inconsistent, conflicting mess; why referee calls are so disputed; and why we can't see our missing keys when we're looking right at them.

We're all so certain that we know the truth, and yet there's no real way we can distinguish between factual reality and our perception of it. Facts may be facts, but we can never really be sure what we saw—or didn't see. We will always default, at least in the moment, to seeing what our brain has been primed to see, just as we will believe what we have been primed to believe.

Short Changed

At its most basic, the Shell Game is about physical perception: how our most vital tool in assessing truth doesn't really exist. Or at the very least, it doesn't work the way you think it does, thus (much like theory of mind) allowing for the subversion of the very system it's supposed to regulate. You can only be tricked because you can see, and therefore believe what you see is true.

Another variation on the Shell Game is a scam called Change Raising.[21] It's a very quick short con that'll earn you a few bucks if you can pull it off. It relies on the same sort of directed mirroring, inattention in the face of too much information, and rapid movement and exchanges exploiting perceptual lag time as Three-Card Monte.

It works like this: you go into a store or gas station and buy something small. You hand the cashier a ten-dollar bill; he will give you back a five-dollar bill, a few one-dollar bills, and some coins. While engaging in the transaction, make conversation, hold eye contact, and fumble through your wallet or bag looking for exact change. Make a confusing mess of different bills and coins on the counter. Keep talking and hold eye contact, except to look down at the growing disarray on the counter. The teller will unconsciously mirror your gaze and look at it too. This gives you time to keep switching bills in between glances downward. More important, seeing so many different combinations of change will confuse the cashier's short-term memory, causing them to lose track of the original numbers every time your eyes direct theirs (via mirroring) to look down at a growing pile of different bills and coins.

While you're talking and rummaging and making eye contact, a line will start to form behind you. This will divide the cashier's attention (to the extent that attention can ever be successfully divided), making them increasingly hurried and confused, causing neurological stress that enhances the cashier's natural bias to believe whatever they are presented with. Still talking, you start counting your change amid the crumpled money mess you've made.

As the line gets longer and the cashier gets more distracted and anxious, change the terms: ask, "Actually can I give you these one-dollar bills and this other one for another five-dollar bill?" Of course you can; no one says no to that. As he starts to exchange the bills, you interrupt him midcount and say, "Wait, give me those ones and I'll give you this five and four more ones." (By this point, customers behind you are complaining, or at least audibly groaning—increased stress, increased honesty bias.) "And then, um, you can just . . . give me a twenty?" (Keep moving your money in and out of your purse or wallet, hold eye contact, and don't stop talking.) "Yep! We got it"— and like that, you've just floated the suggestion that this was his math, priming him to agree that it's correct.

By this point the cashier will likely hand you whatever bills you suggest just to move the line along because it's become so stressful— and because he's completely lost count, but mostly because one five-dollar bill and four one-dollar bills comes to nine dollars. That *sounds* right in the instant, because he already had the number nine in his head. It was your original change on the ten-dollar bill. If he doesn't immediately acquiesce, you defuse his potential mistrust by correcting yourself; you say, "Wait! That's wrong. . . . Here, I'll give *you* the ten dollars. No wait . . . you give me, uh . . ." and start again with more bills and some coins. You keep going in this fashion until the clerk is thoroughly flustered, can't remember what the original change was, and is so eager to get you out of the line forming behind you that he just hands you exactly what you request.

When done correctly, you can walk out with a free $1.50 purchase and twenty dollars in "change." But what I'm describing isn't just a quick way to make twenty bucks; it's the very essence of how perception is not what we think it is.

Change Raising, while still the same basic con, goes a step or two beyond the requirements of a shell or card game, which primarily exploits delayed perceptual cognition, and a little bit of inattentional blindness. Just like the rubber-ball trick, Change Raising employs a significant amount of *behavioral priming*. From where your eyes tell their eyes to look to the fact that gas-station attendants expect to be robbed with a weapon, not a smile, you are exploiting the mark's neurological blind spots while simultaneously engineering their responses to what they *do* see.

Although at this point, you're probably wondering why I'm telling you so much about my hobbies. The thing is, it's not just *my* hobby; the CIA likes to play a very similar game when waging covert wars.

Watch Closely

These basic cons, these fundamental lies, are with us all the time. They're woven in and out of our lives—in our brains, in our beliefs, in the butterflies in our backyard. These simple deceptions underpin our very society in ways you've never noticed. Have you ever wondered why "shell companies" are called that? It's because they're used like overturned shells—not so much to hide money but to *move* money from one place to another in a misleading and deceptive fashion. So, really, more like those clear cups than shells. Because you can see the money the whole time, but the deception still works; you watched the whole thing and yet somehow you have no idea where the money went or how it got there.

The Shell Game comes in all shapes and sizes, but no matter how large and elaborate it becomes, at its heart it's always the same.

Watch this one: in 1979, under shell number 1, there was a violent "revolution" in Iran, in which the authoritarian—but U.S.-friendly—shah and his family were deposed and exiled and a great many Iranian citizens were killed. Western hostages were taken, people were hung from cranes, and eventually Ayatollah Khomeini consolidated power and declared Iran a caliphate. The United States is *really* not into caliphates (or hostage taking, which was another factor in our bad breakup with Iran), so this understandably caused a rift between the two countries.

But you know what the United States is *very* into? Arms dealing (just by the numbers, war is actually one of our primary exports), as well as double-dealing.

You see, before the revolution, the United States was the single largest supplier of weapons to Iran. So when regime changed, as regime often does, and Ayatollah Khomeini severed all ties with the United States, we retaliated with intense sanctions, including a weapons embargo against Iran called Operation Staunch.* This weapons embargo was our idea. That fact is important. And we not only embargoed them, labeling the new regime a terrorist state, we lobbied, urged, and (in some cases) squeezed every other country that we had any kind of sway with to likewise sanction Iran and refuse to sell them weapons. And we were pretty successful.

Of course, this great success became a problematic state of affairs, because the new Iranian caliphate would have to buy weapons *somewhere*, especially after they entered into what would become a ten-year-long war with Iraq in 1980. And while that sounds a lot like an Iran problem, not a U.S. problem . . . it actually was an issue. It occurred to the National Security Council that if we refused to supply them, Iran would most certainly buy those same weapons from the Soviet Union, broadening the Soviet sphere of influence and gaining the Soviet Union an ally. And during the height of the Cold War, we

---

*You cannot make this stuff up.

couldn't have that. So regardless of our formal position, we had to keep Iran supplied with weapons somehow—if only to stop them from making flirty eyes at Russia.

Now, that same year, 1979, on the other side of the globe under shell number 2, the more or less democratic government of Nicaragua was overthrown by revolutionaries of its own: the Sandinista National Liberation Front. The Sandinistas were less religious fanatics, more socialist/fascists. And if there's one thing that freaks out the United States more than theocracy, it's the specter of communism.

Public opinion in the United States was strongly against starting a war in Nicaragua, but the Sandinistas' enemies, the counter-revolutionaries, or Contras for short, were happy to do the ground fighting. This is where covert war comes in handy. Because, for reasons that passeth understanding (mine anyway), the newly elected U.S. president, Ronald Reagan, had *big* heart-shaped eyes for the Contras, likening them to America's founding fathers. So instead of sending troops to fight the Sandinistas in South America, we sent money. *Lots of money.* In 1980 the Reagan administration quietly authorized the CIA to "assist" the Contras with funds, weapons, and training.

Where did they get this money? Certainly not from Congress—because the whole affair was super illegal. Congress even passed the (first) Boland Amendment in 1982, which barred "the use of funds for the purpose of overthrowing the government of Nicaragua or provoking a war between Nicaragua and Honduras." You can see, they were quite specific: *Don't do that!* So instead, the CIA skimmed from the military budget and secretly continued to sell weapons to Iran—to raise cash to fund the Contras. The same Iran the United States had convinced most of the world to agree not to sell weapons to. So how do you sell weapons to an entire country secretly? Well, this is a Shell Game, you need a third shell—a middleman. In this case, Israel.

The United States gave Israel (shell number 3) the arms (ball number 1), Israel sold them to Iran (shell number 1), and then Israel (shell number 3) gave the United States the money (ball number 2)—which the United States subsequently funneled to the Contras (shell number 2) to fund the covert war (ball number 3) expressly forbidden by the Boland Amendment. Are you still watching closely? This international sleight of hand was repeated over and over and over again, in an operation now known as the Iran-Contra Scandal, which the Reagan administration just called "the Enterprise."

Coincidentally, "the enterprise" was also what Soapy Smith called his Shell Game racket.

Eventually it all leaked, and both houses of Congress had a complete meltdown. And by then the Enterprise had gotten even more convoluted, when the Contras began providing actual tons of cocaine to be sold in the United States to generate additional funds. In 1984 Congress passed the second Boland Amendment in an attempt to make it all stop. But you can't actually vote to end a covert war, since it doesn't even officially exist, *Congress*. And the Reagan administration continued to not so totally secretly carry on with this guns-for-money-for-guns-for-coke-for-money-for-guns Iran/Israel/Nicaragua Shell Game for years.

Good luck keeping your eye on *that ball*.

DON'T BUY IT

Goldbricking and the Often-
Misleading Nature of Facts

The closer to the truth, the better the lie, and the truth itself,
when it can be used, is the best lie.
—ISAAC ASIMOV

There's nothing more deceptive than an obvious fact.
—ARTHUR CONAN DOYLE

THE BAIT AND SWITCH

There are countless versions of the Bait and Switch, and they all have their own colorful, descriptive names: salting, goldbricking, upselling, a pig in a poke. But at their core they're all the same basic con. The short version: you promise your mark one thing, then deliver something of lesser or no value. This isn't as simple as offering something that doesn't exist or telling an absolute falsehood. Unlike the Big Lie, which is fake through and through and relies on its own simple lack of plausibility to confuse you, the essence of the Bait and Switch involves using honest evidence to do dishonest work.

The Size of Lies

Sleight of hand and the cognitive fallacies it exploits are always effective. There's no way to avoid falling for it—it's just how our brains are wired. But while that approach works great for magic tricks and street hustles, it only really exploits that one-tenth-of-a-second delay in cognition, so on its own it only works for very short cons. The Big Lie, on the other hand, sells visibly, persistently, and absurdly enormous fictions, which is, ironically, how those lies become credible.

But how do you tell a medium-sized lie? Because that's the size of most lies.

The answer is that you have to use both. It's not always enough to lie to someone with what you're saying and count on their theory of mind and reliance on objective reality. Sometimes you have to further press that objective reality by manipulating legitimate facts around the falsehood—concrete evidence and things that they (ostensibly) know to be true, things they can see with their own eyes to support the lie.

Goldbricking, for instance, involves coating a lead bar in a just-thick-enough layer of gold that it can be scratched or filed by a buyer and still appear to be solid gold, at least until it's melted down. There's a lie at the heart of the exchange, but everything else about it is, technically, real. The mark initially trusts the (often too-good-to-be-true) deal because they've seen some sort of compelling proof. Unfortunately for the mark, once the transaction is complete and you're long gone, that proof either went with you or, like the gold coating on the lead bar, turns out to have been "real" but wholly misleading.

People will always believe proof. If they believe their own eyes and they also believe not only what they're seeing but other facts they already know, then it's just a simple miscalculation on their part to believe the conclusion you've presented them with.

And besides, they *want* to believe you. But we'll get to that later.

The Golden State

Long before it was Silicon Valley, the Bay Area was famous for a different element: gold. The city of San Francisco sparked and then expanded like an explosion; and then, just as now, it was teeming with people looking to strike it rich. Some of them did, most of them didn't. But anywhere there's possibility, there's hope; where there's hope, there's always fraud. And in the years following the California gold rush of 1848, fraudulent gold mines sprang up all over the west.

One of the most common gold rush scams was the Bait-and-Switch practice of "salting" barren claims. Salting a mine involved planting an otherwise insignificant amount of gold in an area to create the illusion of native gold deposits. A worthless claim or barren mine would be sprinkled with particles of gold dust or flake to make the mines appear as though they were rich in untapped ore. With the Colorado silver rush of 1859, the practice spread there too. There was plenty of real gold and silver to be found out west. But anywhere there's a boom, there are people looking to get rich quick and ready to believe almost anything—and anywhere they go, professional purveyors of fantasy follow, happy to accommodate. Kentucky cousins Philip Arnold and John Slack—ex-49ers who'd made a modest living prospecting over the years but had never really struck it rich—were two such individuals.

In 1872, Arnold and Slack put a very interesting spin on the gold-salting Bait and Switch when they managed to convince not just a few other dubiously educated prospectors of the gold content of a mine in gold country but, rather, to convince an abundance of elite capitalists, bankers, and gemologists (among them, Charles Lewis Tiffany) to invest vast amounts of money in a worthless *gem* mine in the northwestern corner of Colorado that Arnold and Slack didn't even own. Having been duped into believing that the barren stretch of land would yield a mother lode of diamonds, rubies, emeralds, sapphires, and garnets, the money men were more than happy to oblige.

All this in a region of the world that yields few of those minerals, never in abundance, and *never* together. The "Great Diamond Hoax" (which wasn't actually a Hoax, so much as a Bait and Switch) was the most infamous mining swindle of the gold rush era, without ever even involving gold.[1] It embroiled a U.S. representative, the former commander of the Union Army, prominent lawyers from both coasts, and the most well-connected bankers from California to London.

All That Glitters

As eager as the popular imagination was for gold in the nineteenth century, the South African diamond rush had whetted the American appetite for something more. Stories relentlessly covered by the press told of vast diamond finds under South African farms, just waiting for prospectors to dig them up; of giant gems being pulled from the Orange River like fish; and most of all of the massive fortunes being made overnight. You might even say American prospectors were *primed* to believe finding diamonds was an inevitability. The reality was less promising: while the stray diamond had been found here or there, no diamond deposits of quality or quantity had ever been found in North America.

Of course, that stopped no one's imagination, and Arnold and Slack played their con like pros.

They arrived in San Francisco late one night, a pair of dirty and road-weary prospectors, allegedly new to town. At least that's how they presented themselves when they arrived at the office of a prominent local businessman named George Roberts. He was rich and well connected, but known to play fast and loose with both the facts and the law. The seemingly ragged prospectors came knocking rather late, clutching a small dirty leather bag, which they hoped to deposit for the night rather than hold on to themselves, since it was "of great value."[2]

The two men deliberately acted nervous and shady, anxious to see the bag safely locked up for the night but unwilling to disclose the nature of its actual contents. They told Roberts that they were only asking to deposit it in his safe because the Bank of California was already closed for the night. Of course, Roberts was curious—if not licking his chops—and wouldn't stop asking them questions, which they affected an uncomfortable desire to avoid. Finally Slack, "the dumb one," let slip that it was a bag of uncut diamonds. Naturally, Roberts wanted to know *everything* and wouldn't take no for an answer. The two con men feigned panic at their own disastrous slip of the tongue and bolted—completely according to plan.

As soon as they were gone, Roberts went and told his friend William Ralston, the founder of the Bank of California, about his deeply suspicious—and terribly exciting—interaction with the two idiots and their bag of diamonds. And then he sent a cable to a financier friend in London named Ashly Harpending, who was working on floating a silver stock offering on behalf of Ralston when he got the news. Harpending was so sure that they "had got something that would astonish the world"[3] that he dropped what he was doing and booked it back to San Francisco.

By the time Harpending arrived in May 1871 (several months *was* booking it, in the nineteenth century), Arnold and Slack had convinced Roberts that a second trip to the still-secret location of their vast gem mine had yielded sixty pounds of rough diamonds and rubies. The second score was worth at least $600,000—according to Roberts, who claimed to have had the rough stones appraised by a local jeweler. Maybe he did; maybe he didn't. But apparently his word on the subject was good enough to ensnare a major mining investor named William Lent and a U.S. general, George S. Dodge.

Ralston's entire crew agreed by this point that it was vital to get Arnold and Slack out of the way for good, so Ralston tracked them down and demanded they talk business. Ralston assumed he was dealing with a couple of drunk prospectors—rather than one drunk prospector and one major-league con artist who had spent most of 1870 neither drunk, nor prospecting (as he claimed) nor on his modest farm with his wife and children back in Kentucky but working as a bookkeeper for the San Francisco Diamond Drill Company, which made industrial-diamond drill bits.

Philip Arnold had learned a great deal about uncut diamonds.

And when Arnold left the employ of the Diamond Drill Company in November of that year, he left with a small bag of uncut, rough, diamonds. They were not particularly valuable, being industrial-grade diamonds, but they *were* diamonds. And all diamonds look a little scuzzy before they're cut and polished. At some point he obtained a handful of small uncut garnets, rubies, and sapphires and added them to the bag as well. Of course, no one knew any of that the night he and his cousin "arrived" in San Francisco.

Bigger Crooks

Roberts, Ralston, Lent, General Dodge, and their ever-expanding gang of well-heeled thieves and thugs started with the carrot, offering to buy out Arnold and Slack and take over the whole thing, as they really were better equipped to fully capitalize on such a history-making windfall. At first both men refused to be bought out of their own claim—to which, they argued, these moneymen had *no* actual connection, beyond their own greed and desire—which was one of the very few true things anyone in this story said to anyone else at any point. But like any good goldbrick, it was just a thin layer of truth coating the larger con. Just as he had been the one to *accidentally* say the words "rough diamonds" in front of Roberts that first night, John Slack *seemed* to buckle under the mounting pressure to sell and finally agreed to accept $100,000 for his half of the claim.

Ralston paid Slack $50,000 for half of his interest in the mine up front, with another $50,000 guaranteed on further verification of the gems. Arnold would not be bought so easily, and instead agreed to possibly discuss it again, later in the year, once he had returned from a third trip to the secret location he was about to undertake.

In reality, Arnold and Slack weren't headed for their secret gem mine, they were headed for a boat. They snuck away to London, where they used the $50,000 Slack had been paid to buy an assortment of uncut, gem-quality diamonds and gemstones, some for use in Ralston's verification process, most to use in salting their barren land.

The rough stones they bought were far superior in quality to the industrial rough they'd been passing off as the product of their diamond and gem mines thus far. They returned from London, their would-be partners were none the wiser, having believed the two had spent the previous months working their claim, wherever it was. They made a quick trip to their location as soon as they returned to California, but only stayed long enough to salt the claim with new, better jewels. After they finished, they returned to San Francisco with the remainder of the newly bought gemstones, pretending to return from the mine with a new yield, this one worth approximately two million dollars.

Meanwhile, Ralston's crew had grown to include two Civil War generals, George McClellan (who ran for president against Lincoln) and Benjamin Butler (a U.S. representative whose job was to smooth over any legal issues that might arise in Congress since the diamond and gem mine was on federal land), and Horace Greeley, the editor of the *New-York Tribune*—who, incidentally, was about to run for president himself. The London-bought stones were swiftly taken to New York for authentication and appraisal. Ralston and his group convened in Manhattan at the home of New York lawyer Samuel Barlow with an assortment of prominent, albeit dodgy financiers to meet with the one and only Charles Tiffany himself, the founder of Tiffany and Co. Tiffany dumped out the huge bag of diamonds, as well as some garnets, rubies, emeralds, and sapphires, onto Barlow's parlor billiard table, where he "viewed them gravely," inspecting them one by one, holding them up to the light, examining their surfaces, weights, and other qualities.[4] After a dramatic wait, Tiffany declared them real, perfect, and worth a fucking fortune.

At that point, Ralston set about maneuvering to bargain, swindle, or outright steal the two prospectors' ownership of their jewel mine, an endeavor complicated by the fact that no one else had ever *seen* the actual claim. Not one of them actually knew where it was or how to find it. Ralston insisted to the two prospectors that—no offense—a professional needed to survey the area. He convinced Arnold and Slack to take a mining expert named Henry Janin to their secret site—blindfolded, of course, so that they would be assured he couldn't give away its location before terms were reached. John Slack was sent, without his cousin, to help the expert and his team locate the claim.

When the expedition returned, they came back elated. Janin reported that the claim really was there, and really was loaded with diamonds, rubies, and lots of other precious gemstones. The problem was that Henry Janin was allegedly a mining expert, of some sort, but he was certainly neither a *diamond* nor a *gem*-mining expert. Either would have looked for the telltale *context* of a diamond find, not just the gems. An oil or a coal mining expert, for example, wouldn't have known the difference; he would have expected either to see the jewels or to see nothing. And so that's all Janin was looking for, and all he saw.

But at that point the expedition was considered a huge success, and everyone came back with dollar signs in their eyes—everyone but John Slack. He never came back at all. The official story was that he mysteriously disappeared one night after an alleged argument about "something" with "someone" in the camp. Though no one, it seemed, could recall whom he had argued with or what the argument had been about—just that Slack had gotten angry, wandered off, and never returned.

It's a thin story; it has been since it was first told in 1871. The fact is that John Slack was never seen or heard from again, though the truth of the matter is open to interpretation and, like most truth, will never be settled.

But with Slack gone, Ralston believed they had only one problem left: Philip Arnold. But Arnold, now the sole owner of the claim, seemed ready to give up and finally sell. Ralston paid Arnold a little over half a million dollars to go away, forever—and he did. Arnold lived happily, if ignominiously, ever after in Kentucky, on his farm, with his family (minus his "missing" cousin).

Thereafter, Ralston and his gang formed the New York Mining and Commercial Company, capitalized at ten million dollars, and started selling stock—hand over fist—to investors. Within months, at least twenty-five *other* diamond exploration companies had been formed. Suddenly everyone believed in American diamonds, and so were primed to see them. The whole country was thrilled, particularly the finance sector, and the public imagination was set ablaze. Now, not only was our manifest destiny sprinkled with gold and silver, apparently the American West sparkled with major diamond deposits too.

Really Fake

I'm sure you've heard the common expression "the cat's out of the bag," referring to spilling a secret or spoiling a surprise, but do you know why it means that? It's actually a really old, surprisingly literal expression. In the Middle Ages it was a reference to a uniquely medieval Bait and Switch.

If you'll indulge me a moment: back in ye olde times, people would travel a long way, sometimes days, to sell, shop, and trade at a weekly or monthly market. One thing you could buy, if you could afford it, was a pig in a poke, which sounds utterly filthy, but was actually just a small (but still quite costly) pig in a sack that was tightly tied or sewn shut. As a customer, you'd find a pig seller and choose one of their screeching, rambunctious piglets. Once you agreed on a price, the seller would pop your little piggy into a sack and then sew or tie it closed for you, because pigs are crazy, and impossible to catch if they manage to bolt. You paid, and you got a pig in a poke, an easy-to-transport object, rather than a psychotic runaway piglet. The sack might squeal and thrash around a little, but your valuable purchase would be secure for your long trip home.

Unless you got conned.

In which case the seller bagged your pig in plain sight and then set it down somewhere *just* out of your sight (say, at his feet, behind the counter) for a moment, while taking your payment. Then he picked up and handed you a different but basically identical screaming bag from seemingly the same spot. You wouldn't even see the switch. What made this particular version of the Bait and Switch con so effective was that you would *never* (unless you were as deranged as a piglet in a sack) *ever* open the bag until you were home. When you finally did cut the bag open, now far away from the long-gone seller—rather than a fat little pig, a very angry, freaked-out, and inedible cat would jump out of the bag at you and run away.

At which point *the cat's out of the bag.*

The thing about a Bait and Switch is that it's not as simple as being told a Big Lie and believing it. Like the Shell Game, there's an added element of manipulating expectations and perception. But rather than employing sleight of hand, a Bait and Switch fools you with a different cognitive fallacy: assumption. The Bait and Switch exploits our certainty in both *the accuracy of our perceptions* and *the truthfulness of our cumulative knowledge* (certainty in both of which are required for us to function at all) by offering genuine but deliberately misleading proof.

Real fake proof is a strange idea, but look at it like this: the diamonds in a salted mine are real diamonds, but they've been intentionally taken out of their correct context. Real evidence is demanded and received. But in this case, the evidence, however legitimate, only covers the surface—like the gold coating on a lead brick. Once the evidence is confirmed to be real, whatever claim it was presented to support is also believed to be true, and that halo of truth is extended to the entire scenario—however unlikely it may be. If the surface is confirmed to be gold, the whole bar is assumed to be. In this case, the lie exploits our confidence in what we *already definitely know.*

In the same way that your brain will fill in the missing rubber ball that never went up—because everything else you saw tells you it should have, and thus primed you to see it—your conscious mind makes the same sort of errors as does your visual cortex based on prior experience or available information. Like seeing the pig you purchased go in a bag, carrying around an identical bag with a similarly sized live animal in it, and assuming it's your pig.

Because of the way our minds are designed to extrapolate general principles from individual examples and wholes from mere parts, the smarter you are, the more you know, the more likely you are to fall for it.

Butterflies, Brain Damage, and the Bigger Picture

That's because we're designed to fail (or to succeed) that way, depending on how accurately you manage to extrapolate the whole from only a part. Humans, and in fact most living creatures, must be able to inductively make determinations about the nature of a whole from exposure to a portion. *We're supposed to do that.* Even though it very often leads to mistakes. There's actually something wrong with the visual cortex of a person who can't make those judgments and errors. It's a neurological disorder called cortical visual impairment, wherein a person lacks the ability to do just that: to extrapolate an (even obvious) whole from pieces of it, like a picture of a chair with a few strips erased.

Our ability to make these evidence-based, visual assumptions allows us to function in the physical world. Imagine if you couldn't identify a chair because a jacket was hung on the back of it. It also allows us to spot danger (a flash of snake scales in the grass) or advantage (a flash of fish scales in the water) more quickly. The ability to extrapolate general rules and concrete identifications without seeing or knowing everything confers major evolutionary advantages. That's why everything in competition plays this game.

The aptly named owl moth has dull brown and gray wings patterned like feathers. Each wing bears a large, striking bull's-eye in the center. And while their defensive lie is not as dazzling as the disappearing-reappearing blue morpho butterfly, it works just as well to keep them alive. Unlike the blue morpho's flashing defense, which fools the eyes and allows the butterfly to seem to vanish, the owl moth *wants* to be seen; its wings have evolved to fool the conscious mind by looking deceptively like the face and eyes of an owl. So much so that the animals that would otherwise feed on the moths are frightened away when they see them, having mistakenly extrapolated an entire owl from a pair of eyes.

The ability to see a piece (like eyes) and extrapolate a bigger picture (like a predator) is a crucial skill, but like every advantage, it's also a potential vulnerability. That ability allows us to lie and be lied to and is exploited by predator and prey alike. Some species use misleading evidence, real fake proof, to act as the aggressors, rather than for defensive obfuscation. The corpse flower, a carnivorous plant that smells like rotting garbage (it is not by any means rotting—the scent comes from several adapted chemical compounds produced by the flower, that when combined and gradually warmed on the flower's surface smell, among other things, like decaying meat), which conveniently draws flies and other scavengers looking for a meal to their own death. The scent is real, but it is not indicative of what it should have been. The scavengers caught by the corpse flower have fallen victim to an aromatic Bait and Switch.

Creatures like the owl moth or the corpse flower rely on sensory cues, like sight or scent, to manipulate a mark's expectations based on prior knowledge. Humans do the same thing, but our cons become somewhat more elaborate. Because, compared to most organisms, we have really big brains—and also have that honesty bias allowing us to share collective intelligence beyond individual capacity. And the more you know, the smarter you are—the more vulnerable you become to successfully extrapolating real fake proof into an incorrect bigger picture. Mark Twain put it best: "It ain't what you don't know that gets you into trouble. It's what you know for sure that just ain't so."[5]

Simple Stupid Coincidences

What finally brought Arnold's diamond con to light—as so often happens with the most elaborate and vast conspiracies and schemes—was just a simple, stupid coincidence. On October 6, 1872, that not-so-expert mining expert Henry Janin found himself on an Oaklandbound train with an actual geologist, a twenty-one-year-old kid named Clarence King who was out west leading an exploratory geographic survey of the fortieth parallel.

Maybe Janin was bored on the long ride, maybe he wanted to impress a real geologist, or maybe talking to a kid just made him less cautious than he should have been. In any case, at some point on the journey he started gossiping about the massive diamond field they had discovered in Colorado. He even took some rough crystals out of his bag and *showed* them to King and his survey team. One of King's surveyors, Samuel F. Emmons, wrote in his diary, "suspicious looking characters on the train are returning diamond hunters. Henry Janin showed us some of the diamonds."[6]

Janin's diamond field was clearly within the area King's team had just surveyed, which caused King to panic. In fact, it was alarming for his whole team. If they'd missed *diamond fields,* it was certainly grounds for Congress to declare them incompetent and defund their scientific survey mission, preventing them from continuing mapping the frontier. To cover their academic asses and protect their mandate, King and his team pieced together scraps of information from Janin's gossip, retraced his steps, and, to their credit, *found* the fake diamond field. Because they were real scientists.

Once they arrived at the location, it didn't take them long to inspect the area and realize that the ground had been salted with gems. The diamonds were neatly nestled with the rubies and emeralds at semiregular intervals, like prizes at the world's most glamorous Easter egg hunt. They all noted that the peculiar assortment of precious gems did not belong together. Diamonds are found in the remains of ancient kimberlite pipes—primordial volcanoes that long ago exploded.

Emeralds are found in greasy black shale, in areas where tall mountain ranges like the Andes or the Himalayas were forced upward eons ago. Rubies tend to occur in mountains, alongside marble or quartz. And garnets—which actually *are* often found in the United States—are never found buried in sand alongside other more exotic gemstones.

Even more obviously fraudulent: these deposits were only found in disturbed ground. When King and his team dug deeper trenches to better investigate these little jewel nests, they recovered no further evidence of gems. In fact, they found nothing at all once they dug more than a few inches into the ground. The jewels were only on the surface, or just barely half buried in loose, sandy ground, free from any rock matrix, which they should have been embedded in, or at least attached to. Finally, and most bizarrely, King found that a few of the diamonds bore *jewelers' cut marks*. It was clearly an elaborate scam.

And once King realized that, Boy Scout that he apparently was, he rushed back to camp and wrote a letter to his boss in Washington to try to stop the New York Mining and Commercial Company from selling any more soon-to-be-worthless stock. After that, he made the long journey to San Francisco to track down Henry Janin. When he found Janin, he spent the better part of an entire night explaining what they'd found, what was wrong with that picture, and what they'd concluded, until he'd "at last convinced him of its correctness."[7]

And that was the end of the New York Mining and Commercial Company, as well as a lot of the people involved—just not the ones you'd think. The big-money players mostly ended up just fine. Ralston, as the ringleader, lost a lot of investment money, including the half a million or more he had paid Arnold and Slack to go away. But for the most part, Tiffany's is still Tiffany's, and the *San Francisco Chronicle* reported extensively about "how the millionaires were victimized." When the fraud behind the New York Mining and Commercial Company was exposed, the subsequent collapse and scandal was so huge it both created and wiped out whole fortunes, careers, and other companies. And it took a few lives in the process. It made headlines across the world for several years.

So, though it's cold comfort, at least there's no way that the *exact same thing* would happen again.

Except of course it did. Frequently.

Stop Me If You've Heard This One

The largest gold-mining scam in the history of the world went down quite recently—about a decade ago. It was just a more modern version of the same old con, but this time a shady prospector named Michael de Guzman used a gold wedding ring to fake the existence of six billion dollars' worth of gold in a mine that didn't exist in the jungles of Borneo. Everyone from Lehman Brothers to the government of Indonesia fell for it, and when the Bait and Switch was finally exposed, it was a multibillion-dollar scandal.[8]

In 1994 Michael de Guzman claimed he'd found gold. His partner, "explorer/geologist" John Felderhof, decided to find them an investor (much like William Ralston) "who had a hunger for risk and wasn't going to be asking questions."[9] They found that investor in a Canadian businessman named David Walsh, the owner of a Canadian penny-stock mining company called Bre-X. After convincing Walsh to back their venture, Felderhof advised Bre-X to buy the mining rights to the entire region of Borneo. Felderhof made this wild recommendation to Bre-X based entirely on samples from the mine that he received from Guzman, which seemed to be filled with gold. They even passed an independent lab inspection.[10]

The problem was that Guzman was producing "crushed core" samples from the mine, meaning a lot of broken, mixed-up rock and earth, which are used to assess the general composition of the ground in an area and project the presence and quantity of anything valuable. In other words, to take a small portion and extrapolate a larger whole. Crushed-core samples are a very legitimate way of assaying a potential mine. But Guzman was cheating. After the samples were crushed up, he used a tiny file and flaked gold dust from his own wedding ring into the small samples, salting them, to make it appear as though the samples themselves came from earth rich in native gold deposits. The only reason the samples passed inspection was that the lab, just like Henry Janin, lacked the context to draw an accurate conclusion. They were looking for gold particles, saw gold, and said, "Yes, I see gold particles. There's definitely gold in this sample."

Which was technically true. But still incorrect. As soon as they got formal confirmation they could use from the lab, Guzman, Felderhof, and Walsh collectively sold off a portion of their stock in Bre-X for around one hundred million dollars—which doesn't exactly scream innocence—but investors were too excited about the money to look closer.

In 1994 Felderhof initially projected there might be 136,000 pounds of gold in the area, but within a year the estimates had been revised to one million pounds. As the estimates grew ever larger, the stock price just kept climbing, and Guzman just kept salting the samples as new assays were required. And just as Arnold bought more diamonds in London, Guzman spent the next two and a half years paying locals for gold flake to add to the crushed-core samples, because eventually you run out of wedding ring. But fraud can be a delicate craft, and Guzman salted a little too much.

By 1997 the projected volume of gold had reached five million pounds, making it the largest gold deposit ever purchased. The final estimate given to JP Morgan was thirteen million pounds of gold. By this point, though there was still no actual mine, an entire mining town—replete with homes and a church—had already sprung up around where it would or should be, and Lehman Brothers was freaking out about the "gold discovery of the century."[11]

As soon as the banks got involved, the sums of money ballooned so rapidly that the mine attracted all sorts of attention, including the attention of other grifters. In 1996, as Bre-X stock was rising faster than the gold parts per million in their core samples, the Indonesian government demanded to be cut in.* President Suharto slammed the brakes on the whole enterprise by revoking Bre-X's exploration permits, claiming "red tape." It was the kind of red tape that can only be cut by green paper, so a deal was eventually worked out with Suharto that split the gold proceeds between Bre-X, their investors, and "Indonesia." The deal with Suharto, finalized in February 1997, left Bre-X with only 45 percent control of the mine and new problematic partners.[12] Both factors caused the stock to take a tumble, but mostly the part where the extremely corrupt president of Indonesia suddenly owned controlling interest.

That's when the whole con fell apart, fast. To boost the stock price, Guzman upped the gold content of the samples even higher. Which

---

*They didn't really have any valid reason to be cut in, but kleptocrats gonna klepto, I guess.

worked, in the sense that the price skyrocketed still higher, but there was still no gold mine. And with Suharto satisfied and Bre-X's permits restored and all the grifters more or less copacetic (or at least resigned) about their cut, it was time to actually *start mining* the gold. But Bre-X, a small company, wasn't really capable of a mining endeavor on that scale, and their partners—unaware that Guzman had been salting the samples for years—insisted on involving another party. A second, larger mining company, Freeport-McMoran Copper & Gold, was brought in to do the actual work.[13] As soon as the bigger company got there and tried to, you know, *mine* . . . they quickly realized that there was never any gold at all.

Guzman, Felderhof, and Walsh ended up in remarkably the same positions as Slack, Arnold, and Ralston. Michael de Guzman was found dead in the jungle about a month after the deal was formalized with Suharto. Supposedly, he was so upset about the fraud he had perpetrated that he threw himself out of a helicopter in midair, on his way to meet with his partners.* John Felderhof was acquitted of insider trading, despite selling over eighty thousand dollars' worth of his Bre-X stock just a few months before the fraud was exposed. I guess just to be safe, he moved to the Cayman Islands, which may or may not be nicer than Kentucky, but *does* conveniently lack an extradition treaty with Canada where financial crimes are concerned. He lived out his life there with his new wife and family until he died quite recently.

The similarities don't end there. For his part, Walsh claimed to know absolutely nothing about the scam, despite being in it from

---

*Clearly scamming the Indonesian government is worse for your long-term prospects than conning Wall Street.

nearly the start. He moved to the Bahamas and died of a heart attack two years later.[14] Bre-X declared bankruptcy and folded in 2002
without ever being held accountable for so much as negligence. The
banks were fine, of course—never even blamed, really—and the corrupt government officials slinked away and continued to do whatever
it is they do.

Gold Bricks and Mortar

We just keep falling for the same gold brick, over and over. And *knowing that* makes no difference, because a Bait and Switch exploits what
you already (think) you know, so the smarter you are, the bigger your
blind spot. In fact, the twenty-first-century global economy was arguably laid low by the same gold-rush swindle when the 2008 banking
crisis began with mortgage-backed securities and turned into the subprime debt crisis.

The housing market of the early 2000s was a lot like the gold
rush. The conditions were just right, coming off a decade of economic
growth, so that everybody felt a little rich—and therefore, behavioral
economists would tell us, morally impaired (but we'll come back to
that). There seemed to be money and opportunity everywhere, and
this led to a fair amount of magical thinking. More important, property
values were genuinely going up and up, without signs of slowing. This
made it a great time to buy a home—interest rates on mortgage loans
were low—and a great time for banks to lend, because who cares if that
guy defaults on his mortgage next year? We get to keep the house and
it'll be worth twice as much! These two lines of reasoning led lots of
people, both those who could and those who could not afford one, to
get a mortgage—and lots of banks to sign off on them.

These conditions made for two kinds of mortgages: prime and sub-prime. If you could afford your mortgage and would probably make the payments, you were prime. If you couldn't, if you had bad credit or no job and would probably default, you were subprime. But property values just kept going up, which made all the properties, even those houses belonging to subprime borrowers, worth more every month; and that's tempting. So on top of borrowing to buy a house, a lot of people took *second* (or third, or fourth) *mortgages* on their original collateral—the first and not-yet-paid-for property, making even the prime loans into subprime loans. And it's worth mentioning that a lot of these subprime mortgages carried variable interest rates that escalated from standard to crushing: a Bait and Switch in itself.

In fact, almost *every* part of that story could be considered a modern Bait and Switch, not just the interest-rate come-on, but let's think bigger. In the same way Philip Arnold salted worthless ground with diamonds to create the illusion of a valuable asset, the banks holding these mortgages combined them, good and bad (and really, really bad), into mortgage-backed securities. Mortgage-backed securities were bonds that the banks sold to investors. The MBS were supposed to be composed of mostly excellent loans, with a few subprime loans mixed in, but in reality the MBSs were mostly filled with really garbage loans (the subprime ones) and just enough diamonds to get a sparkly rating from the necessary credit rating agency.

They basically put these mortgages, good and bad, into a blender—metaphorically speaking. What they had were *representative samples,* like Guzman's crushed-core samples—the very few prime loans were sprinkled into a lot of junk loans, just like his gold flakes were sprinkled into the crushed-core samples, thus misrepresenting the larger pool's value. Alfred Lord Tennyson famously said that "a lie which is half a truth is ever the blackest of lies," and that may or may not be true—but it's also the most effective lie. Ironically, the *factual* information was there all along, just like Arnold's diamond field or Guzman's gold mine, but at the time no one ever bothered looking into it, in part because we are designed to extrapolate a whole picture from a small sample and in part because confirmation bias makes us see what we are already primed to believe.

The banks took these MBSs and sold them as low-risk, high-reward investments to investors—people, businesses, and institutions—all over the world for many years. The fraud wasn't exposed until the unthinkable happened and the value of property started to go down. When it did, individual people started defaulting on their individual mortgages. When enough people defaulted on their loans, the mortgage-backed securities became worthless, and suddenly everyone could see—that there had never been anything there at all.

Because America

It's hard to feel bad for anyone in the story of the Philip Arnold diamond swindle. Arnold and Slack bought some uncut diamonds, salted a barren strip of land, and conned the founder of the Bank of California into thinking they were dimwitted prospectors sitting on a fortune. That banker and his sleazy financier friend fell for it, then tried to con the prospectors out of their diamond mine. The former general / current congressman wasn't a professional con man, per se, but he was in Congress, and he did make a lot of money unethically, if not illegally, greasing the skids for the rest of them to privately mine diamonds on federal land. Then there was Tiffany, whose job it was to authenticate the diamonds, which sounds pretty legit . . . until you consider the fact it was also his job to then *price* the diamonds, and to *both buy and sell* the diamonds. At which point, his participation starts to look like a pretty neat vertical monopoly.

Everyone involved in the Philip Arnold diamond swindle was working somebody, and when you read it straight through, the whole thing is pretty transparently bonkers. Which raises the obvious question: Why did *any* of them buy this horseshit? Greed, it turns out, is confusing, and money messes with your mind—literally.

Just the specter of it impairs our judgment and rational thought. A recent experiment using fake cash—participants played a game with something akin to Monopoly money—showed that even subtle reminders of wealth enhanced the subjects' tendencies toward personal agency, as expected, but also evoked unreasonable emotional responses.[15] Once in contest with one another, even in a simple game, we become hyperaggressive. Instead of prompting us to be our most cautious (or even most calculating) selves, exposure to money "does the opposite, leading to druglike mental states and irrational choices."[16] In other words, just thinking about wealth, even in the abstract, is enough to kneecap our thought process and make us behave irrationally.

Money also impairs our *moral* judgment. Researchers at Harvard ran an experiment in which subjects played a series of games. But before they played, half the players were unwittingly exposed to money-related words—like bank, diamond, investor—while the other half were not. When they subsequently played the games, the players exposed to money-related words—having been subtly primed to think about wealth—were more likely to lie or cheat.[17] It seems as though the more directly exposed we are to money, wealth, or reminders of same, the more narrowly our own thought process is whittled down to a sort of zero-sum ethics.

And it cuts both ways: thinking about a lack of money is just as mind-altering as thinking about excess. Another study measured the cognitive function of a group of farmers both before and after a harvest—that is, when they were at their least and most financially secure, respectively.[18] It turns out that a lack of adequate resources proves *measurably* cognitively taxing. The results showed that on average, a participant's individual IQ score was nine to ten points *lower* right before harvest (when they were broke) than it was right after harvest (when they were flush again). To be clear: they *did not* actually gain IQ points when they got paid, because you can't buy extra IQ points with money (unless you pay someone else to take your test), but you *can temporarily lose them* to exhaustion, distraction, and anxiety. And that's *exactly* what happened; those nine or ten points missing from each participant's IQ *before harvest* are approximately the same temporary net loss you see in a person's score when they're forced to stay awake all night before a test and are subsequently too tired to think straight the next day. Anxiety of any kind, including economic, is as cognitively taxing as sleep deprivation. Ease that anxiety, and evidently you free up cognitive ability.

And it's not only your IQ that's impaired by material concerns: your EQ suffers as well. A series of UCSF studies asked hundreds of participants to analyze the facial expressions of strangers in photos. The results showed a striking correlation: the wealthier the participants were, the less able they were to read those faces or to judge their intent.[19] Stranger still, when coached to merely *imagine* being in a less financially and socially secure position, those same participants became more adept at detecting and deciphering other people's emotions and intent. It appears that wealth and power—or even just imagining one possesses it—temporarily diminish one's theory of mind and ability to successfully mentalize—that is, to think about what someone else is thinking.

Another experiment, using completely different methods, showed the same outcome: that power impairs your theory of mind. In that study, participants were asked to write for five minutes about a situation in which they felt powerful; other participants were asked to write for five minutes about a situation in which they felt powerless. Meanwhile, candy was handed out to the subjects as they wrote. The subjects who were asked to write about feeling powerful were given candy to keep and/or hand out as they pleased, whereas the other group could only *ask* the first group members for some of the candy and hope they got some. At the end of the exercise, all the participants were asked to quickly snap their fingers five times and write the letter E on their foreheads. The subjects primed to feel powerless—through written memory and unfair candy distribution—*were three time more likely* to write the letter backward on their own head—so that others could read it.[20]

So, greed impairs your reason, judgment, and moral compass, while thoughts of wealth or power diminish your theory of mind, and excessive anxiety about money can actually (temporarily) knock ten points off your IQ—and that's just one person, in a vacuum. Add a second person and you have competition, which induces extreme aggression and irrational behavior. More unsettling still, it *doesn't matter* whether you're winning or losing that contest—because both scenarios fundamentally undermine your ability to think clearly, particularly about what might or might not be true. Now, how did all of these people in the middle of the gold rush, frothing at the mouth over giant piles of diamonds and gems, simultaneously scheming to cheat one another out of an untold fortune in jewels, fail to notice one another's fairly transparent prevarications? Got me . . .

There's also the fact that they were all actively lying to each other, which—frighteningly enough—diminishes our ability to even *believe the truth we already know.*

According to the National Institutes of Health, lying actually alters your memory. Danielle Polage, a psychology professor at Washington University specializing in memory research, conducted a sweeping study into the effects of telling a lie versus just planning a lie on our subsequent belief in the truth. She wanted to know if you have to actually *tell* the lie or if conceiving of it is adequate. Turns out, you have to tell a lie in order to believe it—and, in fact, once you *have* told it, it permanently alters your feelings about the truth. In her own words, "the intentionally deceptive component of lying, not just the creation of the lie, affects belief in the lie. These results suggest that belief change may occur as a result of a deliberate lie, and that liars become less confident in the truth after lying."[21] That's a remarkable statement. We can prime ourselves to believe all sorts of things, all sorts of ways, but apparently we can also prime ourselves simply through the *act of lying* to "become less confident in the truth."

So, the only thing more confusing than money, the lack of money, or feelings about money is *competition* over money. *Also, making shit up actually rewrites your memory of the truth.* And everyone involved in the Philip Arnold diamond swindle was conning someone—inciting them to be increasingly dishonest while throwing them all into *heated competition* with each other (even as they each believed they were the only operator). This no doubt had the effect of making everyone involved in the scam—and each and every one of them *was running their own scam*—a little less than clearheaded.

And, in fact, in the larger context of that era, almost everybody was running some sort of racket.

When noted behavioral economist Oscar Wilde pointed out that "America is the only country that went from barbarism to decadence without civilization in between,"[22] he had a point. Throughout the nineteenth century, the country was rife with cons of every sort, particularly mining swindles. That era, more than almost any other, really doubled down on the mirage of America. It was the flip side of the railroad, oil, and gold fortunes being genuinely made overnight: the land of opportunity was by necessity also the land of magical thinking. This made almost everyone susceptible to being conned.

To some degree, it still does.

It's said that the best place to hide a lie is in between two truths, which is not just the essence of the Bait and Switch, it might be the story of America itself. It was the American dream (really American delusion) that you could be or have or do anything. And all it would cost is everything you ever had. Your history, your home, your family—sometimes even your name. If you were willing, you could trade away everything you had in the past for anything you wanted in the future. It was implicit in that promise that we were willing to believe fantastical things, no matter how unreasonable. Americans, particularly in the nineteenth century, were especially primed to see opportunity everywhere and believe their eyes when shown diamonds and jewels lying on the ground.

Now, if you were watching closely, you might have noticed that we've slipped over from talking about how we use priming (one of the practical mechanisms of deceit) to tell a lie, to how priming itself (one of the practical mechanisms of belief) might also be part of what *makes us lie in the first place,* and finally to the idea that what primes us to believe and what primes us to lie are one and the same. If you caught that sleight of hand, good for you. But don't jump ahead; I'm just priming you to hear next about the fundamental connection between deception and belief.

We can lie only because we believe. And just as teeth beget scales, as soon as we believe . . . we begin to lie. It is obvious that the lies we tell each other are inextricably bound up in the lies we tell ourselves; particularly the first and most central lies, about the nature of truth and our physical and cognitive capacity to even evaluate it.

Without that one Big Lie, we couldn't believe anything at all.

Faith, Fraud, and the Funny Thing About Belief

Only one deception is possible in the infinite sense, self-deception.
—SØREN KIERKEGAARD

My fake plants died because I did not pretend to water them.
—MITCH HEDBERG

THE FUNNY THING ABOUT BELIEF IS THAT IT CUTS BOTH WAYS. We've all heard that seeing is believing. Why else would anyone ever demand to see proof of a claim, let alone fall for a card trick? But just as surely as your senses can fail you, so can your sensibilities. And just as often as seeing is believing, *believing is seeing*.

Whether we are subject to the placebo effect, led astray by our own greed, or taken in by the reassuring promises of one who can help or save us—once you've convinced yourself of the truth of a lie, you may find the lie starts to function like fact. These next chapters explore how and why we come to believe and whether it's possible to reverse our capacity for self-deception by examining three very old cons and their very contemporary counterparts.

In the first chapter, we'll look at the impact and influence of the Guru Con, which exploits the softest of human weak spots—emotional need. From Rasputin to Steve Bannon, from Jim Bakker to Joel Osteen—there have always been, and will always be, willing sheep ready to be sheared . . . in exchange for promises of all kinds, particularly the intangible. It seems that to the right crowd (and we're *all* the right crowd), hope is a commodity you can sell for almost any price.

Next, in chapter five, we'll look at the expansive history of the selling of Snake Oil, which started as a railroad hustle in the Wild West, launched the craze for so-called patent medicines, and ended in a Victorian opioid epidemic. The newly minted FDA and its subsequent crackdown was intended to protect us but, instead, led us in a blindfolded circle through the "wellness" industry, new-age medicine, and finally right back into the opium den of prescription drugs. Is the story of Snake Oil really about gullibility, or does the strange science of placebos tell us more about the biology of belief than we realize?

Last, in chapter six we'll look at Pyramid Schemes—from Bernie Madoff to Bitcoin—which have the unique power to be utterly transparent and still totally effective. Is it because the real trick is just tricking you into thinking that you got in on the ground floor of what you know is almost certainly a scam, or because you don't always see a familiar institution for what it is? Or could it be that Pyramids are so ubiquitous that the better part of civilization is built upon them?

You see, there's a trick to belief: *you have to want it*. Because at the heart of any belief lie not just cognitive shortcuts, but emotional ones. Whether it's fact or falsehood, demonstration or deception, wildly improbable or reasonably plausible, mostly people simply believe what they *want* to believe. The truth is that belief shapes our lived reality as often as our lived reality shapes our belief.

To what degree are we lied to, and to what degree do we allow ourselves to be lied to? How much of an agent are we in our own manipulation? This second part, Lies We Tell Ourselves, explores the biology of belief and the effect of consensus and confirmation. Somewhere in the tiny but devastating difference between truth and fact is the answer to the question *Why do we believe?*

HOLY SHIT

Charlatans and Other
Authority Figures

When you choose your holy man, you surrender your will.
—FYODOR DOSTOYEVSKY

I'm not a businessman. I'm a *business*, man.
—JAY-Z

THE GURU

The Guru Con is by far the most mean-spirited con. It preys not on ambition and hope, but on their emotional opposites: fear, desperation, and unhappiness. The Guru claims to possess some special knowledge, authority, or power to help, protect, absolve, or guarantee happiness or success.

And all it costs? Blind loyalty, absolute devotion, and unquestioning faith in and adherence to whatever code of conduct the Guru mandates.

And, of course, *money*.

Mean Spirits

The specifics of the Guru Con vary depending on the circumstances of the grift and the medium in which it works. It may take the form of Ouija boards, psychics, fortune-tellers, spiritualists, televangelists, or cultists, but all have the same foundation: the promise of special knowledge or divine ability, wisdom and authority that defies rational understanding and thus, conveniently, defies the need for rational proof.

Its targets become totally dependent on the Guru, and in a vicious little circle, their belief in that reliance makes them believe, increasingly, *on* their own reliance. The more they believe, the more they have to continue to believe; otherwise, their whole worldview is at risk of coming apart.

The Guru Con demonstrates the often tragic impact when two of our cognitive traits work in tandem: the ability to suspend our disbelief (and, in fact, our natural proclivity to do so) and the urgent desire to avoid *cognitive dissonance,* or the collision of our emotional beliefs with our rational ones.

Overkill

If you know only one story about "the mad monk" Rasputin, the peasant holy man and Svengali of the Romanov court, it's most likely the story of how he was killed—or failed to be killed, according to legend.[1] In 1916, a group of Russian aristocrats led by Tsar Nicholas's brother-in-law, Prince Felix Yusupov, tried to murder Rasputin. First, they fed him huge amounts of food and wine doped with cyanide. As he gorged himself and the night wore on, the conspirators began to fear that he was protected from the poison by some dark magic. So they just shot him.

According to Yusupov's later account, they thought they'd left Rasputin dead in the basement, when a few hours later he seemed to come back to life. He stood back up, to their horror, and fled across the palace courtyard, where they shot him again. As dawn neared, they inspected the body to find him still alive, dazed but conscious. At that point, the panicked would-be murderers set upon Rasputin en masse, repeatedly stabbing and bludgeoning him, and yet the terrifying mystic refused to die. Finally, they dragged him to the Neva River, where they dumped him. When his corpse was eventually found, the lungs were full of water, suggesting his actual cause of death was drowning.

Spooky.

But how did the most famous monk in Russia, and the most influential man in the Romanov court, end up frozen in ice, in the Neva River, rope around his neck, stabbed, shot, and beaten to a pulp with a bellyful of cyanide? Outside of a Dan Brown novel, who stages a coup to assassinate a monk? Beyond its being a bit much, don't most corrupt clergy just die from gout? Why so much drama?

Rasputin, of course, wasn't just a monk. Actually, he wasn't a monk at all. He may or may not have been sincere in his bizarre beliefs, and he even may or may not have been an actual psychic. But one thing he definitely was—*a hustler*. And an ambitious one. He ended up in that icy river a decade into running a failed Guru Con on the Russian royal family.

Or, perhaps, just an overly successful one.

The Mad Monk

Grigory Yefimovich Rasputin was born in 1869, in the very ordinary Siberian village of Pokrovskoye, where he grew up in a very ordinary peasant family. At eighteen he married a woman named

Praskovya Dubrovina and had three children: Maria, Dimitri, and Varvara. He worked on his family's farm. He was a drunk and a letch, and occasionally in trouble with the authorities. But not that much trouble, probably owing to his strange personal charm and powerful natural charisma. He didn't make a big name for himself, either as a holy man or a con man, until he came to the attention of Tsarina Alexandra, the wife of the last Romanov tsar and the mother of the fatally ill male heir, Tsarevich Alexei.

Later retellings would claim that by the time Rasputin was twelve, his "mystical gifts" were evident—in the form of vague prophecies, healing prayers, and (my personal favorite) adamant tales of how the family cows produced more milk when he was around—although, of course, people tend to remember these things differently and more dramatically after the fact. This is known as the false-memory effect, and it is the cornerstone of (fake) mystical experiences. We'll be coming back to it.

Tsarina Alexandra believed every word Rasputin said and became increasingly certain that only he could save Alexei. This irrational belief—Alexandra's misplaced faith in Rasputin—would be not only her own undoing but also her family's and her country's as well. It would have more impact on world history than anything else she, her husband, or any other Romanov ever did. Such is the power, and horror, of genuine faith: we believe what we believe, not for any rational reason, but simply because we need it to be true. And in the process, we fail to see what's right in front of us.

One image of Rasputin that was consistent throughout his lifetime, long before he achieved fame and fortune (and a cult-like following, complete with a harem of women) as the tsarina's closest confidant, spiritual adviser, and all-purpose magical BFF, was that of an outrageously drunken, outlandishly hedonistic young man known for lying, stealing, womanizing, and generally unholy behavior.

He was also noted for his genuinely hideous appearance and personal hygiene, or lack of it. He cut a remarkable figure, given his massive size. His long, dirty, tangled black hair and his beard didn't do enough to cover a genuinely frightening face that included a broken nose, rotten teeth, and cartoonish, demonic eyebrows over his most famous feature: pale, mesmeric eyes, featuring pupils he could allegedly contract and expand at will. He actually seemed to take pride in his disgusting appearance—once returning from a pilgrimage having gone six months without changing his clothes. One man claimed he smelled like a goat.

So what exactly made him so irresistible, let alone able to claim spiritual authority?

The answer lay in an apostate sect within the Russian Orthodox Church that believed, conveniently enough, that the only way to reach God was through great sin.* Just like that, Rasputin had found his people. He never took holy orders—probably because he was a married man with three children—but after spending a while at the monastery, he began wearing the robes of a monk. Preaching that "without sin, there is no repentance,"[2] he wandered the country, sinning everybody's brains out. In fact, he claimed that he could take on the sins of women (hot ones, anyway) by sleeping with them, thereby supposedly helping them find the "grace of God." Essentially, sex with him was an act of religious purification.

---

*Which is just so Russian . . .

Of course, cult leaders from time immemorial have used this line in every language.

The history of the twentieth century might have unfolded very differently had Rasputin stayed in the sticks, seducing country girls and grifting other peasants. But he didn't. He moved to Saint Petersburg. Once there, he quickly caught the eye of the Grand Duchess Militza, Tsarina Alexandra's cousin, when he publicly proclaimed in a *sort of* church service in 1903 that the tsarina—who was getting old and already had four daughters—would finally give birth to a son.[3] He even put an expiration date on his prophecy: the child would be born within a year.

And then in 1904, against all odds, he was!

Not long afterward, Alexei, the infant heir to the doomed Romanov throne, was diagnosed with "the royal bleeding disease," or, as we know it, hemophilia. In the early 1900s, hemophilia was essentially a death sentence, and as such Alexei's medical condition was a closely guarded secret. Alexandra, who'd been really tightly wound to begin with, became prone to alternating episodes of hysteria and despair. Increasingly desperate, she lost faith in doctors completely and began looking for a spiritual solution. In other words, Alexandra was ripe for a con. And unfortunately for her, cousin Militza was a moron. Not for being vaguely impressed by Rasputin's prediction—it was vaguely impressive. But Militza sort of collected holy men, as well as fake mediums, pseudo-psychics and so-called mystics, which were all the rage among the aristocracy of the time.

Worse? She liked to introduce them to her cousin.

You might expect that Rasputin's generally revolting appearance and behavior would have been off-putting to the overly precious tsarina.

But actually, like her cousin Militza, Alexandra was also very into fake holy men. That, combined with her isolation and desperation over her sick child, and maybe also a weird, faux-humble reverence for peasantry that was very much in fashion, made for an instant fascination when the grand duchess introduced Rasputin and Alexandra.[4]

Rasputin had already found success in the capital, in the form of recognition and a small but devout following. Once the grand duchess had him summoned to appear before Alexandra, he was in the big leagues. He quickly insinuated himself with the royal family and began to move in Saint Petersburg's aristocratic circles, all the while maintaining his man-of-the-people shtick, from illiteracy to eating with his hands. He even referred to the tsar and tsarina as "Mama" and "Papa." Undoubtedly the royal couple felt really cool having their very own, salt-of-the-earth, peasant holy man—complete with magic powers.

He may or may not have been an actual psychic, but either way he put on a pretty convincing show. Alexandra was sold. And what really sealed the deal? Alexei fell down while playing one day and nearly bled to death. Somehow, Rasputin succeeded in stopping the bleeding, after which he earned Nicholas's goodwill and Alexandra's unwavering devotion. The story goes that he came to the room and put his hand on the kid's forehead and then kneeled by the bed and prayed for quite a long time, and as he did so, the bleeding gradually stopped.[5] As magic tricks go, that's pretty damn good. It was hailed as a miracle and cemented his mystical reputation *beyond question*.

Except for the *obvious* question: Ruling out the actually miraculous, how'd he do it?

Vague Miracles

There were witnesses, so it's not an exaggerated myth that's developed, and the kid lived, so it wasn't just a temporary illusion or a trick. The most likely scientific answer is a little boring, as scientific answers tend to be.* He probably just calmed the terrified little boy down with his presence—the implicit promise that all would be fine, now that he and his big magic were here—which would have slowed his pulse and dropped his blood pressure, mechanically slowing down the bleeding. That could have given even a hemophiliac the extra time necessary to form a clot. But for it to work, for him to go from the terror of imminent death to so calm his pulse was barely ticking, would require a powerful sedative.

Have you ever heard of the placebo effect? We'll talk more about it in chapter five, but in short: if you believe strongly enough that something is physically affecting you, often the actual chemistry of your body is altered as though it really were. Can the placebo effect be a powerful enough cure or temporarily reduce the effects of seemingly irreversible conditions? Indeed, it can. Legitimately healing yourself is not as common as simply feeling better, and far harder to explain. But the ability of the body to heal in response to a major, forceful belief that it will be healed—be that by a drug or a miracle—is just a more exaggerated form of placebo effect. And it is very real, if unusual and barely understood.

Because they're so susceptible to suggestion, people searching for imaginary cures are already more primed to believe in them. And

---

*Except when they're not. In that case, they tend to lean toward the horrific. We're gonna talk about a few of those scientific answers as well.

fervent belief and desperate need are a natural resource that Gurus and faith healers have been exploiting forever. Remember, these are the lies we tell *ourselves*: as such, the Guru isn't really working as hard as you'd imagine to make their interventions appear miraculous. The mark is doing all the belief-based heavy lifting. The Guru just frames things in a way that helps them believe whatever it is that they already want to believe. That's the whole trick. The fact that Alexei and those around him were so certain Rasputin could effect a magical cure may have actually affected its own cure.

On second thought . . . that is vaguely miraculous.

Cult Leaders and Cognitive Dissonance

Within a few years, Rasputin was giving more than spiritual counsel; he was giving political advice and recommending individuals for advancement or ruin. All based on his infallible psychic ability, of course. As the mad monk's star rose with the Romanovs, so, too, did it rise in Saint Petersburg. His small following became massive. Crowds, hundreds deep, wrapped around his home, waiting to see him, touch him, potentially be healed by him, and leave flowers or gifts. Or, in some cases, they sought to directly bribe him for a political favor, as he had not only the tsarina's ear, but her heart and mind as well. By 1911 a number of high government positions had been filled by his appointees. The situation gave him enormous influence over matters of state,[6] in addition to the personal control he already exerted over the tsarina. His corruption, financial and political, was becoming as well known among his ever-increasing number of enemies, as were his drunkenness and extreme debauchery—which were already legend.

The aristocracy did not care for this situation.

As increasingly obscene rumors began to spread about Alexandra's alleged sexual relationship with Rasputin (she didn't have one), both her and her husband's public credibility were radically diminished.[7] Rasputin, filthy and lecherous and wasted as ever, but now drunk with power as well, actually began to brag loudly and publicly of these very rumors. During one of his drunken nights carousing, he exposed himself to an entire restaurant and described his liaisons with both the tsarina and her daughters. What's really remarkable is that when Alexandra was told of the event, in detail, by numerous witnesses, she *refused to believe it*. In a spectacular display of denial, first she claimed it was a pernicious lie. As others in her circle confirmed the story, she softened her position to "a mistake."[8] As more and more acquaintances confirmed that the humiliating episode *had* in fact occurred, she suddenly had an epiphany. It was so obvious: someone was clearly impersonating Rasputin! Someone who looked *just like him* was running around Saint Petersburg drinking, lying, and behaving appallingly, all in order to damage Rasputin's reputation. Having arrived at what she felt was this perfectly obvious, and absolutely satisfactory explanation, she would hear no more about it.

As things got worse for the Romanovs, both politically and personally, Alexandra grew more and more dependent on Rasputin. She believed everything he told her—no matter how far-fetched, ill-advised, or brazenly self-serving—because she *had to*; if some of it was bullshit, she would be forced to reconcile that with the possibility that *all* of it was bullshit—including things that she needed to continue believing in order to function. Like the notion that he and he alone could save her dying son. This state of mental conflict in which a person must consciously accommodate two mutually incompatible beliefs is called cognitive dissonance. I mentioned it earlier in regard to the Big Lie: when two ideas or beliefs are in conflict—one of them has to go in the idea shredder. The state is usually triggered by a situation in which a person is presented with new evidence that directly contradicts not an opinion or a misapprehension, but a core belief.

Humans will do almost anything to avoid this mental discomfort—*not by revising their beliefs, but by ignoring or dismissing or destroying any evidence that controverts it*. This act is called motivated reasoning. Alexandra's extreme dependence on Rasputin both drove her to believe everything he told her and simultaneously explains *how* she managed to believe everything he told her. Of course, she was neurotic to begin with and desperate over her dying child; and Rasputin was *her* personal cult leader, he devoted a lot of time to it. But what about everyone else?

How to Start a Cult

How *did* Rasputin convince a handful of otherwise rational people that he had magical powers?

Well, I'd recommend *not* opening with "Hi, I'm a psychic." You can't just present someone with a lie. In the absence of proof of a specific claim, particularly a false one, you have to give people a general framework in which to believe you. Rasputin presented himself as a simple Siberian peasant and a sort of wandering holy man. This was maintained in the vaguest terms possible, probably because he never had any affiliation with the Russian Orthodox Church.[9] Gurus, whether they're fake men of God or fake men of science, are never actually a valid member in good standing of the field they claim not only to represent but also to surpass; it's one of the first tells of a Guru.

No matter who you are, if you say that you're a holy man,* the next reasonable response for the person you've just told is to question, however briefly, if that's actually true. If you call yourself nothing but act somehow in the way they would expect a holy man to act and wait to be called one, then you've made no claim, no obfuscations or omissions—and so there's no room in the transaction for their doubt. It's merely lying by insinuation.

Seeming to stop a hemophiliac from bleeding out is pretty compelling, but Rasputin was well in the tsar and tsarina's confidence by then. And for the most part, how he had gotten there had nothing to do with mystical powers. Long before he was performing miracles or delivering prophecies in a weird trancelike state, he was using intense charisma and weaponized empathy, like any con man worth his salt, to intuit their hopes and their fears and to deduce exactly what either wanted or needed to hear. Early on, in 1906, Nicholas wrote to one of his ministers: "A few days ago I received a peasant from the Tobolsk district, Grigori Rasputin, who brought me an icon. . . . He made a remarkably strong impression both on Her Majesty and on myself, so that instead of five minutes our conversation went on for more than an hour."[10]

This conversation, or protracted grift, would go on for over a decade. And though his act was both perfectly chic in 1906 Saint Petersburg and expertly tailored for the nervous, paranoid, isolated, and coincidentally occult-obsessed royal couple, what really cemented his grip on their faith was a trick everyone has used: he told them what they wanted to hear. He told spineless Nicholas whatever would make

---

*Or anything else for that matter: a doctor, a Canadian, an alien passing for human, a mournful Victorian ghost . . .

him feel more confident; he told Alexandra just the right things to constantly soothe her relentless anxiety. This is important: it's not about sucking up; it's about setting a baseline for reality. By telling them exactly what they wanted to hear—in essence, what they most needed to believe was true, however far-fetched—he *established a basis for being believed,* however fantastic his future claims.

When it comes to the metaphysical, from horoscopes to cult leaders, it's clear once again that believing is seeing more often than seeing is believing. Once an individual wants to believe something—or worse, actually does believe that thing—he or she will look for evidence that it's true and just as surely dismiss any evidence that they happen upon to the contrary. Confirmation bias is that simple. But things get weirder with nonrational belief. Once people feel permission to believe this absurd thing, they will not only see proof of it, they will actually alter the record of events that is their memory to conform with that belief. This strange phenomenon is known as the false-memory effect.

Fortune-tellers, Faith Healers, and the False-Memory Effect

The false-memory effect involves the ability to remember a scenario in which there's room for great doubt, and rather than engage that doubt, to simply airbrush that ambiguity away in a fascinating method of memory adjustment. This is how lies based in nonrational belief, from superstitions to religions, function.

Fraudulent mediums and fortune-tellers exploit this tendency all the time. Go to a tarot card reader or get your palm read: you can watch how they maneuver their way around the big void that is their actual knowledge of whatever you came to hear. First, they play warmer/colder, throwing out statements that sound specific but really could apply to anyone or any situation. Things like "Sometimes you feel alone," or "You've lost something," or "The thing you're waiting for is already happening; you just can't see it yet."

The tendency to believe that these statements are not only true but specific to the listener is called the Barnum effect. This was originally called the Forer effect, but in 1956 it was appropriately renamed in honor of the self-styled greatest showman on earth, P. T. Barnum, when psychologist Paul Meehl noticed how similar the statements being used in the Forer study were to Barnum's own on-stage act. Believing that any of the given Barnum statements specifically apply to you is the basis of how horoscopes work, on the people on whom they work. And apparently some people are naturally more predisposed to see these deliberately vague statements as unambiguous and moreover specific to them. These are also the same people who read their horoscope and like having their fortunes told, so that works out really neatly for the con and the mark.

As these Barnum statements are made, the fake psychic or medium waits to see which ones land, eliciting an emotional reaction, however small—and then works that angle by adding in questions. They're basically playing psychological battleship with you, keeping track of hits and misses. The questions are really more like subject suggestions (love, money, death, career) that the psychic can lean into or away from based on your response. When mediums or clairvoyants do it, it's called a cold reading, but it's really just a fishing expedition.

They ask questions—always in the form of a statement—that will be true no matter what, like "You miss someone" (because everybody does) or "You've been treated unfairly" (who hasn't?). Then they gauge your reaction to each Barnum statement to figure out why you came.

And half the time, you just blurt it out. No one responds to "Something big is happening soon" with a shrug. They answer, "I'm getting married!" or "I think I'm getting fired. Can you tell me if I am?"

If a statement like "You've lost something" makes your eyes widen for a fraction of a second or causes a twitch in that palm they're reading, they know they've hit something, and they start telling you things about yourself, your life, your problems—all Barnum statements, of course, something like "People underestimate you"—and as soon as they start, you join in, either to agree with them ("My husband! He thinks I'm blind") or to correct them ("I don't know . . . I just got a promotion"). At this point, they know work is good but marriage is not. Since they got a hit with "You've lost something," naturally the next step is to dazzle you with the revelation that you lost your husband recently—and if they see the slightest flicker of *huh?* they can quickly pivot to "No wait . . . you *feel* like you've lost him. You don't trust him."

If their first guess wasn't right, then their second one almost certainly will be. Either way, you'll *feel* like they got it right and start to confide in them. At that point, all they have to ascertain is which story you came hoping to hear: that he's a lying cheat, or that it's all in your mind and everything's going to turn out fine.

The false-memory effect comes into play later, when you remember the interaction as strange or remarkable; you can't understand how they could know so much. Everything they knew about you was so accurate, specific, and profound. . . . How could they know so much about you? About your feelings, your problems, your past, your future? It's because you told them, *and then you quite literally forgot that you did.* You forget about all the misses, and you only remember the hits (which is called survivorship bias)—and you definitely don't remember the fact that you've almost certainly offered up exponentially more information than was revealed in the reading.

Unless you've run into an actual psychic—in which case, I promise you, they were not working as a fortune-teller.

It's All Fun and Games Till Someone Loses Their Mind

Although it does beg the question: Why have we all met so many *fake* psychics? And mediums and fortune-tellers and clairvoyants and the whole spectrum of spectral specialists? Has creeping people out always been a profession? Who decided any of that was real enough to be worth faking in the first place? All these supernatural-flavored grifts are built on our underlying belief—however slight or grudging—that some of it *might* be real.

And that belief is much more recent than you might think.

Have you ever been to a séance? Or played with a Ouija board? Or stood in the bathroom flossing your teeth, silently debating the pros and cons of saying "Bloody Mary" three times into the mirror?* These childhood games and traditions grew out of a movement in the early nineteenth century called Spiritualism (not the kind where you keep a crystal in your glove compartment to protect your debatable transmission and try to be a vegan except on weekends). At the time of its emergence, Spiritualism referred to ghosts and mediums and the occult. In fact, most of our modern ideas about ghosts and mediums and all things supernatural and postmortem are really just holdovers from the Spiritualist movement of that era.

It was sort of spontaneously started by three young girls in Roches-

---

*Oh, good. I was worried that was only me.

ter, New York: Kate, Margaret, and Leah Fox. The basic idea underpinning Spiritualism was that ghosts are real and certain special people (like these sisters) can communicate with them. The Fox sisters were among the leading proponents of the Spiritualist movement, owing to their alleged ability to do just that. The girls would talk, and the "spirits" would respond through a system of mysterious snapping and knocking.

Rather suddenly, trying to commune with the dead became everybody's weird new obsession.

Obviously, there was something weird going on in Rochester, New York, at that point, because the small town had become a hotbed of odd new religions, including Mormonism and Seventh-Day Adventists, but by far the most popular and glamorous of the new nineteenth-century cults was Spiritualism. You're probably wondering how three girls, two of whom were ten and twelve years old, started their own religion, let alone such a creepy one.* They did it by accident when a prank got out of hand. They were bored kids, pranking their parents by—supposedly—popping their toe joints. If that sounds stupid, it's because it is. They pretended that their house was suddenly haunted, and would talk to the spirits, who would reply in strange clicking, snapping sounds. It scared the bejeezus out of their mother, who sent them to live with their married older sister in Rochester. Once there, the whole lie kind of spun out of control.

At the time, Rochester was a one-industry town, and, as I mentioned, in 1848 that industry was starting cults. And inventing breakfast cereal—which was also sort of a cult at the time—but, strangely enough,

---

*If you're not, *why not*? Be more curious. Unless it's because you're thinking, "Oh yeah—I remember that time I started my own macabre, for-profit religion. As a child." In which case . . . kudos, I guess.

that actually belongs in the next chapter. When two little girls (whose proven ability to commune with the dead was so apparent and tangible that it had scared their mother into banishing them) arrived in I-invented-my-own-for-profit-religion-Rochester, obviously the local culty experts wanted to hear everything. So they just kept going with it.

Soon they were declared the real deal and eventually had over a million followers. More important, they had *backers*. They were taken to Gilded Age New York, where they made appalling amounts of money holding séances for wealthy people, which over time became more and more elaborate, incorporating table tipping, flickering lights, auto-writing, possession, and occasionally even apparitions. Spiritualism was embraced by many, including Sir Arthur Conan Doyle, yet vehemently rejected by others, chiefly Harry Houdini. Houdini was all for a little entertainment but he took the Spiritualism fraud very personally and obsessively debunked alleged mediums. Nevertheless, the rise of Spiritualism became a global phenomenon, and the girls kept the lie going and growing for forty years.

And then quite suddenly in 1888, Margaret Fox, all grown up and a little bit of an alcoholic, appeared at the New York Academy of Music, where she publicly denounced Spiritualism. She was paid $1,500 to do so, but her primary motivation was a feud with her oldest sister, Leah, a leading Spiritualist. She confessed to the audience and the journalists present: "My sister Katie and myself were very young children when this horrible deception began." She further explained that "a great many people when they hear the rapping imagine at once that the spirits are touching them. It is a very common delusion."[11] She even gave a demonstration, in which she took off her shoe, put her foot on a stool, and proceeded to create the bizarre but familiar rapping sounds.

The New York Herald reported, "There stood a black-robed, sharp-faced widow, working her big toe and solemnly declaring that it was in this way she created the excitement that has driven so many persons to suicide or insanity. One moment it was ludicrous, the next it was weird."[12]

With due respect to *The New York Herald,* I'm pretty sure the whole thing was weird.

But then, the whole latter half of the nineteenth century was weird. Really weird—between electricity, automobiles, and world's fairs, you can kind of forgive people for encountering something bizarre and saying, "Well, yeah—okay." Science was new, magic was old, everything was strange, and it was probably hard to tell the difference. And by the way, this was at about the same time Rasputin was putting the whammy on the Romanovs.

So, obviously the uncertainty of the times, the strange new world emerging around everyone, played a part in people's willingness to believe this pile of stupid. But mostly this is the kind of fraud where you want so badly to believe it that you make up most of it in your own mind. It's a little bit like seeing the rubber ball that never left the magician's hand, except instead of physically seeing or feeling things that didn't happen—like Ouija board movement, a cold spot in the room, a spirit tapping your shoulder (though that can occur as well)—the false-memory effect induces you to *recall* things that didn't happen. Or to conveniently forget them. It also works a little like the placebo effect, in that you want to believe it, because you already believed it.

But in the case of religious, spiritual, or supernatural scams, there's an added dimension that can backfire very badly. Because their need to believe is so strong, the exposure of a fraud can make people very, very angry.

Magic Versus Spiritualism

Harry Houdini had a serious hate-on for fake mediums. It started when his mother died. They were very close, and in a state of deep grief he did what a lot of people do and turned to spirituality—or in his case, Spiritualism. He went into the process more than open-minded: he was ready and willing to believe all of it, if it meant that he could talk to his mom one more time. He was in exactly the right frame of mind to believe the lie. Unfortunately, although truth may be subjective, *facts are not,* and Houdini was one of the greatest illusionists in the world. As much as he wanted it, séance after séance, he couldn't fail to see the tricks of the trade everywhere he went. Accepting that the mediums he met were mostly frauds, and clearly none could speak to the dead, his hope soured and turned to anger.

In a seemingly disproportionate rage, he spent the rest of his life seeking out and publicly exposing various Gurus, psychics, and mystics. He became a relentless crusader against Spiritualism, especially studying its methods and claims, and was particularly obsessed with exposing what he called "vultures who prey on the bereaved."[13] He was so obsessed with these vultures, that he trolled individual fake mediums by attending their séances incognito and observing their act. As soon as he spotted the trick, he'd reveal himself to the other would-be believers present and expose the scam. Usually in brutal detail. Eventually, he spent most of his time and energy aggressively discrediting them, in newspapers across the country and in public appearances, where he'd project images of specific mediums, name and shame them, and denounce them as frauds. Then, just to make his point, he would reproduce their alleged paranormal abilities for the crowds. He even wrote a book, *A Magician Among the Spirits,* published in 1923. After it came out, he traveled the country but replaced his magic act with lectures explaining and debunking mediums. In 1925 he went on a national tour to sold-out houses. He offered ten thousand dollars to anyone who could exhibit legitimate supernatural phenomenon or psychic abilities that he could not reproduce.[14]

Houdini's vicious obsession sheds some light on the powerful grip belief has on us, once it's taken hold, both to make us adamant followers and ardent opponents. You can't make someone that angry unless they did, indeed, believe the lie, even just briefly. People really lose their sense of proportion when they realize they have been genuinely taken in by nonsense, not because the lie itself is so devastating, but because *having believed it* is. It fundamentally destabilizes one's sense of objective reality. If they really believed that lie and it was not true, then what else do they believe that might not be true? Is anything they believe true?

There's an entire emerging field of science looking at how difficult it is to change someone's perception and emotional opinion of fact once they've accepted that something *is* fact, even after they're provided with incontrovertible evidence to the contrary. What it mostly boils down to is more cognitive dissonance: they become incapable of processing new information, and more often than not they just can't accept that the first fact was a lie—at least, not if they really bought it.

The trajectory of confirmation bias (wherein you believe something and thus begin to see evidence for it everywhere you look) followed by cognitive dissonance (where you dig in your heels and believe something more the more it's disproved) is a powerful emotional response and a form of recursive cognitive error that subverts objective reasoning. And this looped failure to see (or even be able to see) reason occurs because it's not about what lie they believed, it's about whether or not someone could make them believe it. Processing new and contradictory information becomes entirely about a desperate need to believe—offset by an equally desperate need not to discover that one's beliefs are false. It turns out it's actually easier to convince someone (anyone) to believe a lie (any lie) than it is to convince that person that they have been lied to—once they've come to believe the lie.

And because it's so far-fetched, the Guru Con can be one of the more difficult lies to make a majority of people believe, but it helps that the very people seeking out this sort of guidance are already in a frame of mind to accept it. It's magical thinking, which makes people ready to simply accept the unbelievable. If they were not, then they wouldn't even have entertained the idea in the first place. And it doesn't hurt that because Guru Cons often involve the supernatural—unless, like Houdini, you can expose the physical mechanism by which the Guru is manipulating physical reality (for example, a rigged Ouija board or hidden fan)—it's almost impossible to expose them as scams. When the con doesn't involve physical objects, when it's entirely faith-based or nonsupernatural, it's actually impossible to expose.

And people will do some truly amazing mental gymnastics to avoid confronting the fact that their Gurus are frauds—like Tsarina Alexandra's insane conclusion that Rasputin had some mysterious, malicious impersonator making him look like an obscene, drunken liar all over Saint Petersburg. Maybe she was just crazy. Then again, try reasoning with an extreme devotee of a TV ministry and you'll see what I mean.

Televangelists and Other People Going to Hell

Guru Cons come in all shapes and sizes, and with the addition of televangelists: SUPER SIZES. These hustlers are, like Rasputin, political-favor-trading, wealth-accumulating, self-appointed religious figures who, more often than not, have no real credentials or official affiliation with the organizations or entities they claim to represent. That's why they have to start their own ministries.* And where better to reach the desperate masses than on television?

They spend hours a day "preaching the gospel." Just not really. There's a little Christianity sprinkled in here and there, but if you listen, they spend most of that time telling their target demographic—and they *do* know precisely who their target demographic is; they make it their business (model) to know—exactly what they want to hear about all manner of things: social, political, personal, and otherwise non-gospel-related. Things like, you're a righteous person, things are gonna get better for you, you really are very put-upon, it's okay that you voted for that guy, and you're also right about that other insane thing you believe, etc. This of course serves to set up that same baseline-for-reality paradox in which to continue to believe what they wanted or needed to hear early on, they must continue to believe that the Guru is infallible. But if the Guru is infallible, then they must believe *everything* they say or fall victim to the unsustainable state of cognitive dissonance.

Inevitably, this leads to the Guru making suggestions that involve . . . money.

---

*Which really should have been a tip-off for their flock.

Sometimes, the money is being collected for a cause; other times, it's just a straight donation for "the ministry," like the money my grandma used to send to the Praise the Lord Club.* The Praise the Lord Club was the brainchild of the original send-me-money television preacher, Jim Bakker. Bakker and his wife Tammy Faye were among the first, and most famous, televangelists in America. It was apparently Bakker's idea to do a "Christian version of *The Tonight Show*," which has been called "innovative"—and that is one word for it—but by far his greater innovation was how he financed the show. Instead of getting sponsors to pay him to run commercials, like most talk shows, the Bakkers appealed directly to their viewers and said if you're with us (send money).

And send it they did; according to former PTL security chief Don Hardister, "we had a cash office and at times there was certainly more money in than . . . I could imagine," he said. "People would send us mink coats, diamond rings, deeds. I mean, we got all sorts of donations."[15] Their show originally aired on a small North Carolina station; then they bought airtime on TV stations across the United States. By 1978, Bakker created a satellite network to distribute The Word more widely. More viewers meant more donations, and within a few years they were filthy (embezzler) rich.

But not all the money went to buy Tammy Faye mascara; the Bakkers used some of it to buy 2,300 acres on which to build a five-hundred-room hotel and water park they called Heritage USA. It was supposed to be some sort of "Christian Disneyland." Because, sure, that's a thing. But bad taste notwithstanding, the trouble started (to

---

*Funniest part of this story? My grandma wasn't even Christian, let alone an evangelical. That's how good these guys are at hustling people. Especially old people.

show, I guess) when Bakker asked his followers to donate a thousand dollars each, which was supposed to get them a "lifetime partnership." A lifetime partnership in what, you ask, besides the Lord? Those donors were entitled to an annual three-night stay at the Heritage Grand Hotel. The hitch: he took thousand-dollar donations from way too many people—more than 66,000 lifetime partnerships. That amounts to around 200,000 *free* nights a year at the Heritage Grand Hotel for his "partners," or at least forty-two more rooms than the hotel actually even had, running at full capacity, for free, forever.

And right at that very inopportune time, as Bakker had also just broken ground on a new hundred-million-dollar (let's say) church, which he tastefully called the Crystal Palace, Tammy Faye had a breakdown. A full-on, raving, hallucinating, naked-in-public *snap*. A couple months later, the Bakkers released a videotaped message in which they explained that Tammy Faye was being treated for drug dependency. Whoops. But when it rains, it pours; and in short order *The Charlotte Observer* published an exposé about Jim Bakker's affair with a twenty-one-year-old church secretary named Jessica Hahn. Then it got worse. Hahn claimed that there was no affair, Jim Bakker sexually assaulted her. He disputed it, but either way the ministry had illegally paid her over $200,000 in hush money. Which doesn't look great.

Bakker resigned and asked his good pal Jerry Falwell to run the ministry until the scandals blew over. Because televangelists are nice people, Falwell later refused to go, saying the Bakkers were not fit to lead PTL. He also exposed accusations that Jim Bakker was gay. For good measure.

But by then the Bakkers had *real* problems, because the government was auditing all of PTL's finances, including Bakker's compensation and their personal spending—and it turns out, to no one's surprise, they were the same thing. "At one point, the Bakkers' vast portfolio included several homes, a private jet, two Rolls-Royces, a Mercedes Benz, expensive clothes and an air-conditioned doghouse."[16] The surreal even-for-the-eighties investigation eventually resulted in indictments for Jim Bakker (eight counts of mail fraud, fifteen counts of wire fraud, and one count of conspiracy) and for all his top guys. On October 5, 1989, Jim Bakker was found guilty on all twenty-four counts, ordered to pay a $500,000 fine, and sentenced to forty-five years in prison. Bakker filed an appeal, and in 1991 was granted a reduced sentence of only eight years. He ended up serving fewer than five.

You'd think that would be the end of Reverend Jim Bakker. But he wasn't in the business of faith; he was in the business of thrall—like all Gurus. As soon as he got out of prison, he launched a new ministry, called Morningside, and in 2003 he started broadcasting *The Jim Bakker Show,* starring himself and his new wife. The new Bakkers raised money for the new ministry by hawking apocalypse merch, like survival gear and five-gallon buckets of freeze-dried food—you know, for "the end of days." And wouldn't you know, they were very successful in this not-at-all-new endeavor—*almost* like their flock had completely forgotten about the greed, the fraud, the debauchery, the criminal accusations, and the hundreds of millions of dollars they had stolen—and all they remember is *Praise the Lord!*

As Salvador Dalí once said, "The difference between false memories and true ones is the same as for jewels: it is always the false ones that look the most real, the most brilliant."

Asking your followers to send money while you live it up is pretty brazen. And criminal. But somehow that open shamelessness makes it seem less hypocritical. It's not like they said send money for a church—for you—our congregation, then locked them out. They just said *send money*. Usually when donations are solicited, they're earmarked for a particular project—like the hundreds of millions of dollars followers donated to build Joel Osteen's 16,800-seat megachurch in Houston, which incidentally locked its doors during Hurricane Harvey (in which tens of thousands of people were displaced) and wouldn't let thousands of those same disciples inside to take shelter.[17] When Osteen was publicly called out for this craven behavior, he claimed the Lakewood megachurch—one of the largest in the United States—was "inaccessible due to extreme flooding."[18] Unfortunately, this was mega not true, and outraged Houstonians wouldn't stop posting pictures and videos on social media of the decidedly not-flooded church. The Lakewood Church finally issued a statement claiming they *had never* closed their doors but also (confusingly) were prepared to open their doors "once the cities and county shelters reach capacity."

When that still wasn't really good enough for a lot of people, Osteen, who happens to preach the "prosperity gospel" (not a real gospel, for the record), which claims that following his Christian teachings will magically bring greater personal success and wealth, defensively insisted that "this is not just an attack on me, it's an attack on what we stand for—for faith, for hope, for love."[19] "Jesus even said, 'When the world hates you, remember: it hated me first.'" And while a multimillionaire, self-help-book-authoring TV preacher (who closed his church to victims of a category 4 hurricane) comparing himself to Jesus *is* pretty remarkable, it's the first part of that statement that's actually interesting, as it was both a message to his flock and a road map to how he manipulates them. When he said, "This is not just an attack on me, it's an attack on what we stand for," in response to criticism of *his* choices, *his* behavior, and arguably *his moral failing,* he equated that criticism to an attack on everything his parishioners believed in. He couldn't have been more blunt if he'd just shouted *"cognitive dissonance"* into a microphone.

But just in case any of the faithful were still questioning his moral authority, he followed that up with a sermon in which he warned his congregation, "You know I really believe in these times of difficulty it's, for me, certainly not the time to question your faith but to turn to your faith because God is the one that gives you the strength to make it through the difficult times."[20] If the first statement was a manipulation, that second was an outright threat: continue to question me and you're questioning not just your own faith—you're questioning God, and you don't want to do that or you might just find yourself without any sort of belief system to get through this crisis.

Yikes.

Who knew that donating money to build a church (let alone seeking shelter in one) could be such an ethical, psychological minefield? And that's when the money is solicited directly, for a specific purpose—like building that church—and then *actually* spent on the project it was donated for. In other cases, televangelists require a cash show of faith *as an act of faith*. In this case, you're not exactly asked for the money directly; it just comes up in such a way that you're excited, and it somehow seems like such a good idea to give, and you're not the only one opening up your wallet, so it hardly seems like a hustle at the time. But the purpose of your donation is far less clear than funds to build the world's biggest and most inhospitable church. You're making a less rational, less specific donation *to the ministry itself,* supposedly earmarked for "a project," or "good works."

In these cases, particularly transparent televangelists preach the gospel of "seed money." Seed money is one of the gospel of prosperity's creepier practices. The idea behind seed money is that you send God, via these televangelists, actual cash.* For no particular reason or project (though it will undoubtedly be used for "good works," right?). To be clear: you don't do this to build a church or even to support their ministry in some undefined way—PTL Club style—but just as an act of faith. And because, they claim, God wants you to do this as a show of faith, if you do, you will be rewarded with many multiple times your investment—er, donation—returning to you. In some form . . . not from them, obviously. They use it to buy drugs and hookers and jets and stuff.† But God knows what you did, and He will see that you reap a commensurate windfall, in some way or other. And if you don't . . . wait longer. If you never do, God probably knows what *else* you did, so you better send more money to smooth things over.

The rational framework involved in believing that you have created a metaphysical outcome (pennies from heaven) via a completely unrelated physical act (like sending that seed money) is built upon the phenomenon of magical thinking. It's a state of mind that's really ubiquitous among compulsive gamblers, but more so among the oppressed, the impoverished, and the otherwise physically or financially desperate. As such, it's a variety of the Guru Con that involves creating the illusion of wealth, control, and power, even as it saps those very things from its victims, who, most tragically, willingly cede them. Consequently, its

---

*They might also take PayPal. I'm not sure.
†I'm not being a reductive jerk; Jim Bakker actually did that.

version tends to work far better on poor people than on rich people, making it characteristically especially nasty.

Which, of course, brings us to politics.

"Without Rasputin There Would Have Been No Lenin"

At least not according to Alexander Kerensky, a key figurehead of the Russian Revolution. Even though the provisional government he led following the Russian Revolution was quickly dissolved by the vicious, incompetent Bolsheviks—shortly after the Bolsheviks had murdered the vicious, incompetent Romanovs—Kerensky called it like he saw it: blaming the royal family's Guru problem for the shocking state of the state.

"Without Rasputin there would have been no Lenin" is an observation worth keeping in mind, particularly since there are no new lies, only new liars. And from playing at being a populist man of the people to being aggressively physically disgusting, Steve Bannon (an ironically self-professed Leninist) is a creepy Svengali in his own right. The story of his rise is illustrative of how the Guru Con works with politicians as well as holy men, because it's *really* not about religion.

It's about control.

And for big-league Gurus it's about getting the ear of the right person (be that Trump, the Mercers, or the GOP) and convincing them that you have special abilities and are therefore both infallible and indispensable. It's about creating the illusion—and eventual reality—of *need*. Once that's accomplished, the mark does most of the actual work of belief. Gurus, dangerous though they are, are nothing more than parasites. That's why they always start by offering their services, seemingly selflessly. It's a foot in the door that allows them access to the mark and time to decipher their wants, their needs, and (most useful of all) their fears.

Once insinuated, the Guru begins by flattering his mark, telling them all the things that they already need to believe are true, then gradually peppering this discourse with their own agenda. Lies and failures are airbrushed away by survivorship bias and the false-memory effect, and no matter how appalling his behavior, once he has your complete faith, the choke chain of confirmation bias demands it be denied or dismissed.

But why those marks deliberately put themselves in a position to be conned in the first place—because they do, and they do it over and over—is a question worth asking. Not only because it's a curious propensity, but because if what you're looking for in your Guru is something a little more intense than a horoscope, a palm reading, or evidence of life after death, then it can have an effect on people and events wider than just the Guru and the mark.

I happen to like horoscopes. But no one's horoscope ever told them to kill someone or tried to dictate foreign policy. Cults, on the other hand, are more direct in their marching orders, and have far more tenacious believers than astrologers. Televangelists absolutely tell people what to do and how to behave in ways that transcend "don't buy anything while Mercury is in retrograde." They tell people what's morally acceptable, what's socially required; in some cases, they even claim to speak for God. And their devotees believe them. That kind of power is dangerous. But televangelists primarily prey on the powerless; the only people their slavish devotion can usually hurt is themselves. Televangelists, for the most part, are not manipulating the kind of people making decisions for the rest of us: people like the Russian royal family, the president of a world power, or an entire political party.

So why do *those* marks, people in a position of power and influence, deliberately seek out Gurus in the first place? Because the truth is, *more of them do than don't.* The answer is still fear and desperation—just like everyone else. While it intuitively makes sense that the genuinely powerless might feel this way, it's strange to think that the most privileged and powerful among us are often the most desperate and fearful. But they are. While desperation is often born of poverty, grief, uncertainty, or actual powerlessness, but ironically it can just as easily be the result of excessive power, influence, or wealth and the anxiety it brings, about everything from how to wield it to how to hold on to it.

Incompetence is a powerful motive to fear the future.

And then there are the true believers—the people who are most profoundly susceptible to Gurus—who are scared, usually, and always desperate to be told what to do. They are more than willing to trade freedom for security. "When you choose your holy man," Dostoyevsky wrote, "you surrender your will"; you don't get to make your own decisions, but on the flip side, you're no longer responsible for the consequences of those decisions. This need to give over agency—and with it, responsibility—is why true believers show so much overlap with religious fanatics and authoritarians. From zealots to fascists, some people just need the security of not being in control of anything, especially if it means someone else is. Even when that person is a monster.

And once in the thrall of a Guru, there's rarely any way out except feetfirst.

BITTER PILL

Snake Oil, Salesmen,
and Subjective Reality

The doctor-patient relationship is critical to the Placebo Effect.
—IRVING KIRSCH

The more medicated, the more dedicated.
—SNOOP DOGG

SNAKE OIL

The Snake Oil con promises people in a state of anxiety a miraculous medical remedy, either a cure for or a protection against whatever it is that ails them. The product is usually pharmaceutical, but may also involve medical treatments, procedures, or testing. At best, the miracle cure has the effect of a placebo. At worst, it may *provoke* or worsen sickness—which then, of course, requires further treatment. This may seem like nothing more than a medical Bait and Switch, but there is in fact a distinction. Snake oil doesn't function based on manipulating hard evidence—the kind you can see, like gold salting. It functions best, in fact, in spheres of human experience that resist the absolute determination of hard evidence. This, in combination with the placebo effect—powerful proof, on its own, of the inextricable connection between realities imagined and subsequently experienced—makes for one of the oldest, and most pervasive, tricks in the book.

Chinese Take Out

Long before Snake Oil became a byword for fake cures handed out by shady salesmen claiming to be spiritual and/or medical experts of some sort, Stanley's Snake Oil was a real product and a very specific con. And for centuries *before that,* on far-distant shores, genuine snake oil was a legitimate medicine. But once that snake oil was found to have actual curative properties, it was quickly co-opted by the burgeoning pharmaceutical industry of the nineteenth century—offering drugs, poisons, and nonsense of all kinds—then branded, packaged, and replaced with, well . . . *Snake Oil* of the more euphemistic variety, and sold to more people than had ever used the legitimate version. The whole era was so rife with hustlers, fake doctors, and commercial "cures" that could kill you that it inspired the formation of the FDA—which is ironic given how much of the modern medical industrial complex is still running the same racket.

This story gets confusing, and *not* just because everyone in it is on drugs, so let's start at the beginning. In the late nineteenth century, around the same time a huge wave of Irish immigrants flooded onto the eastern shore of America, another giant wave of immigrants, this one from China, was pouring into the West and would quite literally meet them in the middle. Between 1849 and 1882 over 180,000 indentured Chinese laborers, mostly from farms and poorer villages in the south, came to America to work on the Transcontinental Railroad. Indentured servants, they were signed to contracts of up to five years and paid almost nothing. They couldn't bring much with them from home, but they couldn't buy much once they got here, either. And among the necessary items most frequently imported to American shores were various traditional medicines, including the now infamous snake oil.

If you looked up a definition now, the *Oxford English Dictionary* would tell you that snake oil is "a quack remedy or panacea," but in the nineteenth century and for long before that, it was a traditional Chinese remedy, and by all accounts a very effective one. It was an anti-inflammatory, primarily used to treat aches and pains, sunburns, and arthritis brought on by the hard labor. The original Chinese snake oil was made from the rendered fat of black water snakes, also called the black water moccasin. It was a transdermal, lipophilic agent with an extraordinary concentration of omega-3 acids, which really did reduce pain and inflammation.[1]

So, despite the modern connotations about "selling snake oil," snake oil was, ironically, exactly what it purported to be and worked really well.

Also, it was never actually *sold*—certainly not by traveling salesmen. It was, however, generously shared by the Chinese workers with their immigrant and non-Chinese counterparts. It was radically effective and completely foreign: no one had ever encountered snake oil, in large part for the simple reason that there are no black water snakes in North

America. But everywhere the railroad went, its builders went—and awareness of snake oil spread gradually across the country.[2] But as the railroad moved on, so, too, did the workers, taking their snake oil with them. As soon as they did, that remarkable Chinese snake oil that people swore could cure a multiplicity of ills was in short supply.

Selling Snake Oil

The next two tidal waves that slammed into each other were drugs and advertising. The introduction of snake oil to American cities and towns coincided with a craze in the late nineteenth century for something called "patent medicines," not to be confused with *patented* drugs as they exist today.* These patent medicines were tonics and cure-alls, narcotics and poisons, and a fair amount of *nothing* mixed with alcohol or syrup. Patent medicines were anything, really; the only real qualifier was that they come with swell branding and very recognizable labels. They were sold directly to the public on the back pages of newspapers and on posters, not unlike the way we sell vitamins, supplements, diet pills, uppers, downers, and a variety of beauty, brain, and sexual enhancers today. But unlike our current beauty, health, and wellness merch, in the 1800s purveyors could say (or not say) absolutely anything they wanted to about their products. And they did.

You'd think all that shameless lying was the primary selling technique, but actually, it was the relentless branding and *selling itself* that did the trick. The way patent medicines were sold—practically every-

---

*They were called "patent medicines," because secret formulas used to make proprietary drugs in England were manufactured under "patents of royal favor," to the makers who also provided medicines to the royal family.

where you looked—served to constantly, subtly, reinforce their believability. It's a cognitive fallacy known as the illusory truth effect, and we'll talk more about it later. The short version is: the more often you see or hear something—no matter what it is—*the more credible it becomes,* simply by means of repeated exposure. Even if you kind of knew, or at least suspected, that it was crap the first time around. Over time anything takes on the illusion of truth. The more you hear it, the more you believe it, the more you see it, the more you trust it.[3]

It's a real thing and it's completely crazy.

On top of which, human susceptibility to authority bias makes us trust people whom we think are *more* than us in some regard—any regard, really. As with most cognitive fallacies, the bias is just the downside of a necessary heuristic. We've developed all these mental shortcuts because we need them to function at around sixty bits per second— which ain't even all that much. One of those shortcuts is extending an assumption of credibility and good intent to any perceived expert. Another is complying more readily with individuals we physically recognize to be in a position of authority. The downside of these shortcuts is, as we've discussed, authority bias, which makes you highly inclined to do or believe what you're told, like electrocute your lab partner, particularly if the person telling you to do so is wearing a white coat. Or a uniform. Or any other signifiers of authority or expertise.

And here we have two more unexpected collisions: authority bias and the illusory truth effect. You see, these rabid consumers of patent medicines weren't initially trusting experts (however self-styled), although every product came with the endorsement of some imaginary doctor, witch doctor, shaman, or expert. Over time they associated the expert with the brand, then the brand with the expert, and then the brand with expertise. Through nothing more than relentless media exposure and repetition, they learned to trust people like self-proclaimed doctor William Bailey, the inventor and distributor of a radioactive patent medicine called Radithor: Certified Radioactive Water. Bailey's tonic was made from distilled water, thorium, and radium.[4]

And it absolutely killed people.

Which you would think customers might find off-putting, but they didn't seem to draw a connection between "Dr. Bailey" and their jaw cancer. And Radithor was hardly an exception—patent medicines were bizarre. Who drinks Borax, lead, and arsenic for dandruff? Or takes Dr. Williams' Pink Pills for Pale People (no clue what was in there) for anemia? People who are neither being looked out for by their government nor their own common sense, I suppose.

Ultimately, consumers were not concerned with science; they were just buying novel (but very recognizable) products that were so extensively advertised, so ubiquitously present, that their very existence took on the illusion of truth. And then one fallacy compounded the other: once these items were accepted as legitimate products, the endorsement of whatever manufactured expert or authority figure they invoked primed their consumers to believe that they worked.

The Rattlesnake King

One such bullshit artist and self-styled expert was Clark Stanley. Stanley was a Wild West showman who called himself the Rattlesnake King—which is both trashy and peculiar—but on the bright side, at least he didn't call himself *Dr.* Clark Stanley. In addition to Wild West shows,

Stanley also claimed to be a real-life cowboy. Though he didn't do any actual ranching, he did shovel a lot of horseshit; Clark Stanley was *the original* Snake Oil Salesman.

At the 1893 Chicago World Exposition, he put on a display so over-the-top (even for the era's prevailing medical circus-show environment) that it involved pulling an allegedly live rattlesnake from a sack in front of the terrified, titillated crowd, slitting it open, and throwing it in a pot of boiling water.[5] I kind of suspect the Rattlesnake King's live rattlesnake was already dead,* and he just shook it wildly, making it seem to wriggle, and making the rattle, well . . . rattle. People expecting a live snake would have seen one—or at least remembered it that way later.

Either way, that snake was dead once it was in the pot of boiling water, where he let it cook while he made his eccentric pitch to the crowd. It may or may not have involved a literal song and dance. He later claimed in an 1897 pamphlet—that he published himself, about himself, his product, and his Wild West exploits—that he had learned about the secret ancient formula of rattlesnake oil from Hopi medicine men.[6] And that tracks, because Hopi medicine men definitely tell random trespassing white people stuff like that. But "when the fat rose to the top, he skimmed it off and used it on the spot to create Stanley's Snake Oil, a liniment that was immediately snapped up by the throng that had gathered."[7] And, just like that: "selling snake oil" was invented.

And people bought it.

They bought it so much, in fact, that we're still talking about

---

*I'm in New Mexico right now, and there's no way dude pulls a live rattlesnake out of a bag and does anything but get bitten and die.

it today, about *selling snake oil*—that is, in the colloquial sense of pitching bullshit. Because that's exactly what he was doing: not making anything like Chinese snake oil. Not only was Stanley using the wrong snakes (rattlesnake fat doesn't contain the same chemical compounds as black water moccasin fat, which has at least three times the omega-3 acids), he was also preparing it incorrectly. Even with the right snake, boiling it in a pot of water would be the wrong way to extract those compounds. But worst of all, his flashy show for the crowds had absolutely nothing to do with what he was peddling in those thousands of bottles. The boiled rattlesnake was just for show—and just for *that show,* evidently.

Really, all Stanley sold his customers when they bought a bottle of Stanley's Snake Oil was mineral oil, turpentine, and a fancy label. But it didn't matter that what was in the bottle had nothing to do with what was on the label, or that what was on the label was almost always crazy, patent medicines like Stanley's Snake Oil were the first really effective experiments in pharmaceutical marketing—a practice that would both be to blame for at least two American opioid epidemics and numerous other mass illnesses, casualties, and deaths; and also be responsible for the wild success of Stanley's Snake Oil and almost every other ineffective or dangerous pharmaceutical in the last 150 years.

While we're on the subject of ineffective or dangerous products, did Stanley's Snake Oil work? Doubtful. And given how much turpentine was in it, thank God no one was swallowing it. But the question of whether or not a drug "works" is a surprisingly difficult one to answer. Because in a lot of ways (and certainly in the 1800s) the only real metric for the efficacy of a medicine was whether or not it made the patient feel better.

And they *did* feel better. And the better they felt, the more they believed it—and the more they believed it, the better they felt.

And that's called the placebo effect.

The Strange Science of Placebos

The strange science of placebos is a tangible object lesson in how belief can be turned inside out—producing actual evidence to support a prior conviction and, more specifically, the queer way in which you can believe in a thing so fervently that you convince not only your mind *but also your body* that it's true.

The placebo effect occurs when a preexisting, conscious expectation is met, resulting in the anticipatory release of specific biochemical substances from one's own body into one's own bloodstream, no drug required. Numerous remarkable studies have been done, first and most famously one including Valium and cellulose pills administered with the manipulation of the patient's expectation.[8] Essentially, half the patients were given Valium and half were given what might as well have been Tic Tacs. But all of them were led to believe that they had received the good stuff. And it worked just like Snake Oil.

That is to say—it worked so long as the patients remained convinced that they had been given the actual drug.

Though maybe more interesting still, researchers at the National Institutes of Health found in a double-blind trial that Valium "has no discernable effect on anxiety unless a person knows he is taking it."[9] Apparently, Valium is a placebo. But Valium is a benzodiazepine, a tranquilizer, generally given to patients who are, let's be honest—*rather suggestible*. Other than things like pupil dilation or blood pressure, there's really no good metric for "are you feeling less hysterical now?" And it's an established fact that one's blood pressure will go up just because a doctor is taking it. All of which suggests that Valium, or any benzodiazepine, might not have been the best choice for the study. So another study was done in 1978, using injury, pain, and narcotics.[10]

In that study, people recovering from dental surgery—in a great deal of physical pain—were told that they would receive either morphine, saline, or a drug that might increase their pain. Some got one, some got two, and some got all three, since the test was done in rounds.

In the first round, half the patients were given morphine and the other half were only given saline. The subjects who got the morphine responded as expected, creating a baseline for the rest of the results. They were then eliminated from the second round. After the subjects who got the morphine were removed from the study, the remaining patients (*all* of whom were administered saline originally but led to believe it was morphine) were divided into two groups: the patients who succumbed to the placebo effect (having been led to believe they'd gotten high) and felt significant pain relief *with only saline*—and those who did not.

Next, they dismissed the whiners, the ones who could still feel real pain on just saline. Now they were left with only the patients who succumbed to the placebo effect and felt real relief from real pain, on fake morphine (saline).

In round two they gave half of those placebo-happy patients a dose of naloxone, and the other half a dose of saline. Naloxone is a drug designed to counteract heroin and morphine overdoses by binding to opioid receptors, making them unavailable for other molecules (heroin, morphine, our own endorphins) to occupy. If you've overdosed, it binds up the receptors, so the drug can't work and—ideally—you don't die. If you have not overdosed, but rather have been given narcotics for pain relief, the naloxone still binds up the receptors, so the drug can't work, leaving you in the same pain you were in before being doped up.

The researchers weren't just torturing recovering dental-surgery patients for kicks—they were trying to ascertain how it was possible that patients experiencing postsurgical pain who only believed that they were drugged could feel just as good as the patients who actually were. The researchers suspected the endorphins created by the patient's own body—in response to their genuine belief that drug-induced pain relief was coming—was, in some part, responsible for the placebo effect. At least, in this case. And they were proved right when the naloxone knocked out the placebo effect and left the patients once again in pain.

Taking the research a step further, the evolving technology of neuroimaging permits researchers to track precisely how a person reacts to a drug (or a placebo) as soon as they take it. In one trial, an injection of saline—which the patient had been led to believe was a powerful new Parkinson's drug—not only temporarily reduced symptoms of Parkinson's disease but additionally induced a reaction called anticipatory release, causing the patient's body to actually *produce* more of the dopamine molecules that have been destroyed by the Parkinson's disease.[11] In other words, just believing they were given a drug not only relieved symptoms like pain or tremors, it actually caused the patient's body to produce a chemical compound that the disease had largely prevented the body from making—and all of this magic was visible via neuroimaging.

They were able to observe and record what quacks and faith healers have known forever: sometimes just believing in a cure can be as effective as the cure itself.

A Brief History of Nothing

If placebos are so great, how did they get such a bad rap?

After all, they are the oldest drug on the market, by about half a million years, and apparently they really actually do . . . something. And yet, they're fairly synonymous with charlatanry and evoke everything from fraud to foolishness. So, unsurprisingly, there's a Guru involved: Lots of them, actually, but let's start at the start with a German physician named Franz Anton Mesmer. Mesmer, an eighteenth-century physician, had become really famous in Europe for a new treatment he called Mesmerism. He believed he had discovered the theory of what he called "animal magnetism," some sort of healing energy (which he called "magnetic fluid") that flowed through and between all living things. He believed blockages in this magnetic fluid were responsible for all illness. It *sounds* bizarre, but he basically "discovered" chi.

Unlike most acupuncturists, though, he would deploy or repair this energy via totally inappropriate touching.

Before long, Mesmer was so famous and sought after that he had upward of two hundred patients a day to fondle, which was obviously just not practical. So naturally he discovered a way to transfer his supposed animal magnetism to inanimate objects, like a weird bathtub he designed called a *baquet*. Mesmer personally magnetized the strange contraption: a large wooden tub filled with iron filings and glass bottles of water, with iron rods extending outward for the patients to rub up against. All this took place in a dimly lit room full of heavy incense and spooky music. His patients, mostly women, often lapsed into convulsions, sobbing, or hysterical laughter. Apparently, that's how you knew it was working.

Things went downhill fast for creepy Mesmer when the husband of one of his more prominent patients, Marie Antoinette, queen of France, decided he wasn't really all that convinced Mesmer was doing anything other than hanging out with ladies in their underwear—and also decided that he was sick of his wife's Guru. As this patient's husband happened to be the king of France, he simply asked the French Academy of Sciences (specifically, Benjamin Franklin) to have a little look into it. So the Academy did their very own version of Mesmer's shtick to see if it worked. To almost no one's surprise, it did not.

They couldn't reasonably test Mesmerism on people themselves to see if it worked, as none of them possessed the alleged ability. So they did the next best thing: they convinced their test subjects that they *had been* mesmerized, and then tested their reaction to that belief instead. They informed one subject that a tree had been "magnetized" using the same technique Mesmer used on inanimate objects like his infamous *baquets,* and that they required him to wrap his arms around it so that they could observe the effects. Having been convinced that the tree was magnetized, he fully expected to be mesmerized when he touched it, and so he was. When the boy dramatically shook and convulsed and practically talked in tongues it was clear that Mesmer's patients behaved the way they did because they *expected* to be mesmerized, to undergo some sort of profound physical and possibly metaphysical experience, not because they actually were.

This was not a perfect experiment, but it was enough to make Mesmer seem like a complete fraud and to forever link lies and placebos in the collective consciousness. That association was an unfortunate side effect of exposing Mesmer's grift, because the mechanism by which these hysterics took place had less to do with lying than it did with with *priming*.

But it would be another 150 years before that occurred to anyone.

Feeling Better?

The placebo effect, like many profound truths, is inextricably linked with a lie. Not the implicit lie told every time a placebo is administered, but a specific lie told to a dying soldier on an Italian beach during World War II. Under heavy German bombardment, Lieutenant Colonel Henry Beecher was tasked with triaging over two hundred injured men. When the morphine ran out, he had nothing to offer the severely wounded soldiers. The nurse working alongside him, in a desperate act of mercy, lied to a mangled young man and assured him that she was giving him morphine and that he would feel better soon. Then, despite the doctors momentary objection (and obvious confusion) she proceeded to inject him with a syringe full of saline. To Beecher's amazement, the saline injection and the nurse's lie not only stopped the soldier's agony, it also prevented the onset of shock.[12]

Dr. Beecher spent the rest of the war attempting to find a correlation between the severity of the soldiers' injuries and the severity of their perceived pain. Which doesn't really sound like an experiment as much as sadism: presumably, if you've broken your ankle, you feel broken-ankle pain, and if you had your entire leg ripped off, you . . . feel more pain. But what he found was exactly the opposite, and he believed it was a result of *expectation*. He found that among soldiers still lucid and talking and expected to survive, the *more* severely injured they were, the *less* pain they believed they were in. Having averted near death, they were in an unreasonably optimistic frame of mind and thus, they believed that they felt . . . pretty good. Better anyway, than they would have felt under less lucky-to-be-alive circumstances.[13]

No one ever remembers the nurse, but Beecher returned to his position at Harvard after the war and published a paper in 1955 titled

"The Powerful Placebo." In it he wrote, "Placebos have a high degree of therapeutic effectiveness in treating subjective responses."[14] What he meant was that the placebo effect, or the doctor-patient rapport, or the patient's expectations—whatever you want to call it—plays a most critical role in any type of medical intervention. He believed that "our expectation can have a profound impact on how we heal."[15]

What Beecher was calling "expectation" we've been calling *priming*.

Stranger still, it seems as if we can be primed to experience the placebo effect through visual cues alone, like the color or shape or size of a pill. As Michael Specter wrote in 2011 about studies of the phenomenon, "The larger the pill, the stronger the placebo effect. Two pills are better than one, and brand name trumps generic. Capsules are generally more effective than pills, and injections produce a more pronounced effect than either. There is even evidence to suggest the color of medicine influences the way one responds to it."[16] Apparently, colorful placebos are better pain relievers, but white pills are the most effective imaginary antacids. Blue pills help people fall asleep faster than red pills, which conversely make the best uppers. Yellow pills make the most effective antidepressants and green the best anti-anxiety drugs.[17] We have conditioned responses to those colors, just as we have to the idea that bigger or more equals faster or stronger relief.

Like Pavlov's dog, our brains can be taught different responses through all sorts of conditioning techniques. Habitual aspirin users, for example, respond to the shape, color, and distinctively nasty taste of aspirin with an expectation of pain relief; because once they think they've swallowed an aspirin, their brain takes over and produces endorphins via anticipatory release.

Robert Trivers, professor of anthropology and biological sciences at Rutgers University, has a particular fascination for deception, and having studied the phenomenon in depth for decades, has done some of the most compelling and novel work. The leading evolutionary theorist believes that this unintentional conditioning we subject our own brains to explains why the placebo effect works so well on pain, anxiety, insomnia, and even diseases like Parkinson's—but *not at all* on Alzheimer's disease—because what the brain expects to happen in the near future affects its physiological state. In fact, Alzheimer's patients seem to be immune to the placebo effect, which Trivers chalks up to the fact that Alzheimer's diminishes the patient's ability to remember the past or anticipate the future. Without those basic abilities, *priming doesn't work.*[18]

Jim Morrison once said, "Drugs are a bet with your mind," but so is everything else . . . the drugs aren't strictly required. The white-coat effect is a known phenomenon in which a patient, with or without any underlying health problems (it makes no difference), will *always* have higher blood pressure when the measurement is taken by a doctor. Preferably in a white coat. It sounds silly, but it's so widely observed as to be considered typical. The white-coat effect demonstrates that the placebo effect is completely effective even without the placebo—because it's your mind that's creating the reality that is, in turn, controlling your body, not the other way around.

And once the placebo effect is set in motion, it's exaggerated by confirmation bias, wherein one already believes an idea and therefore more readily sees or experiences, and more willingly accepts, evidence that the already-embraced idea *is,* in fact, true. Ultimately, it makes for a perfectly self-perpetuating delusion.

Victorian Children Did Way Too Much Blow

But neither the placebo effect nor the faith of thousands of devoted customers could save the Rattlesnake King. In 1917 Clark Stanley was shut down by the feds. Did you forget about him? I told you this story gets a little bit twisty and loops back on itself a few times.

By the turn of the century, patent medicines had become big business. They had also become a big problem for public health, and not just because half of them were absurd, like Dr. Kilmer's Swamp Root (which made the impossible-to-disprove claim that it cured "internal slime fever"), but because the other half were *not*. They were really powerful and dangerous drugs—or, worse, *poisons*—being sold like health food.

Beauty treatments contained mercury and lead to lighten the skin, which they certainly would have done, though without hair or teeth I can't really see the point. Countless nerve tonics and cough syrups and even draughts for "fussy babies" contained mostly opium, morphine, and heroin. Lydia Pinkham's Health Tonic was a concoction of heroin and lead intended for menstrual cramps, which at least sounds fun. Whereas Piso's Tablets—*also* advertised for "women's ailments"—were a frat-party mixture of cannabis and chloroform (which I assume were meant to be swallowed with a tall glass of shut-the-hell-up). McMunn's Elixir was almost entirely opium and alcohol and was marketed as "purely vegetable," which I guess is technically true. Dr Pepper and Coca-Cola were so-called brain tonics; Coca Wine was the thinking man's booze; and Cocarettes were the only thing to smoke if you wanted to "stimulate the brain."* I suppose that much cocaine *would* make you feel smarter. . . . But a lot of people also had heart attacks. One popular patent medicine used strychnine

---

*The makers of Dr Pepper maintain that they *never* included cocaine in their brain tonic, even when it was legal and industry standard, and we'll have to take them at their word, because they kept their formulary a closely guarded secret from the start, long before the 1906 Pure Food and Drug Act required manufacturers to disclose addictive or dangerous ingredients.

as an aphrodisiac. Another used mercury to remove freckles. And apparently Fowler's Solution was that you drink arsenic—for everything.

Which *is* a solution, I suppose. . . . But not a very good one.

A big part of the problem with patent medicines was that no one really knew what they were taking. They were just inundated with products and slogans and logos and doctors and experts and pretty women and cute children and claims and testimonials shouting at them from every corner. According to Harvard University psychologist Daniel Gilbert, who has been studying the neuroscience of deception for over two decades, human minds "when faced with shortages of time, energy, or conclusive evidence, may fail to un-accept the ideas that they involuntarily accept during comprehension."[19] In other words, the relentless firehose-like advertising created a state of such cognitive exhaustion that people couldn't keep track of the claims; sooner than you'd think, they stopped even trying to and just accepted that whatever was on the label was the truth.

This resulted in two decades of Americans confidently self-medicating with everything from the hardest of drugs to toxic (even radioactive) substances to straight up poison. So in 1906 Congress enacted the Pure Food and Drug Act, which eventually led to the formation of the Food and Drug Administration. Over time, the FDA's mandate expanded, and the law was strengthened and revised. But the original Pure Food and Drug Act of 1906's primary purpose was to ensure that products were accurately labeled.

There were (for some reason only) ten substances deemed addictive or dangerous by the Pure Food and Drug Act: alcohol, morphine, heroin, opium, cocaine, eucaine, chloroform, cannabis indica, chloral

hydrate, and acetanilide. The 1906 law required that products containing any of these ingredients be labeled in a way that clearly listed them on
the package—*if they were in fact in the product.** The law, basically the
No Roofies / No Duds Act of 1906, also strictly prohibited advertising
the presence of any ingredients that were *not* present in the product—
like actual snake oil in Stanley's Snake Oil. As government legislation
goes, it was hardly draconian, but it was enough to put Clark Stanley
out of business. In 1917 federal investigators seized a shipment of Stanley's Snake Oil and, upon testing, found that it contained mineral oil, 1
percent capsaicin, and turpentine—but no actual snake oil of any kind.

The Rattlesnake King pleaded no contest, paid a fine, and went
out of business.

But by then it was officially open season on patent medicines. A lot
of other patent-medicine companies were also put out of business by
the newly empowered FDA. Many more complied with the Pure Food
and Drug Act and listed their formulas on the package but found their
customers unwilling to drink clearly labeled turpentine or rat poison.

In that regard, the law and the FDA itself were both fairly effective. But it's never stopped anyone from buying or selling potentially
dangerous (or simply useless) nonsense. The FDA may be able to control how nonprescription substances themselves are or are not repre-
sented, but it is not entirely able to control representations of what
those substances do or how effective they are. In fact, it can't even dispute false or misleading claims; the most the FDA can do is withhold
its endorsement.

---

*The FDA didn't require a complete listing of all ingredients in over-the-counter products until
1938. The 1906 law only included those (random) ten substances. I have no idea how radium
failed to make the cut. Or arsenic, or strychnine.

And so it turns out that almost every multivitamin, beauty treatment, superfood extract, or supplement you've ever swallowed, slathered on, or inhaled was not, technically, FDA approved. Because the FDA was never empowered to stop anyone from selling endless variations on Snake Oil, only to prevent purveyors from deliberately lying about the contents of such products.

It's All Right Cause It's All White

Of all the self-perpetuating delusions that people have, my favorite is the delusion of *novelty*.

In 1895 approximately 1 in every 200 Americans were addicted to either morphine or opium powders.[20] But this wasn't a problem of crack houses or drug cartels; in fact, it was all entirely legal. Hell, you could actually buy *cocaine and a syringe* from the Sears, Roebuck catalog.* America's per capita consumption of drugs like morphine, heroin, and cocaine tripled between 1870 and 1880, largely in response to over-availability, shoddy regulation, and *advertising*—by 1889 Boston physician James Adams estimated that about 150,000 Americans were "medical addicts."[21] It was nuts, and it was doctors and pharmacists who were driving America's out-of-control drug addiction.

Opiates and narcotics were in a lot of over-the-counter patent medicines, and the availability of these drugs in a totally unregulated marketplace suffused with advertisements was partially to blame. But this opioid epidemic wasn't exclusive to the idiots swigging heroin for hair loss or putting babies to bed with morphine drops. Most of the fault lay with real doctors. They massively overprescribed even

---

*And if they still sold things like that, they might still be in business.

larger amounts of narcotics like morphine and heroin to their patients for any and every complaint they might have short of "I couldn't find parking."

As Erick Trickey notes, in 1888 opiates made up 15 percent of all prescriptions dispensed in the city of Boston—and they were dispensed for *everything*. Opiates were given particularly frequently to women for every possible discomfort, both their own *and* those they inspired in others. "Nervous complaints," exhaustion, menstrual cramps . . . even morning sickness was treated with heavy narcotics. It was so extreme that before 1900 the average opiate addict in America was a middle- to upper-class white woman.[22] And that doesn't include children; they were even more overmedicated but uncounted, because practically every medicine—prescription or not—for babies and children contained morphine or cocaine.

And I've just blamed the doctors, but there's blame to share; the reason the whole country was so high was that the drugs were not just being pushed *by* the doctors, they were being pushed *on them* as well.

At the turn of the century, pharmaceutical companies didn't market directly to the public; it was a distinction between pharma and patent medicine that the pharmaceutical companies took pride in. But what they left on the table with direct-to-consumer marketing, they made up for in the ferocity with which they marketed to physicians, who no doubt responded to the firehose of advertising they were subjected to with the same cognitive exhaustion that their patients experienced in response to patent-medicine and its onslaught of advertising.

Morphine tablets were available by the mid-1800s, eliminating the need to shoot up at home or at work, and conveniences like that were a huge selling point, just as they are now. Even as medical journals were filled with articles warning doctors of the danger of opioid abuse and addiction, the same journals were filled with ads for morphine tablets and hypodermic syringes. The pharma industry made sure to keep doctors constantly apprised of every new development, every new convenience—and, of course, all the infinite ills that could be treated successfully with narcotics, from teething babies to sullen women to short children who stubbornly refused to grow. And as I said, all of this—pharma companies pushing drugs on doctors, over-the-counter patent medicines pushing the very same dangerous and addictive drugs on consumers—was not only completely legal but also relatively respectable.

The *only* reason the makers of Coca-Cola ever took the cocaine out of their soda—which they touted as a stimulant for the body (code for libido) and the mind, an "intellectual beverage" enjoyed by well-off white Americans who knew *exactly* how high they were—was because of a sudden and intense backlash when Black people were able to buy it as well.[23] In 1899, Coca-Cola started bottling their product, selling it for the first time outside exclusively segregated soda fountains, making it available to everyone, at which point southern newspapers became hysterical (and delusional), writing of violent "negro cocaine fiends"[24] high on Coke (yes, the soda pop), burning down buildings, and raping white women as the police looked on, powerless to stop them. I guess they'd all gotten so high they forgot it was a respectable "brain tonic."

Cocaine wouldn't even be made illegal until 1914, over a decade later, but in 1903 Coca-Cola quickly removed the cocaine from their product, replacing it with lots of caffeine and additional syrup.[25] As the whole country reached peak hysteria about Black "cocaine fiends," it was in complete denial about white heroin addicts—which had become a larger and larger slice of the population.

The only reason any of the laws, let alone attitudes, about America's out-of-control drug problem ever changed, was that *demographics* did. By the turn of the century opium dens were competing with pharmacies for the largest crowds of drug addicts—who were no longer just well-off white ladies—but now included those same Chinese immigrants whose snake oil had helped start the craze for patent medicines in the first place. As soon as there were opium dens in cities and towns across America (And who gets to make money on those black-market drugs? That's always an important question.), *non*pharmaceutical versions of the same narcotics became increasingly popular, particularly with a new demographic; younger, more impoverished white men. At which point, you can imagine, the problem was suddenly taken seriously. In 1914 the Harrison Narcotic Act was introduced. The Act was the beginning of an effort to legislate American narcotic users into a state of near prohibition, all in a frantic attempt to keep the white kids clean. Which of course didn't work at all. The only forces great enough to stop the rising tide of addiction were World War I and the 1918 flu pandemic.

But by then, the long-term damage was already done: direct-to-consumer drug marketing had made its way out of Pandora's box of truly awful ideas and into the mainstream—and it was *never* going back, despite the fact that marketing drugs directly to people has been one of the most harmful experiments in modern medicine.

Big Wellness

But there's always backlash or, at least, what looks like backlash: at the same time that most of the country was high as a kite, an increasingly large, generally wealthy demographic had become obsessed with their own health and "wellness." Don't misunderstand: they were just as crazy, and just as swayed by advertising and groupthink as the drug-addled portion of the country. In the very beginning it was just spa towns, bathing, and "taking the waters," but it got so weird, so fast. And ground zero for this new madness was Battle Creek Sanitarium, a "health reform institute" started by Dr. John Kellogg.

Dr. Kellogg—yes, the guy who invented your cereal—was kind of the Gwyneth Paltrow of his day, but somehow scarier. He was a real doctor (unlike, say, Dr. Bailey of Radithor fame), but you wouldn't know it, the way he eschewed narcotics, alcohol, and lead paint chips. Instead, our celebrity wellness doctor went 180 degrees the other way. He was obsessed with purity and "clean" living. Kellogg was an adamant vegetarian (when he ate *at all*) and deliberately celibate over the course of his forty-year marriage.

Battle Creek Sanitarium was the place to go—if you could get in. At the height of the wellness movement, the Battle Creek Sanitarium wait list included Henry Ford, Amelia Earhart, Thomas Edison, and Sojourner Truth—for such forward-thinking treatments as electric-light baths, sinusoidal-current therapy, continuous bathing, fifteen-quart enemas, and my favorite: masturbation cures. The electric-light bathing didn't involve bathing so much as it did getting in a wooden casket lined with lightbulbs to cure insomnia and depression. Which is marginally less insane than it sounds when you consider that both are treated with "light therapy" today. Just not locked in a box. Continuous bathing actually *was* bathing (you know, in water) but for days, weeks, or months at a time—definitely not to be combined with sinusoidal-current therapy, which involved applying electrical currents of various strengths directly to the naked body, via a device Dr. Kellogg cobbled together from old phone parts. Kellogg believed that sinusoidal-current therapy could treat lead poisoning, obesity, and even vision problems if applied directly to the eyeballs.

The fifteen-quart enemas are exactly what they sound like, but worse: it was fifteen quarts *per minute,* as "more people need[ed] washing out than any other remedy," according to Dr. Kellogg. There were violently vibrating wooden chairs to "stimulate the bowels," beating and slapping machines, and intensely weird rules about food, sleep, exercise, and unclean thoughts. Masturbation cures involved, among other things, mutilation. So you can see how all this "wellness" wasn't really any healthier than buying an eight ball from the Sears, Roebuck catalog.

Battle Creek Sanitarium and the wellness movement marked the beginning of what would just get worse, if not weirder, and would be more aggressively marketed as the "Wellness Industry." The wellness movement began in an era that had touted the health benefits of alcohol for infants, random poisons and hardest of drugs for everyone and then flipped and brought us everything from medical cleanses to yogurt enemas to expensive health oriented staycations. It almost understandably evolved in rigid opposition to the lazy indulgence of narcotic overprescription, but then went full-speed crazy in the other direction. As the rigorous abuse and glamorized self-deprivation and self-absorption—I mean self-care (not to mention fun swag!)—of "wellness" proved both popular and profitable, it exploded into the mainstream, until finally, two centuries of medical quackery culminated in Goop suggesting you supposit a jade pool ball.

The FDA might have shut down most of the most bizarre hokum the nineteenth- and early-twentieth-century marketplace had to offer, but the law creating the FDA had no effect on what there's a market *for.* People will always want to believe in magic diet drugs and happy pills and boner pumps and beauty creams, so it's all just been replaced with newer, shinier, more useless, and often more dangerous Snake Oil. At this point there's everything from new age practitioners to anti-aging specialists, shilling everything from fake cancer cures to useless supplements that will endow you with nothing but *very* expensive pee. There are annual conferences—ACAM, A4M, countless others (I've visited them)—of hundreds of thousands of physicians and pharmacists, all looking for the next new product *to sell to you*.

We've come full circle, like a snake eating its own tail and "wellness" has actually fused to some degree with the medical pharma model it sprang up in opposition to 150 years ago. In other words, the Snake Oil industry is alive and well.

Pick Your Poison

Thank God for *real* medicine, right?

Not so much . . . some of it works. But then, some of the crazy stuff works too. But most of it, in double-blind trials, only works on a small percentage of people. It's been determined that only about 10 percent of patients taking SSRIs (selective serotonin reuptake inhibitors, like Prozac) actually respond to the chemical components of the drug. Or it works pretty well, about as well as the placebo. Which is why *more than one in ten* patients taking SSRIs will tell you that they really do feel better.

The culprit, once again, is priming.

In 1997 the FDA changed its advertising guidelines after a century and decided to let pharmaceutical companies market directly to us, the consumers, combining the two worst ideas they ever had. The result of direct-to-consumer pharmaceutical marketing was a huge surge in spending on television and other media advertising on the part of the drug companies—and a commensurate uptick in prescriptions sold. Prescriptions for OxyContin grew from 670,000 in 1997 to 6.2 million in 2002[26]—and that was before we even started referring to it as an opioid epidemic.

Purdue Pharma, the makers of OxyContin, funded more than twenty thousand educational programs designed to "educate" doctors about the many ways in which they could prescribe opioids outside the usual justifications and then they funded groups like the American Pain Society to lobby for people's right to buy pain pills by the bucket. They courted those same doctors with free thirty-day supplies of OxyContin, as well as with paid trips, various swag, and patient referrals. Within 4 years sales of OxyContin topped $1.1 billion.[27]

This dubious choice had an obvious outcome: America ended up right back in the same opioid epidemic that Dr. Kellogg tried to slap us out of a hundred years ago. But there was another less obvious, more interesting outcome as well. It seemed unrelated, and it would take almost ten years to make sense of, but when it all came together, *it really all came together.*

In 2002 a rival pharmaceutical giant, Merck, had a problem, and though they didn't know it yet, their problem was with placebos.[28] As five of their most lucrative patents were set to expire, they pinned their fortunes on the development of an experimental new antidepressant code-named MK-869. After great early success and much hype, MK-869 crashed and burned. It couldn't even surpass a placebo in later stage trials. Merck was at a loss; they couldn't explain MK-869's sudden failure, so they dropped their new antidepressant and compensated for their lack of a splashy new lineup by reissuing their older drugs under new patents for different uses, to stall for time, since they had no new drugs to market. This practice is known as off-label patenting.

But it turned out that this was *not* exclusively a Merck problem. Around the same time, Eli Lilly broke off testing for a much-hyped new schizophrenia drug when the volunteers showed a response twice as favorable *to the placebo* as in previous testing. Eli Lilly was having exactly the same mysterious problem and so were most of the other pharma companies trying to develop new "CNS-regulators," drugs which act on the central nervous system to alter thought, emotion, and behavior, like antidepressants or mood stabilizers. They just didn't know it was a weirdly universal phenomenon at that point. (Pharma companies, as you can imagine, aren't big on sharing research data with their rivals.) But between 2001 and 2006 a huge portion of their new drugs had begun failing those same double-blind trials against placebos. That portion rose by 20 percent in phase II and another 11 percent in phase III. And stranger still, it wasn't just the new, exciting CNS-regulating drugs—the kind they were all racing to develop that were failing the trials, but also the old tried-and-true drugs—the drugs they'd been selling for ten, fifteen, or twenty years. Suddenly, *all* the drugs were increasingly failing to do any better than a sugar pill in double-blind trials. It was a broad, confusing phenomenon; old and new antidepressants were failing seven out of ten times and being abandoned without being manufactured.[29] There was nothing wrong with the drugs themselves; it was almost as if "the powerful placebo," as Beecher's seminal 1955 article had called it, was somehow becoming *more powerful*.

It was almost like that, because it was *exactly* like that.

Their problem turned out to be twofold. First, by creating whole classes of drugs to modify emotion and behavior, which is exactly what CNS-regulating drugs do, they had tried, in their own words, to "dominate the central nervous system,"[30] the part of the brain compromised in Alzheimer's—the part of the brain capable of remembering the past and predicting the future—the very part of the brain *responsible for the placebo effect*. It turns out that when you focus all your time and money on creating drugs specifically to affect the central nervous system—antidepressants, antipsychotics, anti-anxieties, sleep aids, sexual enhancement drugs, and amphetamines—they're going to be particularly susceptible to the placebo effect.

I guess that explains the Valium. . . .

The other thing that backfired spectacularly was *the advertising itself.* After years and years and years of television commercials and magazine ads for pharmaceuticals, the pharma companies couldn't find any volunteers for their studies who hadn't *already been primed* by the expectation of what this pill or that pill would or would not do. The tests were rendered meaningless by the contaminated pool of subjects, all of whom had been subjected to a lifetime of drug advertisements. They were no longer the blank slate that drug testing requires. But were the tests really invalidated? Or do they tell a more profound truth about how these drugs work on us in tandem with a century of marketing inundation and acculturation?

Pharma companies claiming that the tests are compromised can take a seat, regardless—because they don't exactly run pure research. When they submit drugs for testing, pharma companies don't always like the final results of their trial and decide they would prefer a different set of results. And just as often, the trial results are all over the map, proving no insight of value about the drug's efficacy one way or the other. At that point, they run *multiples* of the same trial and cherry-pick coherent results. A lot of those companies feel remarkably okay about doing that and only showing the results of those individual tests that ended with their desired outcome.

It seems that when it comes to drugs, whether it's big pharma or "alternative medicine," you gotta just pick your poison and try to believe it works.

Let 'Em Burn

The 1970 Ford Pinto is famous for only one thing: being a hideously engineered, fiery death trap. The way it was designed, if it was ever rear-ended not only would the rear gas tank *explode* upon impact, all the doors would jam shut, locking the passengers in the car to burn to death.

That's pretty bad. Worse? Ford knew that about the 1970 Pinto . . . *in 1968.*

"The Pinto memo," which Ford has tried to keep under wraps for decades, outlined all these structural flaws, and what it would cost to fix them, two years before the Ford Pinto was released, causing thousands of hideous accidents and hundreds of horrific deaths. The 1968 memo also estimates the cost to recall the Pinto—all eleven million vehicles—and fix the flaw preemptively. It would have cost $11 per unit for modifications, adding up to a total cost of $121 million. The problem with the Pinto memo is that there's another column of numbers, one that calculates how many accidents, injuries, and deaths were expected, as well as a breakdown of the cost in payouts for serious injury, burning, and death. And that number only comes to $49.53 million, well less than half of the cost of a recall.[31]

So they released the Ford Pinto, without modifications, in 1970, because it was cheaper to just let them burn.

That attitude, that it might cost less to knowingly harm or kill hundreds, thousands, or tens of thousands of people and just pay out the settlement—is not unique to the auto industry. Big-pharma drugs like Avandia, Resulin, and most recently and grotesquely, Purdue Pharma's OxyContin are frequently released with the blessing of the FDA and the full awareness by all parties involved that they do absolutely nothing. Or worse, that they do something really dangerous. But they generate *so much profit* in the five to ten years it takes to prove that and pull them from the market that even if (usually when) the companies get sued, it'll be worth it once the accounting is settled.

IT'S LOVELY AT THE TOP

Pyramid Schemes and Why You're
Probably Part of One

The more important the subject and the closer it cuts to the
bone of our hopes and needs, the more we are likely
to err in establishing a framework for analysis.
—STEPHEN JAY GOULD

I certainly wouldn't invest in the stock market.
I never believed in it.
—BERNIE MADOFF

PYRAMID SCHEME

In a Pyramid Scheme, the person at the top recruits a small number of people below them in some supposedly legitimate but still too-good-to-be-true investment or business venture. Each person who is recruited recruits more people. With each tier of recruits, the Pyramid grows larger, as does the concentration of money trickling upward to the top levels. Ultimately, though, the only real business or venture is recruiting individuals to recruit still more recruits, all of them shunting more and more money to the top.

But eventually someone too far down the Pyramid will want their money back—which, of course, won't be there. When this happens, the illusion will be broken.

Panic sets in, everyone wants out, and the entire Pyramid crumbles.

The scariest part?

Modern life is lousy with 'em.

How to Build a Pyramid

Pyramid Schemes are all around us, often hard to see, and some don't even directly involve money. At its most basic, a Pyramid Scheme is just a system that promises a lot of something later, in return for very little investment now—in reality, whatever you invest is gone and never coming back.

The Pyramid survives for as long as it does on pure faith that those big returns you were promised are coming . . . any minute now. Where does this blind faith come from? Well, it helps that everyone else involved believes it too, which extends an aura of respectability to a proposition that might otherwise seem debatable.

Mostly, though, belief—in fact or in falsehood—is an act of will. And often enough, the very expectations that prime us to believe lies are nothing more than our own projected desires. As such, they require only the slightest nudge to loop backward into believability.

Money in the Mail

Have you ever heard of a Ponzi scheme? It was named after a con man, Charles Ponzi, who became famous when his "rob Peter to pay Paul" postage swindle was exposed. In the 1920s, Ponzi realized he could buy international postal coupons (stamps, essentially) at a discount in certain countries. This occurred to him when he got one in the mail from Spain. The Spanish postal coupons had been bought in a Spanish post office for 30 centavos. Because of the way international mail worked, that international postal coupon from Spain could be exchanged for a U.S. postage stamp worth 5 cents. Because the redemption rate was fixed by international treaty, and because Ponzi was aware that the Spanish peseta was weaker than the dollar, he realized that buying those Spanish postal coupons in bulk and then redeeming them in the United States would net about a 10 percent profit. Better yet, bulk buying the same sort of international postal coupons in other countries with *even weaker* economies, relative to the United States, would generate an even higher profit margin.[1]

Ponzi decided he would make bank by buying huge quantities of these international, treaty-fixed postal coupons in certain countries abroad with really depressed economies—this was just a couple years after World War I, so European countries with struggling economies were not exactly unicorns—then ship them to the United States and redeem them at full price for a profit. He surmised that he could do this all over the map, just by determining which country had a stronger currency than another at any point in time—buying in the former to redeem in the latter.[2]

Now that's not a scam. That's actually a pretty decent business model, and Ponzi managed to sell thousands of investors on the idea. What made it a fraud was the same thing that made it so wildly successful. First, he lied about the profits. Not happy with the modest 5 percent profit on his product that he was reliably generating for his investors, he claimed an investment in his scheme would return a 50 percent profit in only forty-five days. Next, he skimmed most of the money his investors gave him and just kept it himself.

The way he stole the money wasn't even as creative as the original business plan, and that's a shame.

He took money from investors, telling them he had a vast network of agents across Europe out buying these postal coupons. When he owed them dividends each month, he took new money from new investors and used it to pay the previous round of investors. When the second round of investors (as well as the first) wanted their dividends the *next* month, he just took more new money from even newer investors and used it to pay the earlier ones. He repeated the process over and over. He kept it going for quite a while, paying thousands of investors with the proceeds from subsequent investors he signed up, all while keeping the majority of the profit.

And there was no vast network of agents across Europe buying anything. In fact, he very quickly stopped buying the international postal coupons *at all*. He just paid out the earlier investments with newer investors' up-front cash. After he got busted, a final audit of his company's assets turned up about sixty-one dollars' worth of stamps.[3] By the time his Pyramid collapsed, it had become so vast, and so many people lost so much money, that we still call this sort of Pyramid Scheme a Ponzi scheme.

Money for Nothing

Charles Ponzi was a pretty big thief. In fact, he even stole the idea for the scam. About thirty years before Ponzi, in 1889, a quiet twenty-four-year-old named William Franklin Miller was living in Brooklyn, doing a very modest business as a bookkeeper. He was generally liked and seen as an upstanding guy. He was a member of Tompkins Avenue Congressional Church, and at one time the president of its charitable branch, the Christian Endeavor Society. He even taught an adult Bible-study class on Sundays. He hardly had Charles Ponzi's swagger, but he did have the idea first.[4]

He'd never swindled a day in his life, although he *did* try to work on Wall Street for a while. But he never really had the capital to get going and had to constantly borrow from friends. His credit was amazing, though, because he consistently paid them back. The first lesson he learned on Wall Street was that you can keep your credit rolling by borrowing new money to pay back previous loans, seemingly forever.[5]

In March, he confided in three men—well, boys, since they were all between seventeen and twenty—with whom he worked at the Christian Endeavor Society. He told them that he had an inside man at the New York Stock Exchange, and he could invest money for them with a promised 10 percent return rate. That might have even been true, but it quickly metastasized into something else. The first boy, Oscar Bergstrom, invested ten dollars on March 16 and was given a little paper receipt for "speculation in stocks."[6] And every week, through April, Miller paid out the 10 percent he owed.

Then, one day, without explanation or warning, a sign appeared in his window. It read:

W. F. Miller

Investments

The way to wealth is as plain as

the road to market. —B. Franklin

The next week, when he showed up to teach a Bible-study class, everyone wanted to know what the sign was about. He told them "It's not fair the Morgans and the Goulds and the Vanderbilts are making so many millions, while us little people are making so little. I've decided to do something about it."[7] His friend could vouch for him, as well as several others. Someone asked what kind of return they could expect on their investment. The 10 percent he quoted was *five times* what the bank paid . . . and then he delivered the jaw-dropping clarification that he meant ten percent *a week*.

That was 520 percent a year.

Unless Miller had found a real diamond mine or started running drugs, there was *no way* to deliver that. But his Bible-study class didn't know that, and a lot of them were eager to invest, though most of them had very small sums of money, as little as five or ten dollars. At that point, he held up his hand, like a painted saint, and said, "I'll accept no investments on the Sabbath."[8]

In grifting, this is called the takeaway. You show somebody something, they kind of want it, and then you tell them they can't have it and they *really* want it. It also eliminates the suspicion that you might be trying to sell them something. Despite his lack of experience, Miller was obviously a natural.

On Monday evening when Miller returned from work, there was a line of investors waiting outside his house to give him money. At the end of the week, he gave them the return on their investment, and many of them invested more, and many more people invested; eventually, they were even rolling over their *interest* into further investment as well, so he didn't have to pay them at all. This continued for weeks. Eventually, the entire neighborhood was invested.

By August he had hired employees. By October he had expanded beyond his tiny office at 144 Floyd Street, taking over the whole building. He had also decided to incorporate as the Franklin Syndicate and replaced those little paper receipts with letterhead engraved WILLIAM F. MILLER, MGR. FRANKLIN SYNDICATE, BANKERS AND BROKERS. STOCK EXCHANGE, DAILY FROM 10 AM TO 3 PM. It also read, along the top: "An Investment of $10 will Net You a Profit of $52 a year," earning him his nickname 520 Miller. By November he had twelve thousand investors, most of whom invested far more than $10, and more often than once. The Franklin Syndicate received between $20,000 and $63,000 in daily deposits. *Every day.* Business was booming; one day the line— well, crowd really—to deposit money was so huge that the stoop in front of 144 Floyd Street actually collapsed under the weight.[9]

520 Miller had expanded way beyond Brooklyn, in part because everyone who wasn't reinvesting their interest payments really was getting paid every week, and in part because he spent over $32,000 placing ads in newspapers all over the country. He also paid to plant articles in all those papers with headlines like "Wall Street Astonished. William F. Miller's Franklin Syndicate a Big Winner," seemingly reporting on the Franklin Syndicate's mind-blowing success.[10] People were actually sending him cash in envelopes. Within a little over nine months, Miller had generated a massive fortune. Ironically, there's no exact accounting of how much money the bookkeeper made, because bookkeepers keep bizarre books—especially when they're cooking them—but it is known that in one month alone in 1899 he made $430,000. Over the year he ran his con he's thought to have made somewhere between $2 and 3 million.[11] Today that would be just shy of $1 billion.

But, as the Notorious B.I.G. put it: "Every true hustler knows that you cannot hustle forever. You will go to jail eventually." And after nearly a year of cash farming, Miller was starting to get cocky. All those newspaper ads he ran all over the country—and those planted headlines about Wall Street's "New Wizard" at the Franklin Syndicate? Yeah, they were a bad idea. They did get him noticed, but not exclusively by dupe investors. Real Wall Street heavies had *questions*: Who the hell was William Miller? What the hell was the Franklin Syndicate? Where was the money coming from? What kind of investment yielded 520 percent annual returns?

And so, eventually, did the police. An investigation turned up the fact that the Franklin Syndicate applied for incorporation on November 20, 1889, in New Jersey, but the corporation had no officers, no manager, and no board of directors. They weren't even really able to do business legally in New York. It turned out Miller was never a member of the New York Stock Exchange and had no license to trade.[12] *Had* he actually been investing the money, rather than building a giant Pyramid with it, that would have been illegal also.

The morning of November 24, the *New York Times* headline simply read: "Desert Miller's Company." The article was even worse, outlining all the questions and, even more disturbing, some of the answers about 520 Miller and the Franklin Syndicate.[13] By that evening, Miller was in Canada.

No Honor Among Thieves

He left in such a hurry that when the police arrived at his offices, they found $4,500 just lying on a table next to four hundred dollars' worth of stamped envelopes. His office staff had no idea where he'd gone. The police spent the next two and a half months searching for him in New York, the rest of the United States, and abroad. Finally, on February 8, 1890, he was apprehended by Captain James Reynolds while walking down the street in Montreal. And I say *apprehended* rather than arrested, because he was not arrested until he reached U.S. soil. He was just strangely willing to go with the officer, even when Reynolds made his intent known.

According to Maria Konnikova's excellent account of their meeting, around seven P.M. on a Tuesday evening, Reynolds "spied him in the crowd. 'Hello Miller. I'm Captain Reynolds of New York,' he said as he walked up to the fugitive. Miller doffed his hat. 'Why, how are you Captain?' he replied. They shook hands, Miller smiled, and the Captain informed him of his impending travel plans back to the states preferably with Miller at his side."[14] Miller went with him, which, when you think about it, he didn't necessarily have to do. It was seven in the evening, in Canada, in February—it would have been fairly dark. And the street was crowded. He was a twenty-five-year-old man; he could have run, or tried to give Reynolds the slip in the dark or in the crowd, or both. Hell, it was 1890, he could have just denied being William Miller.

And it got stranger when they arrived at Grand Central Terminal. "'Well, Miller, we are in New York now,' Reynolds said. 'I will have to place you under arrest.' Miller smiled. 'Certainly. I understand.'"[15] Miller bothered to flee to Canada and hide out in November, but by February he jauntily accompanied the fuzz back to the scene of the crime.

It was weird, frankly. It was almost like he left something behind.

You see, Miller was getting ready to disappear *before* the *New York Times* article came out; that's probably how he managed it so quickly and effectively. Being a bookkeeper, he realized that, though his Pyramid was getting bigger and generating more money every day, it was only doing so by accumulating *more investors* every day. He did the math and saw that he was rapidly approaching the tipping point where he would no longer be able to pay out everyone's 10 percent every week. That's when he confided his predicament to his very criminal lawyer, Colonel Robert Ammon. Ammon asked how much money was left, and Miller told him there was about $255,000 at that moment, which was certainly a lie. The morning the *Times* article dropped, the Franklin Syndicate had $1.2 million in investments.[16] Even if he had paid out 10 percent that week, he would still be left with over $1 million. Who knows why he lied to the criminal lawyer he went to for help, but upon hearing only $255,000 was left, Ammon strongly suggested Miller skip town before the next payments were due. As his lawyer, Ammon offered to hide the money—lest Miller be caught fleeing the country with it—and send it to him once he was settled in his new life in Canada.[17]

His neighborhood Pyramid was the first and only con Miller had ever run, and he was exhausted. He thought retirement with a million bucks sounded like a great idea. He could slip away, have Ammon send him the $255,000 in pieces, and in a few years, when the heat was off, he could retrieve the rest.[18] Before he left New York, Miller signed "all of it" over to Ammon—at least, all $255,000 in cash and bonds that *he claimed* existed.[19]

It wasn't a great idea, though.

Beyond the *Times* article that he wasn't expecting and the investigation that he didn't know about, two things became apparent within a few weeks of his flight to Canada. First, that Ammon had stolen all the money that he was supposed to hide for Miller and had disappeared with it. Second, that Miller's many investors (and the police) had realized he'd skipped town and that all their money was probably also gone. And just like that, Miller became a penniless, wanted man.

A few weeks later, he was merrily accompanying Captain Reynolds back to New York, where Miller was indicted on one count of first-degree grand larceny and one count of second-degree grand larceny. He was convicted that April and sentenced to serve ten years in Sing Sing. He didn't, though. He was released early, when he rolled on someone else, a con man the cops had been trying to nail a lot longer than Miller. It seems Miller had been marked by an even bigger grifter than himself: Colonel Robert Ammon.[20]

After he was released from prison, Miller returned to New York and resumed his previously quiet little life as a working stiff—under an assumed name, obviously. Then, one day, several years later, without warning, he packed up and disappeared and was never heard from again. With at least one million dollars of his swindle still missing.[21]

Charles Ponzi wasn't the first Pyramid builder, nor for that matter was he the last. In fact, his predecessor, Miller, claimed he discovered the basic principle of the Pyramid Scheme during his brief stint working on Wall Street, where Pyramids are still all the rage and just keep getting bigger.

The Great Pyramid at 133 East 64th St.

During his trial, an infamous American con man named Joseph "Yellow Kid" Weil made the extraordinary suggestion that his victims were actually as guilty as he was. He said, "I never cheated an honest man, only rascals. They may have been respectable, but they were never any good. They wanted something for nothing. I gave them nothing for something."[22]

He makes an interesting point. *Nobody's* clean—no matter how many charcoal pills and CBD scrubs they may ingest to clear toxins from their bodies or limiting beliefs from their minds. In fact, the success of modern Snake Oil has much in common with the persistence and popularity of Pyramid Schemes: both depend on tricking not human senses but *sensibilities*. Often people believe things because they've been fooled by their own perceptual glitches or cognitive fallacies. But just as often, people believe things simply because they want to.

So. Did investors learn their lesson after Ponzi went to jail?

Um, not exactly.

In fact, it's kind of weird we're still calling it a Ponzi scheme one hundred years later. Especially when he didn't invent it, didn't pioneer it, and didn't even go out the biggest. That dubious honor belongs to Bernie Madoff, who was busted in 2008 for running the biggest Ponzi scheme in history, to the tune of $65 *billion*.

Bernie Madoff was born in Queens, New York, in 1938, the son of a plumber. He briefly attended Brooklyn Law School but decided Wall Street was the place to make real money, so in 1960 he founded his own firm, Bernard L. Madoff Investment Securities LLC, where he continued to work for nearly five decades, until he was busted by the feds. Supposedly, the wealth-management arm of his firm had been trading in blue chip stocks for decades, managing massive investments for extraordinarily wealthy clients. In reality, the firm, which employed his brother, his niece, his wife Ruth, and his two sons, Andrew and Mark, did absolutely nothing. After he pleaded guilty, he admitted that neither he nor his firm had actually done any real trading since the 1990s.

It was, by Madoff's own admission, a straight Pyramid Scheme.

When Henry Ford said, "A business that makes nothing but money is a poor business," he doubtless had something more ethical or at least philosophical in mind, but it describes the Pyramid Scheme perfectly: there is no product or service, just shuffling money around—mostly upward. And that works for as long as the Pyramid keeps growing. The scheme started to unravel in 2008 when banks began to falter and loans started drying up. Madoff scrambled for months looking for new investors and presenting banks with financial instruments for large-scale investment in his fund. But in those panicky, final days, nobody was buying.

He held it together for as long as he could, which wasn't that long. When Pyramids collapse, they fall *fast*. But we'll talk math in a minute. Madoff accepted, at last, that the jig was up. At that point, he called his sons and asked them to come over. Once they were there, he confessed to his family that the enormous financial institution he had headed for decades was in fact "one big lie." He insisted, even from prison, that they never knew a thing. Though that claim begs the question: What did they actually *do* in those offices all day, if they weren't trading? What did they *think* their business was?

At that point, Madoff believed that he still had time to shuffle money around, to make sure he took care of friends and family. Because the money wasn't actually *gone,* he'd just reached the point, like Miller, where he knew his Pyramid had gotten top-heavy and was about to tip over into insolvency. He planned to slice up that pie to feed his nearest and dearest before that happened. But he had *a lot less* time than he thought. As soon as he confessed to them, his horrified sons—in an act that was either admirable or despicable, and I'm honestly not sure which—dropped a dime on their dad.

The feds arrested Madoff on December 11, 2008. Three months later, Madoff pleaded guilty to eleven federal crimes and to running the largest private Pyramid Scheme in history—if you don't count monarchy, the church, or banking writ large.

One Big Lie

Madoff ran the same con as Miller, but he put the opposite spin on it: instead of taking tiny amounts of money from tons of his low-income peers, Madoff would only take huge investments from obscenely wealthy individuals and institutions. And no—not because he was secretly a really good guy all along. He liked the stability of great wealth. He particularly liked institutions, like charities and massive-scale pension funds, because they were so much less likely to ever withdraw their initial capital.[23] As a result, his Pyramid included millionaires, billionaires, movie stars, captains of industry, and a lot of other people with offshore bank accounts. Suffice it to say, when his Pyramid crumbled, we all heard about it.

To catch a big fish, you need the right bait: the way he caught these big fish was *with each other.* Just the sheer sums of money and name recognition of his existing clients were enough to reassure his new investors that this was a real investment, and a really good one. He salted his crumbly Pyramid with the rich and famous the same way Philip Arnold salted his worthless mine with a few real diamonds. But it worked, because it always does, because our brains are wired to extrapolate a bigger picture from a smaller glimpse. Even when we're being deliberately misled.

That sounds crazy, because it is. But the way in which your mind works *is* often crazy. And there's more than one kind of crazy

at play here: remember Gregor MacGregor and the imaginary country of Poyais? The bigger the lie, the more brazen the liar, the more
likely people are to believe it.

If someone asked you to invest $100 in a sure thing and a couple of
other random people were also investing, you'd have good reason not
to believe them—or at the very least to question the wisdom of the
investment. But if this stranger didn't ask you for the investment—if
you had to be referred by one of your peers, and you recognized (and
maybe admired) the names of his other clients, and he wouldn't take
less than maybe $500 million . . . suddenly it's like making up a
country. And of course you believe it, because *who lies that big*?

Although it seems not everyone believed Madoff. In an interview
from prison in 2011, he was bitterly adamant that some (unnamed)
hedge funds and banks *did know,* or at least suspected, what he was
doing and were thus complicit. After all, he was making a lot of people
a lot of money for a while—quite a lot, for quite a while. He said, "They
had to know. But the attitude was sort of 'If you're doing something
wrong, we don't want to know.'"[24]

He acknowledges his own guilt but suggests there's lots to go
around. The last six or seven years have borne this out, to some degree. Only since he began serving his 150-year prison term, he claims,
has he learned about the e-mails bankers were passing around prior
to 2008, clearly expressing doubt about the validity of his "results."
And, indeed, e-mails have surfaced—warning one firm or another to
steer clear or indicating that certain banks would *loan,* and therefore
profit, but *not invest*. He says, "I'm saying that the banks and funds are
complicit in one form or another."[25]

That's a hell of an accusation—and makes his claim that his sons, who worked with him, *knew nothing* even harder to take seriously. But the fact remains that executives at major banks expressed outright suspicion, not once, not occasionally, but for *years*. And then there are the regulators. Sure, Madoff intended to deceive them while running a multibillion-dollar Ponzi scam. But at several points, different concerned stakeholders raised red flags to the SEC, and yet for some reason these concerns were never investigated and were promptly dismissed— there were even individual investors who began making big withdrawals in the last few months before the scheme started to truly unravel.[26]

This suggests that on some profound level, *they all knew*. And what they didn't explicitly know, they chose not to see. They were complicit (as is anyone who invests in a scheme promising what are obviously impossible financial returns) *in choosing to believe* it was all on the up and up, because it stood to benefit them. Madoff claims that their "willful blindness" to the obvious problems and discrepancies in his regulatory filings made them just as guilty as he was of malfeasance. While this is classic narcissism at work—"it's their fault, not mine"—"Yellow Kid" Weil was at least a little bit right.

Nobody's clean.

Bad Math

If all the system, or Pyramid, needs in order to function is growth, and all it needs in order to grow is for people to believe it's going to work, then believing the lie *does,* in fact, make the system grow. This is just one more example, like the placebo effect, of the kind of alchemy that can transform our desires and beliefs into actual events and physical reality. Until that reality collapses. But what doesn't eventually?

So why did it crumble? Was it just the 2007–08 economic downturn? Doubtful—Madoff's Pyramid lasted for twenty or thirty years, through a couple recessions—so that seems wrong. In fact, his $65-billion fake-out was such a disaster that when it was finally exposed, it actually hastened some of the banks' and hedge funds' woes, not exclusively the other way around.

Warren Buffett once said, "You never know who's swimming naked until the tide goes out." And that was certainly an accurate description (if hard to unsee) of a lot of Wall Street in 2008. The same global downturn and panic that exposed the mortgage-backed securities fraud certainly pulled back the curtain on the Madoff Pyramid by choking off any source of new capital. But even in an imaginary, never-ending bull economy, it was always doomed.

Ponzi and Pyramid Schemes always fail eventually. Which is strange, because they're actually, for a long time, a fairly tenable, if fraudulent, business model.

Hear me out: on January 1, ten people each give you $100 as an investment. You have $1,000 working capital. But they each expect 10 percent interest—or $10—back at the end of each month. Even if you pay up, without doing anything, you've made $900 in January. If, over the course of January, you can get another ten people to invest the same, that's another $1,000, so now you've got $1,900 and only owe an additional $200 in interest at the end of February. That leaves you with $1,700 working capital. Do it *again*, and you have thirty paid investors at the end of March, and you only owe them *all* another $300, leaving you with $2,400. And on and on and on. You're not just covering your debts every month, you're increasing the size of the pot that you retain.

It sounds like it should work, right? It does work. Until you run out of new people willing to invest new capital. Or until enough people want their initial ($100) investment back at the same time. People are fickle. Or somebody panics and whispers *"Pyramid Scheme."* Then you're screwed. At that point *everybody* wants all of their money back, which you don't have, even if *you* never spent any of that pot, because you've been paying out interest every month.

But even if nobody ever withdraws capital, the reason it works, *math,* is *the same reason* it can't go on forever. Nobody ever bothers to do the simple math. Even if you kinda know you're in a Pyramid Scheme (and most people kinda know when they're in one, they just hope, or believe, or *choose to believe* that they got in early enough that the money's trickling up *to* them, not up *from* them), the way the math works out, if you're not in the first several rounds of investors, no matter how many subsequent rounds of investors there are, you're just giving money to other people. And that's if you're the investor.

If it's your Pyramid, you have a different math problem: the pot is technically increasing, but so is your number of investors. It only *looks* like the pot is growing, because the total excess each month, after payout, is a bigger number. But that's just arithmetic; you need to look at the derivative, not how much bigger does the pot get each month or even how much bigger do the payouts get each month. You need to look at *the rate of increase* for each, then compare them and you'll see that each month—though the retained sum seems larger—you actually owe a larger *percentage* of it: in January $100 is 10 percent of $1,000, in February $200 is 11 percent of $1,700, in March $300 is 12 percent of $2,400.

If you go on in this way, adding ten investors a month, losing none, and paying out 10 percent interest, it only takes eleven months for your numbers to reverse and for the pot to start shrinking. In October you owe 100 investors $1,000 out of $5,100, leaving you $4,100. That's your peak. In November you owe 110 investors $1,100 out of $5,100, leaving you $4,000. That $4,000 in November is less than $4,100 in October, and it just keeps backsliding from there.

The total payout you owe increases each month—and, worse, not at a steady rate. Because the amount you take in and the amount you disperse both *increase at different rates,* you owe 10 percent of the pot at the end of January, but you owe 27 percent of the pot at the end of November, and 31 percent at the end of December. Worse, every month the size of the pot from which you draw those payouts actually starts to *decrease* each month after only ten months, even with ten fresh investors monthly and none lost.

Eventually you'll have so many investors you'll owe 101 percent of your working capital, and like Miller's; your Pyramid will tip over. The only way to stop it from doing so is to add an exponentially larger number of new investors each month—*every month.*

Which is why it's called a Pyramid.

The number of subsequent investors, lower tiers on the Pyramid, necessary to keep the money flowing upward—and thus to keep the middle believing they're at the top—increases exponentially with each round. That is just the mathematical reality of pyramidal structures—whether it's stone blocks, human participants, or dollars of investment capital, the Pyramid can only be supported by exponential growth. If you start with 5 investors, you need 25 to support them. You need 625 investors to support those 25, and that's only three tiers.

By the fifth round, you need 15,258,800,000,000,000 to support the top.

Beyond a certain point, there is no way to support it. That's just how exponents work. It's the same process by which a piece of paper, of any size or shape, folded in half twenty times, would be ten kilometers high—fold it in half forty-two times, and it would reach the moon.

Midcentury to Modern Pyramids

So far, all the Pyramids I've mentioned are on Wall Street—like that's the only place we build them. That is the opposite of the case. Pyramids are everywhere. For the sake of argument, let's say you're a wholesome person who's wholly avoided Wall Street. Congratulations. But if you have a bank account, a mortgage, a 401(k) or pension, credit cards, or a car; if you buy gas; if you use a cell phone or the Internet . . . you're still probably involved in a Pyramid Scheme. In fact, lots of institutions and businesses you deal with daily are Pyramids. You may rely on one, you may worship at one, you may work for one. You may even *own* one. But not all Pyramids are created equal—or are equally predatory.

Let's forget about finance for a minute and focus on some more traditional, wholesome Pyramids.

Are you old enough to remember Avon or Mary Kay? They are cosmetics companies that revolutionized the door-to-door sales model in the sixties by letting their customers sell the products directly to their friends. This model made the traditional door-to-door salesman obsolete. Why bother employing a sales force when Avon customers could simultaneously become reps and sell their friends all the fun, pink, packaged crap—along with the business model itself? Every new rep signed would bring a bonus and a percentage of her sales to the woman who'd signed up the new girl into her sub-Pyramid. That sounds swell until you consider that there are only so many houses in the cul-de-sac, and once they're all reps, well . . . they can't sell it to each other.

This is known as multilevel marketing, or MLM. Rather than one big Pyramid in which everyone at every level pays the top and is paid by the top, MLM is a giant Pyramid made of numerous sub-Pyramids. Each of those Avon reps has to buy product from the mother ship—that's the investment—but they're never paid out from the top. They're never really paid at all. If they want to earn, they have to sign up more reps. They get a commission on each one. They're also supposed to be selling the product, but we've already established that there are only so many houses in the cul-de-sac, so that doesn't really happen.

Because of this sub-Pyramid structure, the larger Pyramid is less prone to inevitable collapse. Even so, the math still ensures that, eventually, the only real money an "investor" can earn comes from bonuses on aggressively signing new sales reps, *not* from selling the actual product, because even the leviathan of Pyramid Schemes is still a Pyramid Scheme. Most people involved in a multilevel marketing scheme make no money at all, and many go into deep debt.

Here's the fun thing about MLMs: they're not governed by exactly the same federal laws or accounting standards as say, a *real business*—so you can't necessarily look up any actual financials on them. That's convenient . . . for a business model that makes almost no one any money and leaves quite a few bankrupt. Moreover, when someone recruits you into their sub-Pyramid, legally, they can tell you *anything* they want to about how much money they're making—and they will, most of it purely fictitious.

Mary Kay is so retro you may have never heard of it. But how about Nu Skin? They're everywhere. And there's a reason for that: they are an aggressive multinational MLM founded in 1984, purported to sell supplements and skin care. But most of what they really sell is selling Nu Skin. They've been at it for so long, they've not only been repeatedly investigated by the FTC but also sued many times over. Just a couple years ago, Nu Skin Enterprises was forced to pay eight figures to settle a lawsuit that alleged they "operated a pyramid scheme in China and made false and misleading statements about its operations in the country."[27] Yes, China. When I said they were everywhere, I literally meant *everywhere*.

Nu Skin has blown up so big that they've reached the unholy grail of MLMs: *market saturation*. Once market saturation occurs, there are (I kid you not) more sellers than there are buyers in an entire geographic area. At this point, the MLM—in this case Nu Skin—instead of folding, rebrands into a new company (for example, Big Planet). They do this so that the same people, currently up to their eyeballs in debt, mistakenly see an opportunity for a new, and hopefully more successful, revenue stream to offset their losses. They don't realize that it's really just a second buy-in on the same Pyramid.

Like Madoff's Pyramid, many MLMs are an open secret. Herbalife, a trusted if not beloved global nutrition company, is a *known* MLM. They sell protein shakes and other weight-loss and health products, but mostly they sell *selling* Herbalife. The primary venues through which sellers try to do this is a setup Herbalife calls "nutrition clubs."[28] These are exactly what they sound like: *clubs*. People go for moral support and dieting tips, and to make friends—or if they're already in the MLM, they go to fish for new recruits. Because a seller's compensation comes not only from the profit margin on what they sell to actual customers, but more often from bonuses related to recruiting new sellers. The catch is that both the original seller and the new sellers have to *buy* thousands of dollars' worth of Herbalife product before any bonus structure kicks in.

Herbalife's president John DeSimone says, "The clubs benefit the community. It's a weight-loss regimen tied to a social dynamic."

Whereas the company's most outspoken and financially invested critic, Bill Ackman, disagrees; he says, "Nutrition clubs are simply a recruiting venue for Herbalife to reach low-income distributors."[29] And it does seem pretty predatory, as they're not only preying on the magical thinking of people who badly need to make money, they're also preying on lonely people who just want to belong to a club. And then they're blurring the cognitive weakness, be it herd mentality or magical thinking, that either needs to influence to the other. After all, everybody needs something. Most people can't afford to pay thousands of dollars (just as an opening buy-in) to not even get it.

But the part that makes Herbalife's network of approximately 3.7 million people in ninety countries (talk about market saturation) a straight Pyramid Scheme is the fact that Herbalife deliberately does not keep track of what percentage of the product they require their sellers to buy, that a seller buys from them but then just drinks, or stores in their basement, because unable to unload it.[30] This is important because *not all Pyramids are illegal*; they're not even all bad. Ponzi scams are illegal because there's no work product; it's just shifting money around (mostly up) until it collapses. No one in a Ponzi scheme is ever paid for anything real or paid with any actually generated revenue. Other companies, like Tupperware, use an "independent sales force," but keep close track of what you sell and pay you accordingly.[31] You're not the one buying all the Tupperware, or conning all your acquaintances into selling it, and you're not paid for inducting everyone you know into the Tupperware cult.

It's this ethical mess—in between Tupperware and Nu Skin—that regulators can't seem to regulate. And why not? Because companies that exist in between don't want them to.

The standard litmus test for legitimacy is the so-called 70 percent rule, instituted in 1979 when courts determined that Amway was not a Pyramid Scheme because it required its "independent sales force" to sell at least 70 percent of the product they bought from Amway—not use it, give it away, or hide it in the basement. Herbalife skirts this rule by only counting product that distributors "hold for resale," which means product bought but not resold—yet. Which means . . . nothing at all. They could hold it for resale until the next century. Much more important, Herbalife doesn't track the number of sales made *outside the network of sellers to nonmembers.* In the same way cash is only ever shuffled around inside a Pyramid, it seems entirely possible these sales are only shuffled back and forth within Herbalife between members. But we'll never know, because Herbalife's then president Des Walsh said, "We don't track this number and we do not believe it is relevant."[32]

This evasion—and the fact that Herbalife's own sales, to its own sellers, are in the billions of dollars every year,[33] and that the company has existed for decades—does create the *illusion* that it's a "sustainable business model," which is the other industry standard used by regulators to distinguish legitimate Pyramids from schemes. But that's an evasion as well, because Herbalife loses about half of its distributors each year.[34] It seems it's a sustainable model—so far—but *only* for Herbalife, not for its millions of sellers. And yet, despite having been fined millions of dollars in the last few years, eviscerated in *The New York Times,* and investigated by the FTC,[35] Herbalife is still up and running, because the laws are murky about what constitutes a straight-up illegal Pyramid Scheme.

But consider: 99.92 percent of their sellers *lose* money.[36]

This Will Go on Your Permanent Record

So, you're too clean (you're not) for Wall Street, and you're too smart (you'd be surprised) to fall for multilevel marketing? That's okay, I've got one more. Let's talk about the biggest, sexiest Pyramid Scheme currently going: Bitcoin.

Bitcoin (in case you live in a fallout shelter) is an unregulated, non-physical cryptocurrency based on blockchain technology. Blockchain technology is a snazzy piece of computer programming that allows for the secure and traceable transfer of Bitcoin (or anything else) almost instantaneously. Bitcoin itself is the digital currency that is "created" when so-called miners (really, nerds sitting at their computers) solve complex mathematical problems. As they do, a permanent nonlocalized ledger is created that, like the Book of Life, tracks the existence of every Bitcoin on the planet, from when, where, and how it was created—onward.

Bitcoin is supposed to be the currency of the future. The near future. A decentralized, completely traceable, totally digital, global currency that unites us all and frees us from the shackles of fraud, abuse, monopolized finance, and also . . . regular banking. You know, like when you have to pay a 2 percent fee or something.

That's cool, I guess. I mean, money hasn't really been real since we went off the gold standard; there's nothing backing it that's not at least sort of abstract. I suppose it's no big deal to exchange one form of imaginary currency for another: coins for paper, paper for plastic, plastic for crypto.

The problem is, Bitcoin isn't actually a currency.

Not because it's digital or decentralized. Unregulated is a problem, but not *the* problem. Bitcoin isn't a currency because it's simply not. Bitcoin fundamentally lacks the basic properties of real currency.[37] Sure, you can use it to buy things, in certain venues—though the same is true of live chickens—but there's no government or entity backing its worth; no one sets prices in Bitcoin; and no, you mostly can't buy things with it (especially now that Silk Road* has been shut down).[38]

That last one really gives away the game: Bitcoin isn't currency because *people don't spend it.* Nobody buys a car in Bitcoin (even if you could) because the car would be worth less than the Bitcoin by the time you got home. Since it has no backing and it's not even a physical object, its worth is based solely on its theoretically limited supply and its popularity,[39] making its value balloon exponentially.

It's not meant to be spent. It's meant to be hoarded.

And that's precisely what a lot of billionaires are currently doing.[40] A company called Xapo, run by Argentine entrepreneur Wences Casares, has spent years persuading Silicon Valley millionaires and billionaires that Bitcoin is the future—exactly what kind of future I guess we can sort out later—but in it they'll need their Bitcoin. And since it can be so easily stolen by hackers, these big coin holders have decided (or Casares has convinced them) that it's safer to keep it in his cold storage. He's holding billions of dollars' worth of Bitcoin, *physically,* on air-gapped, encrypted, unconnected private servers—to which only he and (sometimes) the Bitcoin owners have keys—inside the Fort Knox-like facilities he's built around the world, complete with guards, blast doors, and reinforced concrete.[41] He's basically made high-tech strong boxes, safe and cut off from the digital world, in which to store your digital currency.

I'm just gonna leave that there—but Xapo itself might also be a con.

And although it's hard to say how much Bitcoin is in there, the latest estimate is that Xapo is storing about ten billion dollars' worth. So if

---

*Silk Road was a massive website accessible only through the so-called dark web, on which people bought drugs (and far more nefarious things) in Bitcoin, precisely because it was ostensibly untraceable.

Bitcoin theoretically has a finite supply and its value only goes up, you can see how, as with any Pyramid, you really needed to get in on that a long time ago. Like any MLM, the people at the bottom think they're investing in something that will make them very rich—but as time goes on, there will be fewer, more generally unobtainable Bitcoins, and the people holding vast sums of them in places like Xapo's vaults will have almost all of them—and they'll be worth a fortune, because the rest of us made it so when we bought in.

Hey, look! *A fucking Pyramid.*

And at that point, you have to question whether you believed it because you wanted to or because someone else wanted you to. Or maybe, as with all acts of mutualism that allow for the possibility of cheating, it was a little bit of both. Trust, after all, is a cooperative act, and cooperative acts are always, by design, mutual.

Trust Me

The interesting thing about Pyramids is that we associate them with cash grabs. And for good reason. When we hear "Pyramid Scheme" we just hear *"scheme."* We assume deliberate fraud, probably financial; but Pyramids are all around us, all the time, and integral to our daily life. *Not all Pyramids are bad.* Do you know what follows an amazingly accurate blueprint for a Pyramid Scheme?

Religion.

Authority can also trickle upward, for no reason other than the mass belief that it's real. And for so long, as everyone pretends together that said institution has that authority, it does. The same is true of academia, the military, the art world, the global economy. . . . It's not until someone questions it, introducing doubt—and then panic—that the Pyramid starts to crumble. We don't necessarily recognize the familiar systems and institutions as Pyramids, but they are, and we've built most of the world in that shape.

The vast majority of lies we tell each other only require two parties: one to tell the lie, and another to believe it. And often the lies we tell ourselves don't even demand that many. But a Pyramid is one of the few lies in the world that requires *critical mass*. Pyramids, as a deliberate con or necessary structure, are so incredibly ubiquitous because they both represent and appeal to the centrality of faith (both *in* and *as* a group) to human life. And I don't specifically mean religious faith, though certainly that's one kind. I'm referring to *trust*, a kind of blind faith required of us to function as a group.

Butterflies and corpse flowers may be in this evolutionary race alone (as are we, in some regards), but like many creatures, from bacterial colonies to anthills to wolf packs, humans have also evolved to function together as a superorganism, a sort of larger whole—what, on a good day, you might even call a civilization. And as a collective, we have to rely on other people, all of them possessing their own individual mind-states. Theory of mind notwithstanding, those other people's individual mind-states are *never fully knowable*. Or, as H. L. Mencken put it: "It is mutual trust, even more than mutual interest that holds human associations together."

This makes trust—belief in the absence of proof—crucial to human interaction.

Civilization is impossible without trust, and trust is a voluntary act. We *choose to believe* certain things, like you must stop when the light is red and then trust that everyone else will choose to believe it with you and do the same. We choose to trust, in other words, in a deliberately created, mutually agreed-upon structure for reality.

We all pretend together. We have to—or all our Pyramids would crumble.

Consensus, Control, and the Illusion of Truth

There's a world of difference between truth and facts.
Facts can obscure the truth.
—MAYA ANGELOU

We are what we pretend to be, so we must be
careful who we pretend to be.
—KURT VONNEGUT

A GUY ONCE SAID, "THERE'S NOTHING GOOD OR BAD BUT thinking makes it so." He was being philosophical, but it suggests a more literal question: What weight does opinion have on reality? Facts are facts, but *truth* is a more powerful, and ultimately more nebulous, concept. We've covered how to tell a lie and how to make someone believe it. And now, for my final trick, let's examine how to *make a lie true*.

Before you object, consider the strange story of Snake Oil: if you genuinely believe you've taken a drug, the anticipatory release associated with the placebo effect can result in the same chemical effect in your brain and your body that you would have experienced had you taken an *actual* drug. That means, on a material chemical level, a lie can function as though it's true, simply because you believe it is, biologically transforming the falsehood into fact.

And *anticipation* is only one of many mechanisms by which belief in a falsehood can translate into true impact. Consensus is another; what happens when a lie is believed on a large scale? Not just by an individual, but by a whole city? A whole society? The whole world? If a whole city believes Martians have landed and the end is seriously fucking nigh—the chaos will be *very real*.

Which sort of begs the question: If a lie functions as though it's true, is there really any functional difference?

If a whole civilization believes certain objects have power or value, and everyone behaves accordingly, then for all intents and purposes they *do* possess that value or power. It may be a lie, but a quality counterfeit object still works precisely the same way the real object would . . . for exactly as long as it is *believed* to be authentic. And if a thing only needs to be believed in to be effective, was there ever anything to value or authority other than belief in the first place?

Does believing something make it so? Can you make a fraud real by believing it, or undermine an accepted reality through doubt? Is there anything *but belief* that can create or destroy our experience of reality? And what happens if we stop believing certain lies? Why we lie and how we believe are so inextricably intertwined that there can be no faith without fraud, there can be no truth without lies, there can be no civilization without cons. Whether they're the lies we tell each other or the subtler and more complicated lies we tell ourselves, deceit and belief are two halves of one whole. One cannot exist without the other, and society cannot function without both. We constantly engage in this back-and-forth because it's a built-in feature of organic life. The more complex the organism, the more complex the lies. When that complexity reaches civilization size, the lies start to become truly strange, and in some cases strangely true.

The rule of law, the value of diamonds, the existence of the economy—when we *all* agree to believe certain things, those things, true or false, for all intents and purposes, *become real*. Paper money is just paper, but as long as we all agree to believe it, as long as we honor it as real currency, it has value. We all lie, all the time, and we all agree to name certain lies truth. When we all believe a thing together, that thing takes on the weight of reality.

Perhaps, in the end, *truth* is the oldest trick in the book.

FAKE NEWS

Hoaxes, Hysteria, and the
Madness of Crowds

The truth, indeed, is something that mankind, for some mysterious reason, instinctively dislikes.
—H. L. MENCKEN

Whoever controls the media, controls the mind.
—JIM MORRISON

HOAXING

Though they might seem similar, a Hoax is not a practical joke, nor is it a simple fraud. It's a very specific type of con that involves either disinformation or misinformation, often both. A Hoax is undertaken with either malice or the intention to profit materially or situationally by propagating falsehood and successfully deceiving, at least temporarily, a great number of people. A Hoax is perpetuated by first identifying a target group of people; next manufacturing a falsehood that will uniquely frighten or appeal to them, in some cases manufacturing evidence; and then finally letting the false-hoods spread organically so as to have greater supposed credibility and therefore power.

London Calling

A Hoax is not a lie you tell someone else or one you tell yourself—a Hoax is a lie presented as truth to no one in particular and to everyone who encounters it. For a lie that requires such showmanship, it's really quite passive in its approach—like getting all dressed up, going out, and then sitting at the bar waiting for someone to notice. Anyone who's used that method to get another's attention knows that, when properly executed, it can be twice as effective as the direct approach. So not only are Hoaxes wildly seductive, they're disproportionately powerful. When you dress a lie up and passively present it as truth, it is more credible and more likely to be believed on a large scale. And the more people who believe it, the more credible it becomes; and the more credible it becomes, the more easily other people will believe it. When enough people believe it, the Hoax reaches a sort of critical mass, resulting in mass behaviors and responses that render it further indistinguishable from the real.

Most Hoaxes are particularly absurd to begin with—aliens, monsters, shadow government plots. This is by design. A Hoax gets exponentially more attention by being outrageous (and the end goal with a Hoax is to reach critical mass). More important, Hoaxes exploit emotional reaction. If you find a story scary, shocking, enraging, disgusting, hysterical, delightful, or just somehow titillating, you're more likely to listen, and *far* more likely to repeat it.

Counterintuitive as it may sound, you're actually *more likely to believe it*.

Like the Big Lie, this absurdity factor actually works in the Hoax's favor. Not, in this case, because we share faith in objective reality, but because a lie that elicits an extreme emotional reaction resonates in a different way from one that doesn't. A lie that makes you feel something intensely, whether it's delight or outrage or fear, is simply more addictive and more compelling than any other kind of lie. The intensity of feeling it induces in the listener creates an equally strong need to hear more—and to tell someone else.

Besides, who doesn't like documentaries about the search for Bigfoot? Hoaxes are fun! Except when they're not. Like on the evening of January 16, 1926, when millions of U.K. citizens had their radios tuned in to the BBC, listening to a speech broadcast from Edinburgh. Halfway through, the broadcast was interrupted by breaking news out of London. The alarming report detailed rapidly spreading destruction and violence. A huge mob of unemployed citizens had formed and were rioting in Trafalgar Square. As people listened, the report went from alarming to terrifying, as witnesses described the devastation: the mob, equipped with trench mortars (basically grenades), were destroying Parliament—all 320 feet of the famous clock tower, along with its nine-ton metal bell, Big Ben, had fallen into the Thames.

As listeners across the country reeled, trying to make sense of what they were hearing, the BBC correspondent, sounding quite terrified himself, related that Mr. Wurtherspoon, the Minister of Traffic, had just been spotted and seized by the mob as he tried to escape what was left of the Parliament building. He reported in real time that Minister Wurtherspoon had been dragged away by the mob and had *"been hanged from a lamp post in Vauxhall-London Calling. That noise you heard just now was the Savoy Hotel being blown up by the crowd."*[1]

The entire country panicked. People flooded the streets, jammed telephone lines and train stations, demanded the navy be deployed up the Thames River to put down the riot and stop the destruction. But despite their desperate pleas, they were told that no one was coming to help.

No one was coming because none of it was real.

Nothing was actually happening in London; it was a "radio play," in essence a Hoax, with an easy-to-miss disclaimer at the outset. But it was too late to tell the hysterical crowds. Government statements, repeated announcements by the BBC about the real nature of the program, word from London that all was well—no matter how emphatic the denials of a riot, people could not be dissuaded. They refused to accept the government's reassurances nothing had happened or the BBC's explanations and apologies—not even upon hearing replays of that blink-and-you'll-miss-it disclaimer.[2]

Far from being calmed by official denials or reversed statements, the frantic crowds just became more confused—and then enraged—by the conflicting reports. It was *days* before most of them finally accepted that the whole broadcast was just "a burlesque."[3] After all, they'd heard it on the news.

Did that story sound familiar? I bet it did.

Despite the fact that the 1926 BBC Riot Panic made the gullible British the laughingstock of the United States for months, Americans fell for nearly the same Hoax—on a much larger and more *alien* scale—just twelve years later. And, just as it took days to assuage the British public once they'd heard a frightening fiction on the news, Americans would not be dissuaded by redactions or corrections (or even by the fairly recent memory of that widely ridiculed incident) when they heard an almost identically formatted radio broadcast claiming that New Jersey, rather than London, was being destroyed—this time by "Men from Mars."

The War of the Worlds

The night before Halloween 1938 was the night Earth was attacked by Martians.[4] At the time, most of the listening public was tuned into the very popular program *The Chase and Sanborn Hour* with Edgar Bergan and Charlie McCarthy. Most only heard the news of the attack when the radio program started a long, dull, elevator-music break, at which point bored listeners began to channel surf. What they heard when they skipped over to the other station went something like:

> Flash! Meteor reported landing near Grover's Mill, New
> Jersey. . . . Fifteen hundred killed. . . . No, it's not a meteor—
> it's a flying metal cylinder. . . . Poison gas is sweeping over
> New Jersey. . . . The invaders are flying over the nation,
> raining bombs. . . .

The CBS broadcaster showed significantly more emotion and evident panic than his BBC counterpart had a little more than a decade earlier. A lot of *"oh my GOD,"* and *"this is the end,"* and *"God help us all,"* and you get the drift. People became completely unglued long before the hour-long program was over—if they made it that far. Most people probably lost it somewhere around *"The Martians are using death-rays!"*[5]

Orson Welles's *Mercury Theatre on the Air* was a small, little-known weekly dramatic radio play.[6] Usually the broadcasts were a lot more straightforward, but on this occasion, Welles thought it would be really fun to air an adaptation of H. G. Wells's classic science-fiction novel *The War of the Worlds,* which centers on a sudden, deadly invasion from Mars, beginning with New Jersey and progressing to a rapid decimation of the rest of the world.

The version of the script that Orson Welles used had been adapted to read as a series of increasingly frantic and terrifying news broadcasts over the course of an hour.[7] The vast majority of listeners never heard—or subsequently forgot—Welles's similar blink-and-you'll-miss-it disclaimer that, at the top of the hour, noted the program was a drama.[8] They believed that what they were hearing was real news.

And they lost their fucking minds.

Personally, I think there's almost nothing *not* funny about the phrase "The Martians are using death-rays." That said, here are some less amusing hot takes: this being America, when the people panicked, they went straight for their guns. Looting and rioting ensued. Accidents proliferated. Hospitals were jammed with people injured or killed by other people, hysterical people, people in shock, stroke and heart attack victims—literally scared stiff—and even people who had harmed themselves rather than be captured or killed by the Martians. In San Francisco, people overwhelmed army headquarters looking to fight. In Birmingham, people overwhelmed churches, certain the world was ending. A woman in Indiana burst into one crowded church and screamed, "New York is destroyed—it's the end of the world! You might as well go home and die! I just heard it on the radio."[9] Some undoubtedly did so. A man in Pittsburgh came home just in time to stop his wife from downing rat poison. She sobbed, "I'd rather die this way than like that!"[10]

Still fun?

When the radio play ended on the hour and normal programming returned, it provoked mass confusion. CBS was flooded with scared, confused, and ultimately angry phone calls demanding answers. In short order, the cops arrived at the studio where Orson Welles's *Mercury Theatre* was recorded. They took the entire cast, crew, and anyone else associated with the broadcast into protective custody until order could be restored and the scope of the disaster could be assessed. Though most of the hysteria had subsided by the end of the next day, people were so angry that Orson Welles received threats and went into temporary hiding.[11]

Fake News and Real Consequences

In Quito, Ecuador, a similarly broadcast Hoax was executed in more or less the same way.[12] And though it touched fewer people, the panic it provoked was even worse. Hysterical listeners flooded the streets in terror. When they found out they'd been hoaxed, they were enraged. They rioted, burning the radio station and the newspaper plant to the ground. The military was called in to restore the peace, but long before they could arrive, the rioting crowds had destroyed part of the city, including their only means of disseminating or receiving any actual news and information. And far worse than the massive destruction of property, *twenty-one* people were murdered, including six of the show's participants.[13]

So how real is a riot if it's based on a lie? How real is a heart attack or suicide? Fake facts that lead to real actions have a way of becoming something other than black-and-white. If the world believed that aliens had invaded, and as a result you got shot by a neighbor in the dark or flipped your car trying to get out of town—if you were so terrified you had a stroke—it probably doesn't matter that none of it was *really* real. It was *real enough*.

The trouble with Hoaxes is not in the belief in the story—it's in the action that treats the story as if it were true, which has many of the same consequences as if it were.

In 1898, four Denver reporters, Jack Tourney, Al Stevens, Hal Wilshire, and John Lewis—all from different papers—went to a bar, got really drunk, and made up a story.[14] They all claimed in their separate papers to have met a team of four American engineers on their way to China (who stopped in Denver, for some reason). The engineers, they said, told them that they'd been hired to effectively destroy the Great Wall, at China's request. Supposedly this was being done as a gesture of goodwill and as an invitation to foreign trade.

It was a multiperson Hoax. All four reporters agreed to the same fake story, with slight variations, and ensured that it would run. Anyone who had suspicions or wondered if it was a joke would see that two or three other news outlets had printed the same story—confirming its validity.

The Denver Times headline trumpeted "Great Chinese Wall Doomed! Peking Seeks World Trade!" Initially, the story was quickly forgotten by the Denver public and could have vanished into obscurity. Unfortunately, a few other newspapers picked up the story, and it went viral.[15] Viral news is not, in fact, a function of the Internet; stories (especially Hoaxes) have been going viral since printing became ubiquitous. Back then, papers would often reprint entire stories from other papers, which would be reprinted by exponentially more and more papers.

Within weeks, a major East Coast newspaper did an entire special Sunday spread about the fake destruction of the Great Wall, including elaborate illustrations and further exposition about the Chinese government's historic plan to end their isolationist policy. They even added a few fake quotes of their own, from a Chinese national visiting New York, who confirmed the story.[16] We know that the quotes are fake, because we know that the entire story was made up—but it's not clear that the reporters who faked the quotes knew that. Often, lies snowball, as each person who genuinely believes the general narrative adds their own little flourish.

Because this was a respected newspaper, and because they'd sparkled up the article so effectively, the story quickly spread to Europe. Picking up speed, as viral stories do, it spread to Asia, and of course finally to China, where political tempers were already running high.

All of this took place during the era of Western expansionism (which is sometimes also spelled: colonialism)—in the next year, 1899, Great Britain acquired a ninety-nine-year lease on Chinese territories, surrounding the already captured Hong Kong. French, German, and English invaders, colonialists, or businessmen—depending on whom you ask—had either seized or leased (again depending on your perspective) various Chinese islands, ports, and territories. In some cases, they were turned into colonies; in others, military bases. In response, vehement anti-Christian, anti-Western nationalists called the Boxers were campaigning to drive all foreigners out of China.

To make matters worse, those same major American newspapers had been relentlessly demanding access to the Chinese market for years, insisting on the need to "tear down the wall of Chinese tariffs and protectionism." (In fact, they still do; as recently as 2012 *Forbes* ran an article titled "Tear Down This Wall—The Chinese Tariff Wall."[17])

The preexisting conditions for disaster were already boiling, but when the news reached China that the Great Wall was going to be torn down by Americans as an invitation to foreign trade, it certainly can't have helped. It's very possible that these two separate news stories—that the Great Wall would be torn down by Americans seeking trade with China and that Americans demanded the wall of Chinese tariffs and protectionism be torn down to facilitate trade—one literal and threatening, the other metaphoric and merely entitled, were conflated and confused by the time they reached the Chinese, who were already more than a little angry over numerous foreign encroachments and aggressions.

In fact, this fiction, cooked up half a world away by a team of drinking buddies, was later alleged to have helped catalyze the Boxers rage into action and contributed to the Boxer Rebellion. Like every other Hoax, there was no curing this compelling disinformation with truth: according to a 1939 account of a lecture Bishop Henry Warren gave after returning from working in China, "The story was published with shouting headlines and violent editorial comment. Denials did no good. The Boxers, already incensed, believed the yarn and now there was no stopping them. It was the last straw and all hell broke loose to the horror of the world. All this from a sensational but untrue story."[18]

The story itself was easily traced back to those four reporters in Denver, but they'd preemptively covered their asses in what can only be described as a metahoax: they claimed that *they* had been hoaxed by four strangers who came through town, claiming to be engineers. In reality, they had made up both the story and the alibi: that night, before running their stories, they went to the Windsor Hotel in Denver and forged four overnight registrations under the names of their made-up guests. They also somehow persuaded the night clerk to agree that, when asked, he would say the guests were real and that he heard them say they were engineers leaving in the morning for California. The Hoax secure, the Four Horsemen of this particular Apocalypse went and celebrated with more drinks.[19]

Why they did this in the first place is a mystery. They can't have thought it would advance their careers, since, best-case scenario, when the truth came out that the Great Wall absolutely was not being demolished, they would simply seem incompetent. Worst-case scenario, they would be exposed as frauds. It doesn't really make sense at all. Then again, they were pretty drunk. They swore to one another that they would never tell the true story while the others were still alive. A good choice (seemingly their only one), seeing that their Hoax was later blamed for a (probably inevitable) rebellion. It wasn't until decades later that Hal Wilshire, last man standing, finally told the truth about their messed-up, made-up story.

Whether they incited it or merely exacerbated it, the Boxer Rebellion of 1900 was a destabilizing violent disaster that hastened the decline of the Qing dynasty. It had lasting consequences, both in China and abroad, and seriously and permanently affected relations between China and numerous other Western countries. So, you know, it was a pretty big deal.

The point of *my* story is not that these men were drunks, though they were, or that a single fake news story from a few local Denver papers may have radically altered the course of twentieth-century Chinese history—although it did. It's that the rebellion occurred just as it would have *had the news been real*. The cause may have been fictitious, but it had the same effect as its truthful parallel. Reality, in other words, is circumstantial. In the greater scheme of things, it matters less whether or not a thing is actually true than whether or not it is believed to be.

The Contagious Nature of "Facts"

Napoleon referred to history as a set of lies agreed upon. Because he was French and a little bit emo, he made it sound like we're all doing it deliberately because we're corrupt and empty inside. But that opinion notwithstanding, the man had a point. Not because no one cares what's true—but because, once accepted, it seems to be almost impossible for us to unbelieve a falsehood.

Take the history of the bathtub.

In 1917 H. L. Mencken wrote an article titled "A Neglected Anniversary" for *The New York Evening Mail*.[20] It was a satirical history of the bathtub in American life, written in celebration of the seventy-fifth anniversary of our nation's first bathtub—which he claimed had been purchased by one Adam Thompson and installed on December 20, 1842, in Cincinnati, Ohio. The imaginary bathtub was lined with lead and weighed 1,750 pounds.

Everyone who read Mencken's story accepted it as fact. They did so because *The New York Evening Mail* was a reliable, established paper; because Mencken was a respected journalist; because it was an exceedingly dull, detail-filled article about a bathtub; and most of all because it was just such a stupid thing to lie about.

But he *was* lying, and he didn't just make up the man and the purchase of the bathtub. He went into great fictitious detail about why Thompson bought it and how forward-thinking he was. He detailed the massive public backlash Thompson received at the time. Mencken even invented hostile criticism from the medical world, which had allegedly proclaimed bathtubs a menace to public health. Mencken quoted the *Western Medical Repository*'s warning that the bathtub "softens the moral fiber of the republic." He also reported that Philadelphia and Boston had tried to pass a law forbidding the use of bathtubs for health reasons and that various states levied taxes on bathtub installation as a deterrent.[21]

Mencken made up the "fact" that President Millard Fillmore, a firm believer in the health benefits of bathing, was responsible for installing the first White House bathtub, and despite all the bath bashing, took the first presidential bath. Mencken satirically claimed that soak as an act of political courage in the face of "opponents [who] made much of the fact that there was no bathtub at Mount Vernon, or at Monticello, and that all the Presidents and other magnificoes of the past had got along without any such monarchical luxuries."[22] Mencken wrote that Fillmore's stance on bathtubs had set the tone and was responsible for the American institution of the "Saturday night bath."

Mencken assumed, of course, this was all too stupid to be taken seriously, but he seriously underestimated the stupidity and credulousness of the average person.

By far the weirdest part of this very, very weird story is that Mencken's history of the bathtub was accepted as just that, the legitimate *history* of the bathtub in the United States, for almost a century. Not because no one checked to see if it was true, but because, thereafter, no one would *believe* Mencken when he himself insisted that it was not.

He later called his own story a "tissue of absurdities, all of them deliberate and obvious."[23] In 1926, just eight years later, his history of the bathtub had become so firmly entrenched in the public consciousness that he felt compelled to publicly state that "my history of the bathtub, printed on Dec. 28, 1917, was pure buncombe. If there were any facts in it they got there accidentally and against my design. But today the tale is in the encyclopedias. History, said a great American soothsayer, is bunk."[23]

Mencken referred to his Hoax as such, claiming, "My motive was simply to have some harmless fun in the war days. It never occurred to me that it would be taken seriously."[24] But it *was*—for almost a century. In fact, with a little digging, you can find Mencken's satirical article referenced in journals and magazines as source material. This "history"—and its relationship to the evolution of the public health sector in America—was taught for years by a Harvard professor.[25] Most disturbing of all, in the 1950s John Hersey reported that, despite having been corrected about the satirical nature of the history, President Harry Truman "seemed reluctant to let go of his belief" that Millard Fillmore had introduced the first bathtub to the White House in 1850. President Truman—the guy in charge of the Bomb, just swirl that around in your mind for a second—insisted on repeating Mencken's "tissue of absurdities" as true fact whenever he gave tours to distinguished visitors to the White House.[26] As recently as 1990, a news program in New York noted the 140th anniversary of the Fillmore bathtub, and in 2001 *The Washington Post* used those same facts in a story they later had to retract.[27]

The history of Mencken's so-called history very literally proves Napoleon (and Henry Ford) correct. History is whatever we agree it is. Once enough people repeat them, lies start to take on the weight of truth. Untruths simply become "common knowledge," repeated by presidents and Harvard professors alike.

There's even a name for this phenomenon: the illusory-truth effect.

In addition to being a cool name for a band, the illusory-truth effect is what turns word of mouth into conventional wisdom. Our brains work with a lot of mental heuristics—those shortcuts like anticipating the motion of a bouncing ball before the motion is actually observed—and most of the time they're helpful.

But when they're not, they're really not.

One heuristic that helps us learn and retain facts is the mere-exposure effect, which conflates familiarity with truth. For example, you don't need a citation to agree with the statement "the moon is smaller than the sun." You've encountered this fact so many times that your brain actually processes the information *faster* than a novel statement.

But then in a circular turn, your mind treats the very speed with which it confirms a fact as *further* confirmation of its truthfulness. Essentially, the more often you hear something—no matter how absurd, pernicious, or banal—the more familiar it becomes. With that familiarity comes a false sense of *reliability*—even to the brain. Mere exposure leads you to *feel* that the lie you're hearing is true on a neurological level, essentially reconfirming that it is, simply because you've heard it before.[28]

That's alarming—but it gets worse. Like digging a groove in a well-worn path, familiar facts and ideas become more entrenched every time you encounter them. A 2002 study by University of Michigan psychologist Colleen Seifert found that when people were presented with evidence that information they'd been exposed to over and over was factually untrue, the attempts to refute it *further entrenched their belief.*[29]

Here's an example: imagine a tabloid story claiming that Meryl Streep has secretly been a man all this time, but no one caught on until now (she's *that* good). Let's say that news became viral—which it would—and you were exposed to it over and over. As silly as it sounded the first time you heard it, with repetition it would take on the illusion of truth. It would start to *feel true*. And when the story is roundly debunked by every reputable news source and human with access to Twitter, something even stranger would happen: the repetitive insistence involved in *the debunking itself* would continue to further cement the initial lie in your mind.

Every time you read a headline like Despite Viral Reports, Actress Meryl Streep Was Never Secretly a Man, or Meryl Streep's Long Form Birth Certificate Proves She Was Never Secretly a Man, or Reports That Meryl Streep Is Secretly a Man Are Fake News, you might accept the new version of the story *consciously,* but on a deeper level, the only key concepts your brain will really hold on to are *Meryl Streep, secret,* and *man.*

Even retracted or corrected information continues to exert unconscious influence over our judgment and decision-making. In other words, you'd know it wasn't true, and yet . . . the next time you saw her on screen, you'd be looking for an Adam's apple.

Breaking News: Probably Permanently

In 2013, Animal Planet ran a rather long, extremely detailed, and fascinating documentary. It was called *Mermaids: The Body Found,* and they hyped it for weeks. There was nothing really outrageous or over-the-top about it, other than the basic premise: that mermaids are real.

Though in this exposé/documentary, mermaids were presented not as sexy ladies with fish tails but as barely recognizable aquatic mammals, evolved from early coastal hominids millions of years ago in much the same way whales and dolphins are known to have evolved from early coastal canids. So, a startling claim, but not without biological precedent. The faux-documentary was detailed and extremely convincing. There were awkward, unattractive actors playing NOAA scientists, it was salted with references to real facts, actual places, and multiple points of (proven) science. It was pretty amazing. It was also, obviously, utter nonsense.

And I have no problem admitting that I fell for it.

Then again, for once I was in the majority. *Everyone* fell for it. It was all over social media and the news. Random celebrities and (more embarrassing) a few world leaders and noted intellectuals were tweeting about it. Not that anyone would admit to that now. Newspapers and magazines were debunking the claims for weeks, even after the network publicly admitted it was fiction. Outlets like *Slate* wrote article after article disclaiming it as a Hoax, running not-so-subtle headlines like: "No, Mermaids Do Not Exist."[30]

Ultimately, Animal Planet had to issue an apology; they had used that very same blink-and-you'll-miss-it fine-print disclaimer for less than three seconds, for just a few frames, after the end of the end credits.[31] No one noticed. People believed they were watching the best scientific exposé ever. Animal Planet tried claiming that they only meant to entertain—hardly credible, in this case. Animal Planet is not known for their entertaining fictional programming. But as someone who readily admits to having been boating a number of times on Loch Ness hoping to see a monster, I was totally riveted.

Everybody has a weakness for some version of you-should-have-known-better bullshit. Some people are gamblers who can't walk past a card game or Pyramid Scheme, even knowing how it works. Others are true believers, desperate for reassurance in the form of almost any narrative palliative, however outlandish, from cults to Goop. Some people will always believe the most upsetting news they hear, while others can't help falling for the newest miraculous cure-all. And I've never encountered a Hoax that didn't capture my imagination. Even though I know it's almost definitely crap, I am powerless to resist an incredible story or insane conspiracy theory.

I know that the Animal Planet documentary was completely fake. And yet, despite knowing that the documentary was a Hoax, I still *feel* like mermaids are *probably* real. And not because a lot of the science was credible—even if the conclusions have yet to be proved (although that's a better reason, and I should probably start using it). It would seem, like Harry Truman, I'm simply "reluctant to let go of my belief," despite correction.

The truth is, I *want* to believe it—*whether or not it's true*.

And while it's no one's business what obvious nonsense I enjoy believing, *wanting* to believe a story, *whether or not it's true* is an important aspect of Hoax belief. Ask yourself: Why would a person want to believe something demonstrably false? The only plausible answer is that they have some skin in the game. The less-obvious angle? Often, said skin is entirely emotional. Mere exposure aside, people will adhere intractably to facts they know have been disproved for as long as they continue to incite intense emotion.

Which is exactly what a Hoax is designed to do—incite intense emotion. Besides, there's no harm in my clinging tenaciously to a private belief in sea monsters or Truman being willfully wrong about the history of his own bathtub. The problem is that from riots in China to suicides in New Jersey, Hoaxes are a category of lie that never—by definition—stays on a personal scale. Once enough individual beliefs reach that critical mass I mentioned earlier, they alter *everyone's* reality.

Take, for example, the 2016 election. According to a recent Ohio State University study, fake news likely swung the presidency to Donald Trump. The study, authored by Richard Gunther, Paul A. Beck, and Erik C. Nisbet,[32] is one of the first analyses of the effect fake news had on voter turnout and their choices, and it suggests that around 4 percent of Americans who voted for Barack Obama in 2012 were dissuaded from voting for Hillary Clinton in 2016 specifically because of the influence of specious news.

To collect the data, researchers inserted three widely reported, and totally untrue, news stories from the 2016 presidential campaign into a 281-question survey. They distributed this survey to their study participants, a cohort of 585 people who had all voted for Obama in 2012. The first fake news item from 2016 was a widely reported story that Clinton was in "very poor health due to a serious illness." The second was a false report that Pope Francis had given his endorsement to Trump. The third was a fabricated exposé about Clinton approving weapons sales to ISIS while secretary of state.

It turns out that about 25 percent of the study's participants had believed at least one of these stories. Of that group (fake news believers), only 45 percent went on to vote for Clinton. The other 55% defected from the 2016 Democratic ticket and either voted for someone else (including but not limited to Trump) or refused to vote at all. Of the 75 percent of the participants who had believed *none* of the fake news stories, 89 percent voted for Clinton.

According to the published study, 2012 Obama voters who believed one of these hoaxes "were 3.9 times more likely to defect from the Democratic ticket in 2016 than those who believed none of these false claims, after taking into account all of these other factors."[33]

That's provocative, but hardly conclusive. People have lots of reasons for how they vote. Hillary Clinton is inextricably linked with Bill Clinton, and not everyone who voted for Obama in 2012 liked Bill Clinton. Donald Trump is very tall—don't laugh, that's been documented to influence voter confidence. He lives in a gold building and has an allegedly sexy wife. Some people feel Hillary Clinton has an irritating voice. And while we're on it, a lot of people just don't like the idea of a woman president. You get the idea.

To cut through this static, the researchers used a multiple regression analysis to control for other factors: things like sex, age, race, income, education level, political leaning, and even irrational personal feelings about either candidate. When they were done, they found that all those independent variables, combined, explained 38 percent of voter defection.

That's a chunk.

But belief in one or more of those fake news stories accounted for another *11 percent*. For voters defecting from the Democratic ticket, falling for even one of just those random three fake news items had a greater effect than any other individual factor, apart from simply being a Republican.

Gunther, Beck, and Nisbet include the cautious disclaimer that "we cannot prove that belief in fake news *caused* these former Obama voters to defect from the Democratic candidate in 2016," but go on to conclude that "these data strongly suggest, however, that exposure to fake news did have a significant impact on voting decisions."[34] In academic speak, this is as close to an admission of direct causality as we are likely to get.

But it's bigger than that, of course—the *very idea* of fake news, aside from being completely oxymoronic, is *itself* a form of propaganda. Not because fictitious news stories don't exist, but because the whole concept of fake news exists to introduce ubiquitous doubt and to cripple your ability to discern which is which. It manipulates external factors to change the light in which you see the lie—and in which you see the truth.

So how do we tell the difference? Unfortunately, there's not an easy answer to that—in no small part because of a simple but enormous stumbling block: to effectively separate truth from lies, first *you have to want to.*

You Love to Be Lied To

A few days after the "documentary" aired on Animal Planet, when somebody broke the news to me that it was a Hoax, I wasn't embarrassed; I was disappointed. I was having so much fun believing it, I was actually angry, not at the initial liars—Animal Planet—but, rather, at the sources that had debunked it and the person who told me. That probably sounds strange. You'd think I'd be grateful someone would take me aside and save me further embarrassment. But I've been waiting my whole life for sea monsters, I resented having my exciting and entertaining new reality yanked out from under me.

And yet here, too, I am not alone. In fact, it's a surprisingly common response—one that reveals an interesting and paradoxical truth about human beings: *We love being lied to.*

Reality is dull, and the truth is often disappointing and, even more often, tedious. Outrage and terror are at least thrilling. That's why rumors and urban legends and hoaxes and sideshows and social media exist, because we love to be lied to. And enchanting or appalling, the more emotionally provocative a lie is, the more powerful it is. It doesn't even matter if you believe it—the more intense your reaction, the more you want to hear it and need to repeat it . . . and inadvertently spread it, to everyone you come in contact with, just like an *actual virus*.

You know that adage, "A lie can travel halfway around the world while the truth is putting its shoes on"? Well, some guys at MIT proved it.[35] According to a first-of-its-kind study of Twitter, fake news stories (rumors, hoaxes, propaganda) spread six times faster and significantly farther than truthful ones.[36] And before you scream *BOTS!*, these results accounted and corrected for their impact. This was all us.

Humans love to read inflammatory lies and pass them along— *even when they know the stories are untrue.*

The study was the brainchild of its lead author, data scientist Soroush Vosoughi. Dr. Vosoughi was a Ph.D. student at the time of the 2013 Boston Marathon bombing. He was deeply disturbed by the volume and fervor of conspiracy theories emerging in the days following the bombings—most directed at a missing Brown student, whose tragic disappearance was ultimately totally unrelated. "These rumors aren't just fun things on Twitter," Vosoughi claims, "they really can have effects on people's lives and hurt them really badly."[37] That's when he decided to shift the focus of his research to the dissemination of misinformation on social media.

He and his colleagues at the MIT Media Lab collected twelve years of data from Twitter, dating all the way back to its launch in 2006. Next they sifted that data for news-related tweets. Finally, they sifted all news-related tweets for only the ones containing news stories and facts that had been confirmed or debunked by six independent fact-checking organizations, including Snopes, PolitiFact, and FactCheck.org.

Their final data set comprised 126,000 news items, shared 4.5 million times by 3 million people. They followed those 126,000 stories across the entire twelve-year-history of Twitter, hoping for some insight into how rumors spread and Hoaxes are propagated.

What they actually found was, in their own word, "scary."

They discovered that "false news travels farther, faster, deeper and more broadly than the truth in every category of information—many times by an order of magnitude."[38] In other words, we all find lies—about anything really—*exponentially* more compelling than the truth; and Vosoughi's team got hard numbers outlining exactly how much we love being lied to.

The data shows that the truth rarely reached more than 1,000 Twitter users, whereas the most malignant and outrageous lies reached well over 10,000—and, of course, it got there a lot faster. The tweets containing "fake news" stories took one-sixth the time to reach 1,500 people as tweets containing accurate information—and not because they were shared by users with a larger platform or disproportionately amplified by bots.[39]

In fact, the study concluded that, unlike us, bots were spreading fake news and real news at an equal rate. Humans, on the other hand, *could not get enough of the lies.* Average people were just more inclined—70 percent more inclined—to retweet the "fake news" tweets than anything remotely true.

And while Twitter accounts that predominately shared accurate information had more followers, they also determined that the crazier a tweet was—no matter where it came from—the more likely it was to go viral.[40] As you'll recall, mere *exposure* creates in us an unconscious truth bias toward the familiar and prevalent—the predicate of all successful propaganda. The problem with virality is that the more brazen and bizarre a tweet is, the more prevalent and ultimately believable it becomes.

The truth about lies is that they're not only contagious—they're almost impossible to cure.

The Illusion of Truth

Orson Welles's *Mercury Theatre on the Air* had only been on the air for seventeen weeks and lacked a sponsor, or much of a future, when he staged his Martian Hoax. Once the public outrage died down, he and *Mercury Theatre* experienced a dramatic and permanent reversal of fortune.[41] Revered as a genius, Orson Welles received a massive sponsorship from Campbell's Soup. His radio show was no longer a ratings dud, and Welles went on to write his own ticket, first on Broadway and then in Hollywood. Welles maliciously Hoaxed an entire country—probably intentionally—and ended up rich and famous.

It seems the truest thing about fake news is how predictably it plays out.

In the immediate aftermath of the disaster, Welles denied the intentionality of the Hoax and made a great show of his own shock and remorse. He vehemently insisted that it had all been a terrible mistake; that the story was too absurd to be believed; and that, besides, there was that disclaimer at the beginning. But that was when people were still angry, the property damage still new, and the terror still fresh. By the time the bodies were buried, he was winkingly suggesting that he had meant to cause all that mayhem. And decades later, ensconced in the money and power his cinema success had afforded him, he even bragged that it had been an intentional object lesson for the American public about the dangers of believing everything you hear on the news.[42]

Of course, no one else would corroborate that particular strange (and frankly appalling) flex—despite the fact that Frank Readick, the voice actor cast as a witnessing reporter, had dug up and studied recordings of the Hindenburg disaster broadcast to get his *terrified reporter* act just right.[43] Or the fact that Welles had changed the pacing of the "interruptions" at the last minute, making them as confusing and realistic as possible. He even told Kenneth Delmar, the voice actor portraying the secretary of the interior (famous for his perfect FDR impression), to make his speech about the government's efforts to combat the invasion "sound presidential." Delmar complied, despite the fact that in 1938 major networks forbade radio shows from impersonating the president, lest they confuse or mislead listeners. And contrary to their protestations of ignorance, CBS was complicit; they had seen a draft earlier in the day. Proof of this exists in a demand from their legal department to assign a less-alarming cabinet member than the one initially conceived of for the role: the secretary of war.[44]

The problem with fake news is that, much like real history, it's forever repeating itself. The next morning, public mea culpas and regrets abounded—even CBS had to issue a public apology. There were FCC hearings, and some meaningless new regulations were passed, and then nothing happened to anyone. Within a few weeks, newspapers were gloating about the "incredible stupidity and gullibility" of the American public, as though they'd had nothing to do with it, but it was columnist Dorothy Thompson who had the most interesting and frighteningly prescient take. She felt that "nothing about the broadcast was in the least credible. . . ." And in part because of that, she concluded that "Mr. Orson Welles and his theater have made a greater contribution to an understanding of Hitlerism, Mussolinism, Stalinism, and anti-Semitism and all other terrorisms of our times than all the words about them that have been written by reasonable men."[45]

"Fake news" is just a new name for an old con, and Dorothy Thompson could see that the most dangerous element of a Hoax is human nature and the tiny cracks it exposes and exploits. The truth that those terrible men knew, that Dorothy Thompson knew, that Orson Welles knew, is a truth that we all know but persistently refuse to believe: that *we love to be lied to,* and in the end the best story wins. People will always get caught up in the excitement of a narrative that's not limited by reality, and when that fiction incites actions with lasting consequences, it ceases to matter if it was ever true.

HOW TO
MAKE A BUCK
True Facts About Fake Things

The greatest deception men suffer is from their own opinions.
—LEONARDO DA VINCI

Would you believe in what you believe in if you
were the only one who believed it?
—KANYE WEST

FORGERY

This is the simplest scam, but arguably the one requiring the most skill—all you have to do is create a replica of something convincing enough to pass for genuine. This can be done with any object that holds value or confers authority: identification, credentials, contracts, currency, works of art, religious relics. And whether it's an FBI badge, a Renaissance masterpiece, or a counterfeit one-hundred-dollar bill, forgeries work exactly like the real thing—just as long as they pass as authentic.

Faking It

True fact: you can counterfeit literally anything—documents, money, art, priceless jewels, or sacred religious objects. You can even counterfeit people—it's called identity theft. You can do this because a counterfeit object is just a faithful copy of something, exact enough to be convincing—or better, *indistinguishable*—from the original. To anyone and everyone who believes the counterfeit is the authentic item, it will have the same value, power, or effect as the original—which rather suggests that an object's value, authority, or effect—*derives from the believer,* not from the object itself.

We make things what they are by believing in them, *not* the other way around. So what makes a thing real?

The oldest authenticated object of confirmed forgery is a third millennium B.C. Sumerian clay tablet covered in cuneiform writing, including the inscription "This is not a lie, it is indeed the truth. He who will damage this document, let Enki fill up his canals with slime." Nice sentiment. Wrong god, though, because the tablet is actually a *second* millennium B.C. Babylonian forgery of a third millennium B.C. Sumerian clay tablet.[1]

As lies go, that one's pretty old. Not as old as it claims . . . but still, respect.

The truth is that I have no idea what the oldest authenticated object of confirmed forgery is; I have no idea how old the *act* of forgery itself is. Neither does anyone else, because most forgeries go undetected—*forever.* But the sheer volume of forgeries that *are* found out is mindblowing.

Take art: every kind of art from every place in every period of history has been forged, from the oil paintings of the Old Masters to the spatter paintings of the twentieth century. Medieval manuscripts have been copied both by modern forgers and by other medieval monks. Shang dynasty bronzes were copied by Sung dynasty artists—during the later forgery-worthy "golden age of Chinese painting." Ancient Roman statues were constantly forged by Renaissance Roman sculptors.

Want to hear a disturbing fact? If you're still reading by chapter eight, I'll assume *yes*. Anywhere from 20 to 30 percent of the art you see in museums is fake.[2] And I don't mean fake as in replicas presented as the real thing for security or insurance purposes, or even necessary reproductions of damaged parts or whole items of significance. I just mean *fake*. Somewhere around one-quarter of all the art in museums the world over was forged and then passed off as the real deal, at various points over the last five or ten thousand years.* Having once been deemed authentic, the pieces subsequently carry the stamp of legitimacy.

Museums, galleries, and other institutions aren't lying on purpose; often they simply can't tell the difference. And neither can you. And if *no one* can tell the difference—how can you be so sure that there even is one, let alone so certain that it matters?

Many Lisas

The *Mona Lisa* by Leonardo da Vinci is arguably the most famous painting in the world. It's inarguably a masterpiece, so I'm told. And I went to art school. Sure, everyone who goes and sees it comes home and says, "Well . . . it was a lot smaller than I thought," and seems sort

---

*And that's actually an extremely conservative estimate; most experts without any skin in the game say it's closer to 50 percent.

of underwhelmed. Nonetheless, over six million people flock to the Louvre to see the *Mona Lisa* every year. One *could* make the argument that the *Mona Lisa* is only a masterpiece because everyone agrees it is so. But let's skip over that for now.

What if the *Mona Lisa* is only **the** *Mona Lisa* because everyone agrees it is?

In 1911, a man named Vincenzo Peruggia, an Italian janitor at the Louvre Museum in Paris, took the famous painting from its frame and simply walked out with it under his smock. He hid it at home, in the false bottom of a trunk, for the next two years. Having gotten away with the crime of the century, Peruggia then (for no apparent reason at all) took the painting back to Italy, where he brazenly presented the stolen painting for sale to the directors of the Uffizi Gallery in Florence. He was, of course, arrested and the painting was returned to Paris on January 4, 1914. He claimed the theft was an act of patriotism—which never made much sense, because the Louvre was full of paintings by Italian masters, many more famous or more valuable than the *Mona Lisa* at that time—and ultimately he went to prison for about six months.[3]

That's the part of the story of the infamous theft of the *Mona Lisa* that everyone knows. Here's the part they don't: in 1908, several years before the *Mona Lisa* was stolen, an Argentine art swindler, Eduardo de Valfierno, used multiple aliases to gain entry to the United States and obtain access to certain exclusive circles in society. He managed to gain the trust of a number of millionaire art collectors, all of them not only wealthy but also possessed of a certain amount of moral flexibility. He told each of them—separately—that he might be able to obtain (i.e., steal) the *Mona Lisa*. Each one agreed to buy the painting if he could indeed get his hands on it—for an astronomical sum, of course.[4]

In the meantime, Valfierno commissioned a French art forger

named Yves Chaudron to make six perfect copies of the *Mona Lisa*. When Chaudron was finished, the copies were shipped to Valfierno. Finally, for the finishing touch: in 1911 Valfierno paid Peruggia to steal the painting from the Louvre.[5]

That's where the story starts over at the beginning: the *Mona Lisa* vanished from the Louvre in a spectacular theft, which remained mysteriously unsolved for several years.*

During that time, Valfierno sold each of his copies to each of his marks, assuring each one of them that they were in possession of the stolen original. It's actually unclear how many copies were sold as the authentic masterpiece in total (estimates range from eleven to sixteen), as he may have used a second forger.[6] Each buyer was aware that the painting they received was stolen, but they were also told that a forgery would eventually be "returned" to the museum, to reduce their chances of being implicated. Still, he advised each buyer to stay quiet; they could own the *Mona Lisa,* but they could never tell anybody they had it.[7]

This explains why Peruggia stole the painting from the Louvre in the first place ("patriotism" was never a particularly coherent motive), supposedly hid it in his flat for a couple years, and then suddenly handed it over to the Uffizi Gallery. He couldn't really have believed that the Uffizi would buy what had, since the theft, become the most famous stolen painting in the world. It was all part of a vast, transatlantic con: Peruggia stole the painting, which made the kind of world news that would reach each of Valfierno's potential buyers. Once they each heard of the theft, they believed Valfierno had successfully stolen it, and were primed to believe the copy they received was the real thing.

---

*The original source for the story of Valfierno's involvement was an exposé published in *The Saturday Evening Post* by a journalist named Karl Decker in 1932. Decker's primary source was Valfierno himself. This has made external confirmation impossible. A century later, with no compelling evidence either way, as many people believe it's the absolute truth as have claimed it's complete rubbish.

All of which has to make you wonder: Where's the original now?

The Louvre would have you believe it's hanging on their wall. But then how would we (or they) know if it wasn't? It was stolen in 1911—before CT scans, chemical analysis, or any of the other modern authentication techniques now employed. And more to the point: If you were Valfierno and you had successfully engineered the theft of the *Mona Lisa,* after commissioning—and selling off—a number of perfect replicas, what are the chances you'd actually *give back* the original?

In fact, we *know* he saved one *"Mona Lisa"* for himself, because he repeated the scam twenty-five years later and closed *five more sales* to eager collectors.[8] The only twist? This time, he informed his would-be buyers that he'd *kept* the stolen *Mona Lisa* and returned a fake to the museum. Knowing nothing of the previous six sales (or one another), each buyer believed him when he said he'd kept it for himself all those decades. And that now, as an old man, he was finally willing to sell the authentic stolen painting . . . to each one of them, of course.

So, where's Lisa really?

It *really* doesn't matter. **The** *Mona Lisa* is in at least a dozen different *very* private collections right now, not even including the Louvre. At best, the painting in the Louvre has a one in twelve chance of being the original. But here's the truth: the *Mona Lisa*—the one that exists in your mind—isn't anywhere, because you made it up.

At this point, the *Mona Lisa* is *an idea* every bit as much as it is a painting. We all know it as the greatest work by the greatest painter who ever lived (whether or not it is). What painting could live up to that? It looms so large in our cultural imagination that the painting itself frequently and famously leaves people underwhelmed when it can't equal their imaginary ideal.

And besides—if you can't tell the difference, does it matter?

It didn't matter to Valfierno's buyers; he sold his fakes at the same price that the real one would have commanded. It doesn't matter to the millions of people who have seen the masterpiece and been moved by it, or spent hours studying it, or waited in line all day and been underwhelmed by it, or bought a postcard in the gift shop so they could remember the time they'd gone to Paris and seen the *Mona Lisa*.

All that *mattered* was they believed they had.

Con Artistry

That there are an abundance of forgeries accepted as authentic is not a modern problem. If anything, it's a problem of accumulation: both accumulated fakes and accumulated acceptance of their authenticity. So much of "fact" is opinion, and so much of opinion is *consensus*. Before you disagree, consider the story of the forger of the *Sleeping Eros*.

In 1488, as a thirteen-year-old apprentice in the studio of the Florentine painter Domenico Ghirlandaio, a talented young boy got in trouble for committing forgery. He had been loaned a valuable and very old drawing to study. After he'd copied it perfectly, he departed from the typical course of training and decided to age his drawing artificially, using smoke and tint, thus replicating the object itself.[9]

He was so pleased with his work that when the time came, he kept the original and returned his replica. He might have gotten away with it, but he couldn't help bragging to the other boys. Eventually, the owner of the drawing heard rumors and demanded the antiquity back from Domenico Ghirlandaio. When the young apprentice was called in to explain himself and return the stolen piece, he produced the drawing he had kept, now claiming that he had lied to the other boys—*his* was the copy. The problem arose when the drawings were inspected side by side: no one could tell the two apart. Not the owner, not the master, not any expert called upon to make a determination. Neither one was clearly the original. (So you can see how that 20 to 30 percent in museums happens.)

Less than a decade later, in 1496, the now former apprentice was working under the patronage of Lorenzo di Pierfrancesco de' Medici. Like most young artists of his era, he found that people with money were far more inclined to buy masterpieces of Roman antiquity than works of contemporary Renaissance artists. So to make a little extra money, the artist carved a marble statue of the *Sleeping Eros,* a perfect replica of an ancient Greek masterpiece. He then buried the statue in highly acidic earth, which stained the stone and lightly eroded its surface, giving the replica both a convincing patina of age and the credible appearance of having been recently excavated.

When his patron Medici saw the forgery, he was so impressed with it that he offered to send the statue to a sketchy art dealer in Rome, Baldassare del Milanese, who would pass *Sleeping Eros* off as a genuine antique. The young artist agreed, and the forgery was sold—fraudulently—as a newly recovered, long-lost masterpiece, to Cardinal Raffaele Riario, a patron of the arts himself and the great-nephew of Pope Sixtus IV—the one who built the Sistine Chapel.

But you know what they say about two people keeping secrets: one of them has to be dead. Whether the snitch was the smug Medici, the cocky forger, or the slimy dealer looking for more deals, we will never know. But somehow, word of the scam got out. The whispers made their way to the Vatican, and Cardinal Riario realized he'd been conned. He was a powerful man and furious with the art dealer, Baldassare. He demanded both his money back and the name of the forger. Of course, Baldassare immediately paid up and rolled on the young forger: a twenty-one-year-old punk by the name of Michelangelo.

Hard Truths

While the pope *was not* amused, Cardinal Riario was impressed by the counterfeit antiquity. So much so that rather than pressing charges, he invited Michelangelo to Rome for a meeting at his palace. He even let Michelangelo keep the commission he'd made on the *Sleeping Eros*. Soon thereafter, Riario became one of Michelangelo's patrons, commissioning two pieces from him over the next two years. Michelangelo remained in Rome to carve the first of the commissions, *Bacchus,* followed by his next assignment in 1498, the *Pieta,* the sculpture that made him famous. Over the next ten years he sculpted *David* and painted the ceiling of the Sistine Chapel. The moral of this story is that the pope should lighten up—the Vatican has bought more fakes than any institution in the world. I'm just kidding, the real moral of this story is that a lot of the "great masters" started as forgers. But also, the thing about the Vatican.

Would it shock you to know that silversmith, engraver, and Revolutionary War icon Paul Revere was also a notorious art forger?[10] (If it does, I'm pretty sure you've been skimming up to this point.) He copied other artists' engravings and slapped his own name on them all the time. Revere's most famous, and massively bestselling image, *The Boston Massacre of 1770,* was a forgery. It was a direct copy of Henry Pelham's original engraving, intercepted by Revere himself on its way to be printed.[11] Apparently, he liked the image so much he copied it, signed it, and sent his own to be printed first. A dick move, sure—but it doesn't really diminish the greatness of his silverwork, or the nine hundred or so giant bells he made, one of which still rings daily in Boston.*

And what about the forgers who never get caught *or* get famous? If they're re-creating masterpieces that pass muster, it begs the question: Who's the master, and how exactly are we defining "masterpiece"?

If *Sleeping Eros* was never discovered to be a fraud or traced back to a young Michelangelo, would it still be considered a masterpiece now? Probably not. It has been retroactively imbued with that status, because it was crafted by a master. The whole circular logic of *a masterpiece* is born of an aesthetic syllogism, one that determines the value of the creation by the value of the creator—whose own value is dependent upon having previously created those same valuable things.

Nothing is entirely real.

But in the history of art forgery, there is an interesting, recurring theme: when they're discovered, more often than not no one is actually *that* angry at the forger. Unlike in the case of financial frauds or religious rackets, the perpetrators of art forgeries are rarely met with rage. Rather, like Michelangelo's rapidly earning fame and fortune, and eventually receiving the patronage of at least three popes, forgers and counterfeiters often achieve great acclaim once discovered.

So, what's so different about this particular kind of lie?

Truth Is Hard

The difference between fraud and forgery is the difference between truth and facts. Say you saw a piece of the true cross in a cathedral, and

---

*In metalsmithing, making a large bell that can ring once, let alone repeatedly (for centuries) without cracking, is a hugely impressive feat.

you believed it was genuine. Then you walked across town and went to the Louvre, and saw a painting that you were told was a Picasso, and you believed that too. Now imagine both are exposed as counterfeit.

The difference is that belief in the cross is simultaneously belief in a whole structure of religious truth. Exposing one element of the truth as a lie, by definition, challenges the rest of it.

The Picasso, on the other hand, you might have just as surely believed was authentic because a curator, brochure, or little plaque on the wall told you so. But you have no skin in the game should it turn out to be a fraud. You didn't believe it was *truth,* just a fact. When the fact proves incorrect, you experience no cognitive dissonance, because your reality is not contingent on its being true. You're not enraged or disillusioned. Just misinformed.

One is a betrayal of truth, the other a betrayal of facts—a dichotomy that is possible *only if truth and facts are fundamentally different.*

And they are.

It may seem obvious, and a little stupid, when you consider that what is accepted as fact is merely *that which is accepted*; but the implications are profound. They're so profound, in fact, that they're largely responsible for humanity's unparalleled evolutionary dominance. It goes all the way back to the idea of collective intelligence—humanity's great advantage, and unquestionable weakness.

Long before the Internet, before books even, humans evolved to harness the power of the collective: by believing in experiences, observations, and conclusions—not our own. We could each wield far more information than any one person could ever discover or reason on their own in a human lifetime: *all we had to do was ask—and then believe the answer.*

Human belief linked consensus permanently to fact, allowing individuals to aggregate knowledge at an astronomical rate. But it's also a sort of mass delusion. It's a lie we all agree to believe, together. It is the basis of civilization.

So how much of fact is consensus? How much of what we know is simply what we agree to believe? And what does truth even mean in this context?

Making Money

Nowhere, perhaps, is a collective fiction more believed, defended, and simultaneously denied—or at least ignored—than in the realm of currency.

Money isn't real, except in our collective imaginations. "Money" is just a word for an IOU—backed not by gold or other commodities, but by tacit agreement and unconscious consensus. Money is also one of the most precarious lies there is: hence the danger of bank runs, stock market crashes, and economic collapses—all of which can only happen when the collective ceases to believe all or some portion of the lie.

All versions of money are imaginary if you examine them closely enough, and they only have value because we all agree they do. But cash—paper money—is a particularly blatant example: it's just printed slips of paper.*

This makes counterfeiting hard currency particularly easy and tempting.

Victor Lustig—the guy who kept selling the Eiffel Tower to people—was also famous for pulling a scam called the money box.[12] The money-box con worked as follows: Lustig would identify wealthy,

*Well, technically linen.

and unscrupulous, marks (probably the same demographic interested in buying the stolen *Mona Lisa*—and, in fact, he was running this con around the same time, throughout the 1920s and '30s).

Eventually, when he had won the mark's trust, he would show them an ingenious invention: a machine that printed hundred-dollar bills on blank paper. He would demonstrate how the machine worked by feeding a piece of white paper in the tray, closing it, and slowly cranking out, via a small slit in the box, a perfectly printed hundred-dollar bill, indistinguishable from the real thing.[13]

That was, of course, because it *was* the real thing. The box printed nothing: it ate the paper and slowly rolled out an actual hundred-dollar bill, already stashed inside. The money box contained only one bill, so when the buyer bought it for about three thousand dollars, that hundred-dollar bill was a minor loss.

Lustig supposedly made over a million dollars on money boxes before he was temporarily sent to prison.* Joseph "Yellow Kid" Weil got busted running a similar scam. At his trial, he had the audacity, or perhaps just lucidity, to claim that his victims were complicit. He pointed out that they had knowingly endeavored to commit forgery and should be on trial themselves.

The money box was not producing forgeries, of course, since the mark couldn't print any more cash of their own. It's more of a Bait and Switch, with successful forgery as its promise: a con inside a con. But what if the box *had* printed money? People do it all the time; paper money is hardly impossible to counterfeit. And the money-box scam is far from dead. Police bunco experts estimate

---

*He escaped by climbing out a window, and when he reached the street, he casually walked away. People saw him, of course, but he seemed so unconcerned by that fact that they assumed he must be the window washer.

that similar scams are currently run hundreds of times a year in the United States.[14] New money, after all, is printed every day. So why not print it at home?

This, of course, brings us to the heart of the matter: *Why not* print it at home?

Let's say that a money box did exist and that it really did print perfect hundred-dollar bills indistinguishable from the real thing. It's not because the U.S. government *printed it* that a hundred-dollar bill is worth a hundred dollars; it's because we all agree to accept it in a hundred dollars' worth of trade, even though it's only paper—trusting the next person to do the same, and the next, and the next. It's an efficient way to transfer value. That arrangement doesn't change with a counterfeit bill—not if it's indistinguishable from an authentic bill.

A counterfeit hundred-dollar bill, indistinguishable from the real thing, *really would* be worth a hundred dollars. Things have value as long as we believe they have value. If the consensus is that said forged object *is real,* it functions as if it were real; in this case, meaning that the fake could also be exchanged for a hundred dollars' worth of goods and services.

And here's the fascinating part: after the counterfeit bill has been spent, at that point *the lie becomes retroactively true*. The counterfeit hundred-dollar bill really was worth a hundred dollars.

This counterfeit bill is functionally no different from a "real" bill—so long as everyone believes it's legitimate, accepts it, and continues passing it around. If it's discovered to be counterfeit, it becomes worthless, not because it fundamentally changes in any substantive way, but simply because it can no longer be exchanged for anything.

Just like a genuine hundred-dollar bill becomes worthless once torn in two pieces. This is the case because the U.S. Treasury says so.

Why does the U.S. Treasury have the authority to say which bill is worth a hundred dollars? Why do they have the authority to say *any* of them (mine, theirs, the torn-up one) are or are not worthy? They're all just equally worthless slips of paper, indistinguishable from each other—and they're equally valuable, as long as nobody notices that one isn't vouched for by the Treasury.

So where does the Treasury get that authority to declare certain slips of paper "money"? Where does that authority lie? Who gave it to them?

The answer is that the authority the Treasury exercises is granted by all of us, when we agree to believe that money is real in the first place. In doing so, in agreeing to unilaterally believe in something that we know is *not exactly true*—like the value of a hundred-dollar bill—we agree to also believe that there is an absolute truth on the subject. In so doing, we acknowledge that we're all pretending together—and must abide by our own equally fabricated rules.

But there's a nasty flip side to this arrangement, one pertaining not to worth, but to worthlessness. If we abandon a collective lie, the value and authority it implies or confers collapse with it. There's a consensus of belief at work in this. Real currency or forged bills—both are just bits of paper backed by belief. We know it's not true, but we all agree to believe that paper money is worth what we're told it's worth, unquestionably.

If we stop believing *that lie,* then none of it—authentic or counterfeit—would be worth anything at all.

Authentic Fakes

Truth and lies are two sides of the same coin: opposites that can never be reconciled but are, by their very nature, inextricably linked. This particular truth has a tendency to inspire resentment. It did just that in Louis Marcy. Born Luigi Parmeggiani in northern Italy in 1860, Marcy was a brilliant craftsman. His craft, specifically, was the making of counterfeit medieval and Renaissance antiquities, primarily caskets, jewelry, and reliquaries.[15]

He was also a vehement anarchist. He even published a newsletter about it, which seems like kind of a nerdy way to do anarchy. Another weird way Marcy did anarchy was by engaging in what's called "subversive forgery."[16] In other words, he didn't counterfeit because he desperately wanted to make art, nor was he in it for money—his forgeries were pointless. Or, rather, pointedly only for the purpose of fucking people up.

In his anarchy newsletter, he wrote articles about how he loathed the "capitalist art market." He knew experts couldn't tell the difference between an original and a great forgery and he was particularly outraged that they all insisted—and believed—that they could.* He resented the arbitrary value assigned to one thing over another and despised the way people, especially so-called authorities on the subject, persisted in claiming authority that they did not in fact possess by arbitrarily assigning value to art they could not differentiate.[17]

His response? Subversive forgery. He flooded the market with perfect fakes. He got away with producing massive amounts of coun-

---

*And I get it, because I feel the same irrational outrage when confronted with people who claim they can taste things in wine like terroir. But I'm not gonna devote my life to anarchy over it.

terfeit medieval and Renaissance jewelry and art for *decades* before he was caught.[18] Which is surprising, given his demented newsletters. His forgeries were so convincing that they've ended up in private collections and in the major museums of Europe.[19]

When he finally got arrested in 1903 (ironically, for being an anarchist, not a counterfeiter), the police found his house stuffed to the rafters with precious art and antiquities so convincingly authentic that the cops assumed he was a fence, not a forger.[20] He did five months in prison. As soon as he got out, he went right back to flooding the art and antiquities market for years. It wasn't until 1922 that his role as an art forger was discovered and subsequently investigated.

In many cases, art forgers have become famous artists after the fact, like Michelangelo and Paul Revere, making their earlier fraudulent work priceless masterpieces by association. In still rarer cases like Marcy's, forgers simply become famous for their forgeries, which, based on that renown, are then—in a circular judgment—eventually deemed "art."

Today, Marcy's forgeries are celebrated as brilliant, and his whole body of work is as sought after as real masterpieces. The British Museum lavishes praise on "the skilled craftsmanship of his materials, and the inspired eclecticism of his design."[21] And as recently as 2008 Sotheby's had to pull an important thirteenth-century buckle from their Old Masters sale at the last moment; though it was at one time considered authentic by the Victoria and Albert Museum in London, it turned out to be one of Marcy's.

It's probable that many of his fake antiquities, fawned over by experts and critics, are still sitting in collections, misattributed. But at least there's motivation to find them: "Marcy Fakes," as they're now called, are so valuable that many Renaissance objets d'art would be worth *more* if they'd been counterfeited by Luigi Parmeggiani at the turn of the century.

And man, would he have hated that.

You Can Hear the Ocean Because There's Nothing There

Sometimes—as in the case of the subversive forgery of Louis Marcy, now highly esteemed by the art world he so disliked—a lie takes on a life of its own and becomes something else entirely, a thing in and of itself, apart from the deception that spawned it. It becomes an object whose value *derives* from the fraudulence of the value it claimed in the first place. In such an instance, the value is the lie, not the deception. In other words, sometimes a forgery becomes valuable not because it passes for genuine, *but because it is a forgery*.

The precious wentletrap is a seashell with a long spiral shape and distinctive ladder-like ridges. Dutch traders first brought them back from the Southwest Pacific and introduced them to European buyers in the 1700s. Much like tulip bulbs, demand for the novelty soon outpaced supply, sending prices sky-high and making the shells unobtainable to any but the wealthiest collectors.

Within a century, the demand was so great that, *unlike* tulip bulbs, Chinese counterfeiters began flooding the market with near-perfect fakes made out of rice-flour paste. Neither traders nor buyers could tell a counterfeit shell from the real thing until it was submerged in water—at which point the fake shells dissolved back into rice flour. When the scope of the fraud was exposed, collectors became skittish and the craze eventually faded.[22]

What makes the story of the precious wentletrap shell more than just a mildly amusing anecdote is the current state of the wentletrap market. As I said, the craze died down. And then, over the course of another century or two, more sources for the shells were found. At this point in time, you can buy an authentic, but not-so-precious wentletrap shell for ten to fifteen bucks.

I just checked.

Those Chinese counterfeit shells, on the other hand, have become a very precious commodity. Just like Marcy Fakes. An acknowledged fraud, once worthless, is now more valuable than the real thing. But neither the real shells nor the crafted ones are precious for what they actually are, or for what they once pretended to be. They're precious for what we've *decided* they are. Is a fake wentletrap shell, an odd, rare specimen of large-scale economic deception, really worth anything? Not really—not *really* really.

But the market has agreed that it is, and so what was once fraud has become fact.

Faithful Copies

While we're on the subject of mass delusions, let's talk about religion—religious relics in particular and Catholic relics specifically.

Relics are what Catholic saints leave behind and are thus holy by association. Actually, they come in degrees of holiness. First-degree relics are pieces of saints' bodies: body parts, bones, teeth, hair, even bodily fluids. Second-degree relics are intimate physical possessions (like a cup, pillow, clothing, or jewelry) allegedly owned by any now-deceased Catholic saint. Third-degree relics—the most abundant type—are pretty much anything the saint is believed to have come in physical contact with during their lifetime. And despite some conflicting doctrine regarding idol worship, these items themselves are venerated. They're either associated with a miracle or believed to be actually able to perform one.

By their very nature, relics are difficult—if not impossible—to authenticate, and so unsurprisingly they're very vulnerable to counterfeiting.

The Middle Ages saw a booming business in fraudulent religious relics, the reason being that the Catholic faith was spreading across the Western world like Beatlemania. More worshippers required more churches. And by the fourth century, that institutional success posed a significant logistical problem: too few relics. The thing about Catholic churches is that each one is technically supposed to be built around a genuine religious relic. It's Catholic doctrine: you can't consecrate an altar in a church without a relic. No relic, no altar. No altar, no church. But there are only so many actual Horcruxes to go around, you know?

So enterprising salesmen in medieval Europe began manufacturing relics. Posing as pilgrims or traveling traders, they would sell the artifacts to the town or village in need. Often they sold them to the local clergy. Sometimes *the clergy* were even the ones doing the selling. It was kind of a five-hundred- to one-thousand-year-long ethical free-for-all. In at least one case, *the actual pope* (Eugenius II) had an "arrangement" with Charlemagne's grandson, King Lothar, which allowed wealthy and elite Carolingian nobles and high-placed clergy to place bespoke orders for precious relics, including whole bodies, like the bones of Saint Sebastian in A.D. 826.

Producing or manufacturing Catholic relics—which could mean anything from standard grave robbing to far more interesting and creative arts and crafts—became, during the Middle Ages, an entire cottage industry. John Calvin once claimed that if all the Catholic relics in Europe were put together "it would be made manifest that every Apostle has more than four bodies, and every Saint two or three." Nobody cared. They believed that theirs was real—even if they did buy it.*

In some cases, even an acknowledged fake relic could *become* genuine, once it was perceived to have performed a miracle. Almost like the miracle of successfully spending a counterfeit bill: once the fake relic did the job, its sanctity became retroactively true.

In fact, there's still a pretty solid market for Catholic relics—more among individuals now than towns or cities—and an accompanying industry counterfeiting them. You can buy a "genuine" relic on eBay (for $2,200 you can buy a piece of the true cross—I just checked that, too), which is fairly absurd and almost certainly fraudulent.

But what about the "real" ones, the relics vouched for by the Vatican, with cathedrals and chapels built around them? The sort of *legitimate* sacred objects saved from the 2019 fire that nearly destroyed the cathedral of Notre Dame in Paris? Even those sanctioned relics are unfortunately suspect. The crown of thorns has never been authenticated, nor has Notre Dame's own fragment of the true cross—though it has been pointed out that all the recognized fragments of the true cross (not including the ones on eBay) taken together would provide enough wood to build a ship. And there are many other, more thoroughly conclusive, examples of venerated Catholic relics that have unequivocally proved to be false—such as the bones of Saint Rosalia in Sicily.[23]

Saint Rosalia, often called the Little Saint, was born in 1130. The story goes that as a young woman she was led to a secluded place on

---

* Sort of like President Truman and his bathtub.

Mount Pellegrino by a pair of angels, where she decided to live out her life in a remote cave, as one does. Supposedly, that remote, secret cave is where she died in 1166 and where her remains remained, undisturbed or discovered, for almost five hundred years, until a plague swept through Palermo in 1624.

It was then that the Little Saint appeared, first to a dying woman and then to a hunter. She told him where to find her cave and commanded him to go and retrieve her bones. He did so, and then, as he claimed the apparition had instructed him to do, had the bones carried three times around the city in a giant procession. After the third time around, the plague *vanished*. Rosalia became Saint Rosalia, the patron saint of Palermo; a sanctuary was erected in her cave; and her bones have been a venerated first-degree relic ever since.[24]

Most of the story of Saint Rosalia's bones makes no sense at all. If she met a pair of angels, left with them, and died alone in a cave as a hermit in 1166, how would anyone know that part of her story? How would we know what year she died, or how many angels were hanging out with her in the cave? That sounds embellished. And if she wanted someone to go get her bones 468 years later, why did she appear *first* to a woman at the moment of her death? The dying woman wasn't gonna climb up the side of a mountain. And since she then promptly *did* die, how do we know Rosalia appeared to her at all?

Problematic origin story, to say the least.

But that's not the real problem with the relic. The story doesn't actually matter. We're talking about miracles. And miracles, much like Hoaxes, are something you simply *choose* to believe (or not), whether they hold up to scrutiny, or not. The problem with Saint Rosalia's bones is that, upon closer inspection, they turn out to be the bones of a goat.[25]

I'm not interested in poking holes in the very holey story of the life, death, and miracle of Saint Rosalia. But I do feel compelled, given how relics are defined, to point out that the object of veneration, the actual relic, isn't an actual relic if it's actually a goat. A valid relic could be lots of things other than her bones: a lock of Saint Rosalia's hair, or Saint Rosalia's left shoe, even Saint Rosalia's Bible (she was in that cave for decades—I'm sure she brought something to read). But, as I understand the rules governing religious relics, random goat bones cannot be a relic of Saint Rosalia—unless there was a barbecue involved.

So, even without quibbling about the rest of the story—there's that.

And *that* is awkwardly common. Drops of a martyr's blood on the floor of another church, venerated for centuries, were revealed to be bat urine. The brain of Saint Peter was accidentally knocked over and turned out to be a large piece of pumice stone. There are multiple skeletons of Saint Valentine, all deemed authentic. At one point there were twenty-one different holy foreskins (which are exactly what they sound like) competing for validation.* The finger of Saint Paul, the head of Saint Catherine . . . not goats, thank God, but ultimately impossible to authenticate. How do we know whose body they really belonged to?

The answer is that, like the many *Mona Lisa*s, it doesn't remotely matter. If it did, fearless Parisians wouldn't have run into Notre Dame while the cathedral was engulfed in flames and beginning to collapse. Catholic relics are the Snake Oil of religion. Maybe they were real once. Maybe some are truly what they are purported to be. But *the effect they have on people* has nothing to do with provenance, or proof, or authentication. It has to do with belief. The purpose of a relic is to inspire awe

---

*You cannot buy one of those on eBay. I checked.

and devotion. The bones of Saint Rosalia have done that for centuries. In fact, they *still do*—find the nearest devout Sicilian Catholic and try arguing about whether their beloved Little Saint is, in fact, a goat.

They don't believe it, *and* they don't care. And you will find them *quite* vehement—on both positions, simultaneously.

The Myth of Singular Truth

If a fake relic can stir real awe, if it can draw real worshippers to real churches and cathedrals that it has the power to consecrate as real holy ground—if it can even, according to the many faithful, inspire real *miracles,* just as an authentic relic promises—it's inaccurate to declare it fraudulent. In fact, it's a dichotomy so false that it borders on meaningless. Which is more important to the nature of a relic: that it be a DNA match for a woman born almost a thousand years ago, or that it have the power to heal the sick, inspire visions, and mend broken hearts?

The Shroud of Turin is a particularly interesting case: it is believed by some to be Christ's burial shroud—the cloth that covered his body after the crucifixion. It's stained with human blood at the sites of his recorded wounds. It also bears a compelling (and despite modern efforts, as yet unreplicated) reverse image of a distinctly Christ-like man—somehow metaphysically transferred from his body to the cloth while it covered him. Kind of like a holy carbon copy. Every year, tens of thousands of people travel to Turin, Italy, to see the legendary relic. The faithful come to see what they believe to be Christ's two-thousand-year-old death shroud, imbued with some echo of his divinity. And many others come to scrutinize or study what they believe to be an ambitious medieval forgery.

Most relics can be definitively debunked, like a pumice stone that obviously can't be Saint Peter's brain. Other relics fall into the category of *not* debunkable, just debatable: like the jawbone of fourth-century bishop Saint Nicholas. Oxford University researchers recently tested the bone, and I'll be damned if it wasn't a human jawbone (though whose is anyone's guess) from the fourth century A.D. The vast majority of relics, when tested, either *are* (at least in substance, age, regional origin, or other properties) what they're purported to be—or they *are not*.

What makes the shroud so interesting is that, unlike other relics, it has proved almost impossible to either authenticate *or debunk,* not because we lack definitive answers, but because the definitive answers continually contradict each other. Even the age of the shroud's fabric can't seem to be conclusively identified. Though that failure is not from lack of trying: there have been more examinations done, tests conducted, and histories written on the Shroud of Turin than any other holy relic. Skeptics and believers alike have spent centuries employing both creative and critical thinking in an effort to definitively prove *their* truth.

Though many tests have been done on many aspects of the shroud, let's just talk about one: age. How old is the actual linen fabric?

In 1988, scientists removed a few fibers from the shroud and tried to determine its age using radiocarbon dating. What is radiocarbon dating? I'm glad you asked. Radiocarbon (or C14) is an unstable and weakly radioactive isotope of carbon. Radiocarbon is in everything, because rapid oxidization turns it into CO_2, which is absorbed into the global carbon cycle. As a result, radiocarbon is present in all carbon-based life-forms, and any materials made from those life-forms, and any thing made from them: this paper, wooden floorboards, your lunch, your death shroud . . .

When those carbon-based life-forms die, their unstable radiocarbon content begins to "decay" at a specific rate, called a half-life. Radiocarbon dating measures residual radioactivity—in other words, how much radiocarbon is left in a thing—to determine approximately how long ago the carbon-based life-form (say, a flax plant used to make linen for a shroud) died and began its radioactive decay. Radiocarbon is in everything organic, and all radioactive isotopes have a specific and predeterminable half-life. This makes radiocarbon dating a very precise way of getting a very approximate answer.

Scientists took the fibers to laboratories in Oxford, Zurich, and Arizona, where they conducted identical radiocarbon dating on separate strands. Their results were conclusive and unanimous: it dated from somewhere between A.D. 1260 to 1390.[26] That solved it. The Shroud of Turin was obviously an impressive medieval Hoax.

Not so fast.

Now the 1988 radiocarbon findings are in dispute. They are facing off with an equivalently academic, if novel, experiment—the results of which differ by about 1,200 years. The more recent testing, done by Giulio Fanti, a professor of mechanical and thermal measurement at Padua University, in northern Italy, utilized a combination of Raman and infrared spectroscopy, a different but equally scientific method, in an attempt to determine the age of the shroud.[27]

Spectroscopy studies the interaction between electromagnetic radiation and particles, like molecules and atoms. Infrared light is a low-frequency form of electromagnetic radiation, which can produce changes in a material. Raman spectroscopy is an analysis technique used to get a detailed look at a material's chemical structure, based on the interaction between electromagnetic radiation and the material's chemical bonds. In other words, combination Raman and infrared-light spectroscopy measures an object's interaction with electromagnetic radiation. Fanti is using particle physics to see how long the shroud's fibers have been interacting with light. Not visible light, that's iffy—*any* electromagnetic radiation at all. And his conclusion? Fanti has determined that the shroud is much, much older—dating somewhere between 280 B.C. and A.D. 220. Almost exactly the age it purports to be.

So . . . might it be real? Or just a *really* old fraud? I don't know. I don't care. There's a more compelling mystery. Carbon dating and infrared spectroscopy are both so-called hard science, so how can they give conflicting answers?

Good question.

Here are some good answers: Maybe a sample was contaminated. Maybe the fibers tested were from a newer medieval repair to a more ancient cloth, and that skewed the carbon-dating results. Maybe it was subject to some odd, naturally occurring radiation at some point, altering the spectroscopy data. Maybe a lab tech fucked up. Maybe a test was faulty. Or *maybe* we don't totally understand the complete scope of the fields of science upon which those tests are based or the totality of what they mean. As a math teacher once told me: if you did the math and your answer doesn't make any sense, you probably didn't understand the question.

The fact that two scientific tests yielded totally different results isn't even surprising; that happens all the time. What *is* surprising is how unacceptable that particular dissonance is to people. And it says something critical about *the myth of singular truth*—namely, that *it is* a myth. And it's a particularly universal one.

Thus far, we've mostly discussed the truth about lies, but this myth—that there is only one truth, singular and immutable—is actually a *lie about the truth.*

The idea that there can be only one truth *is* true, so long as it is true—the assertion of the lie is also the assertion of its truth. This is nothing more than a weak syllogism. And yet we let our belief in this lie, this myth of singular truth, *circumscribe the entirety of our mental schema,* from the story we tell about ourselves, the world, and other people in it, to our politics, our beliefs, our sense of equality, of rights and freedoms, of reason and reality—it colors our reactions and feelings about everything we see and hear.

It's a broad and reductive lie, but also a dangerous one. Has anything in history caused more war, upheaval, and suffering than intractable faith in *one singular truth* and the inevitable conflict over its specifics?

The truth is, there is no *one* truth. "True" is not an objective standard, it's not a universal constant like gravity or time. And even those aren't really objective; they also depend upon perspective, which changes with circumstance, observation, and distance.

Of course there are objective facts . . . there are just a lot fewer of them than you probably believe.

But facts are not truths, and truths are not mutually exclusive. This notion, that there is only true and false, real and fake, facts and lies—and the certainty that a thing can only be one or the other—fundamentally misunderstands the meaning, and value, of both. The truth about *truth* is that it's even more complicated and confusing than lies; and often, the opposite of a profound truth is not a falsehood, but a *completely different profound truth.*

Even in opposition, two conflicting truths can still be true: an object can be definitively scientifically dated as being both five hundred years old and two thousand years old. A hundred-dollar bill can be valuable legal tender and, at the same time, a dirty piece of paper. By the same token, a *counterfeit* hundred-dollar bill can be both worthless and worth a hundred dollars. A work of art can be a sought-after, recognized fake—or a forgettable forgery crafted by a master.

As a relic, the Shroud of Turin is both true and false, relic and fraud. Few relics have ever served their purpose so consistently and completely: to fuel faith and enhance preexisting belief . . . even when we believe more than one thing at a time.

The Catholic Church has no single, official position on the Shroud of Turin's authenticity. Nor do they need one: at this point, both believers and skeptics alike believe more than ever, though in somewhat different (and conflicting) truths. Every time the shroud's authenticity is "proved," it renews religious faith in the devout; every time it's "disproved," it reaffirms the triumph of reason over superstition for the skeptical.

Truth, like most universal constants, depends on relative position.

WAIT FOR IT . . .

At Long Last: The Long Con

The truth is rarely pure, and never simple.
—OSCAR WILDE

In the end, everything is a gag.
—CHARLIE CHAPLIN

THE LONG CON

The Long Con is an elaborate, multiperson con job often targeting multiple people, or entire institutions, as marks. Unlike a short con, there is no immediate payoff. The Long Con requires a significant amount of time, operators, and investment. Elaborate and operating like clockwork, the Long Con involves multiple different short cons that are run simultaneously by different, seemingly unrelated operators who will later share the take. The Long Con is deliberately convoluted and deeply dependent upon two things: gaining the mark's trust while hiding the *scope* of the real con and successfully disguising the connections between seemingly unconnected events or ideas—thus subverting the mark's experience of reality.

Sanity Is Absolutely Statistical

Truth is an act of consensus: we all agree together on what is or is not accepted as true. It's the most vital, if tacit, clause in the social contract. If 99.9 percent of people believe paper money has intrinsic value or that the *Mona Lisa* is priceless (and actually in the Louvre), then it makes no practical difference if these things are factually accurate: they are accepted as true and thus comprise "reality, the name we give to the common experience."[1]

The Long Con weaponizes the communally dependent nature of truth and falsehood in human society. It relies on not only your fundamental bias to trust your perception, memory, and judgment but also on your evolutionary bias to trust that the larger group isn't attempting, *en masse,* to subvert your sense of reality.

In other words: because humans make communal judgment calls about what is and what isn't true, sometimes a community can deliberately fuck you up. That's what a Long Con is: it's an orchestrated effort by a group to subvert, manipulate, alter, or even negate your experience of reality. And it's disturbingly effective.

It's also, as you'll see, the underpinning of the whole world.

Strangers with Candy

The Long Con is the quintessence of grifting, not only because it employs so many of the different cons and individual techniques we've discussed so far but also because the very scale of the deception—not the size of any particular lie, but the relative enormity of the deliberate, coordinated subversion of your sense of truth and trust in fact—is so unfathomable that if you ever did manage to see the actual fraud . . . you still probably wouldn't believe it.

A classic Long Con involves at least one incident of seeming chance, of luck (good or bad), such as an ostensibly beneficent individual you just happen to meet at exactly the right moment. Often, this person earns your trust by exposing a scam you're about to fall for—and in saving you, creates the illusion of being an honest person. This is called the Good Samaritan play. You are, of course, extrapolating a larger picture of this person's character and morality from a single incident, and in this case the larger picture is incorrect. Thereafter, anything or anyone this Good Samaritan suggests or endorses comes with a protective halo of credibility.

In reality, the Good Samaritan and whatever scammer they saved you from are actually partners. The Good Samaritan's entire job is to exploit your new friendship and sense of trust and to steer you along the predetermined path of a much longer con. Anywhere the Good Samaritan takes you, any suggestions they make for your seeming benefit, and anyone you meet while you're with them—are a part of the Long Con.

A micro-mini version of a Long Con might go as follows: you go into a pawnshop or a small jewelry store to buy, say, a diamond ring. Another woman, a random customer, is browsing the counters (she's the Good Samaritan). When you settle on a piece you like and ask to see it, the man behind the counter (her accomplice) will take it out and show it to you. He will give you the sort of information you would expect to be given before buying a diamond of any caliber: the color, cut, clarity, carat weight, maybe something special about this piece. Once he has told you what you've selected and extolled its virtues, he'll begin to negotiate a price.

At some point during this transaction, this woman, the Good Samaritan, will begin to listen to the explanation as well, looking increasingly agitated. Finally, she'll erupt angrily to end the transaction. Much to your gratitude and relief, it will turn out she's an expert on diamonds and knows that the man is trying to sell you a fake. She'll confront him and accuse him of cheating you. He'll become flustered, angry, and argumentative; he might even throw you both out of his shop.

Now, of course, she's won both your trust and your gratitude. She's also earned your respect—she knows so much about jewelry— and as you consciously defer to her expertise, you begin to *unconsciously* defer to her other suggestions and opinions as well. And she'll keep dropping crumbs of professional insight about the jewelry industry, until you ask her how she knows so much. There will be some very believable answer: she works in the jewelry industry, or her family does, or she knows someone who fell for the exact same scam! After some small talk, she will mention that (or, better yet, *she'll get you to ask her*) if she knows a more reputable dealer. Of course she does! Just around the corner, actually. And she'd be happy to give you his number.

Or take you there—it's on her way anyway.

She'll lead you to a different shop nearby and seem friendly with the owner—this unconsciously extends the trust you've come to feel toward her to her friend—the owner you've just met at the second store. She'll tell him disdainfully about the previous encounter. They'll both lament the gall of that guy and make you feel—again, unconsciously—

that you're all on the same side. Needless to say, the second jeweler is the third accomplice and intends to sell you a fake—for a great deal of money.

Once you see something you like, you'll get offered a "good deal," likely because you came in with the Good Samaritan—a friend of his. If you look like you're hesitating, a fourth shopper/accomplice browsing around the store will notice your potential acquisition, get excited—*it's so gorgeous!*—and try to buy the piece out from under you now that a price has been set. This action is designed to get you in a motivated, even competitive state (and thus not thinking clearly). The competition is intended to elicit your fear of missing out and nudge you into jumping the gun on the purchase—and maybe even drive up the price—while also serving to reassure you about the worth of the diamond in question; if it wasn't worth it, why would the second shopper want it so badly?

At some point in the course of this transaction, a fifth person might arrive, another "shopper," or potentially a professional acquaintance of your Good Samaritan, who will somehow display great expertise while you separately consider your purchase or fight with the second buyer trying to scoop you. The next thing you know, you'll be asking for their opinion. They will, of course, endorse your purchase. And why wouldn't you take their opinion seriously? Not only are they knowledgeable and vouched for by your new BFF, the Good Samaritan, they are neither the seller nor the other customer—so they seemingly have no skin in the game.

If you've been sold a fake diamond ring (at what seemed like a remarkably good price), that's the end of the transaction and you leave happy with your diamond and really happy about what a good deal you got. You'll be less happy somewhere down the line when you find out it's junk—and can no longer find the store where you bought it.

Alternatively, you might not be done in the store just yet—your hustlers might take it up one more level and sell you a reasonably valuable *real* diamond ring—if, by now, they have come to believe that you have both the means and the will to ante up for the better jewelry case. They'll make you feel like a high roller, or an insider, or whatever gets you to the big-ticket rings. And then they will sell you a *real diamond*—at a real discount. But before you leave, one of your new friends will notice that those prongs are a little loose or that it's a little dirty. The shop owner will generously offer to take it in the back and clean it or tighten up those prongs for you—free of charge, of course.

After all, you did just spend a chunk of cash on one of the bigger-ticket items.

Don't be confused. It only takes a few minutes to pop a diamond out of a ring and replace it with an identical cubic zirconia. And (unless it really is your field) don't kid yourself that you can tell the difference. In either scenario, you're leaving with a fake. Once you and your fake diamond are gone, the various operators split your money five ways.

To be clear: this is the *shortest possible version* of a Long Con.

Often, these cons involve many more individual operators, running more than one con each over a significantly longer amount of time. But you get the basic idea. The Long Con is all about manipulating your perception of events, facts, and reality in ways that you absolutely don't recognize at the time—or, ideally, ever—in order to create a different, elaborately constructed false reality that benefits its creators.

The Truth About Diamonds

While we're sort of on the subject, *diamonds themselves* may be the best Long Con in modern history—and not on a microscale, either. Or, rather, the *myth* of diamonds is the best Long Con in history, the myth that says they're special and terribly scarce, rare, precious, and incredibly valuable. The myth of diamonds that says you've always wanted one. The myth that says you'll only know that *you're wanted* when you have one.

But this is just a story—a story you've been told so many times that you've long since forgotten it was never true. The truth about diamonds is that they are neither scarce nor intrinsically valuable. What value they do possess has been carefully cultivated in the mind of the consumer over the last eighty to ninety years.

Diamonds *were* legitimately rare once upon a time. . . . More than a century ago, when they mostly came from the Golconda region of India. Back then, the entire global diamond output was just a few pounds a year. But that was before the South African diamond rush. It started on the banks of the Orange River in 1870 and ended, well, never. At first, the South African diamond rush seemed like a genuine rush—like the gold rush—a flash flood of money that would inevitably tap out. But 150 years later, *it's still rushing,* bringing up diamonds by the metric *ton*. And we just get better and better at mining them every year.

The Golconda diamonds of long ago were alluvial—meaning they were sought and found on the surface, primarily washed up in riverbeds, no mining required. Once we figured out how to mine diamonds from deep in the ground, we discovered they were shockingly abundant—

and not just in South Africa. Diamonds are *everywhere*. The largest diamond mine currently operating, Aikhal, is in Russia. There are more gem-quality diamonds in human hands (meaning cut, polished, in stores, in vaults, in jewelry boxes) than you could possibly imagine. Billions of carats.

The only reason you believe that diamonds are scarce—and thus precious—is that you've been Long Conned into it.

The Gold Standard

A successful Long Con can go on for decades, involve millions of people, and, most of all, be fundamentally ingrained in our reality and way of life. De Beers's diamond cartel created the modern conception of romance, engagement rings, and most of the wedding industry itself to sell their rocks when they realized they had too many. It's so successful, you don't even see that you've been had.

In the last decades of the nineteenth century, back when the diamond rush was expected to eventually tap out, a particularly unpleasant man named Cecil Rhodes begged, borrowed, and stole to gain control of most of the diamond-producing mines in South Africa. When he couldn't get all of them, he merged with a man named Oppenheimer to form the De Beers diamond company.

With 99 percent of South Africa's diamond mines in their possession, it didn't take them long to realize that rather than sitting on the mother lode, they were going to be crushed by it. There were just too many diamonds coming out of the ground. If anyone knew the true magnitude of the supply, no one would believe that diamonds were rare or valuable at all, and prices would plummet—forever.

Price-fixing, when you own the entire market, is slimy—but at least it's direct sliminess. What De Beers did was so much weirder:

they lied, Big Lie style. They simply straight up lied *to the whole world* about their entire (increasingly internationally sourced) output—for decades. They sat on most of their haul, even as it increased year by year, claiming that it *simply didn't exist.*

Oppenheimer actually stated that "common sense tells us that the only way to increase the value of diamonds is to make them scarce, that is to reduce production."[2] It was market gaslighting on a global scale—and it's ongoing. This deliberate manipulation of other people's reality was bold, well executed, and immensely effective. People went on believing that diamonds were rare, and therefore diamonds went on commanding exorbitant prices.

But that in itself isn't quite a Long Con, it's just a really Big Lie. It takes more than one kind of lie to run a Long Con. Luckily, De Beers had no shortage of them.

In the early days of De Beers's Long Con, diamonds weren't quite as desirable as certain other colored stones, at least not the smaller, white diamonds that were most ubiquitous. So the De Beers diamond company, which had rapidly become something closer to the De Beers diamond cartel, hired an advertising agency to *sell the idea* of diamond engagement rings (which were, themselves, not so common) to the entire Western world—particularly the newly enriched, post–World War II American middle class.

And, together, De Beers and that ad agency, N. W. Ayer, didn't just invent the standard diamond engagement ring as a marketing tool: they crafted the entire modern concept of marriage and romance, pioneered product placement (in the movies, in all other media, in person on socialites and movie stars), consumer education, and market testing. They influenced culture and fashion and shaped the wedding industry forever in the process. They convinced not only generations of women that a diamond engagement ring was the only way to be engaged but also generations of young men that a diamond was the only respectable way to propose; they made diamond rings not only an economic but a *social* necessity.

And they did all this over the course of about a century, simply to sell gemstones so abundant that they were in danger of being seen as nearly worthless, if very pretty, semiprecious stones.

Diamonds have been an extremely successful Long Con. So successful, in fact, and so fundamentally ingrained into our reality and way of life, that we walk through this world—imagining, associating, wanting, and if we're lucky getting—this most precious stone, and we never see the con at all. And even when we do, we don't necessarily believe it. Stranger still—like Saint Rosalia's bones—we simultaneously *don't necessarily care*. The manufactured reality (one hundred years in the making) is so powerful, so pervasive, so . . . *accepted* that it's overwhelmed and effectively *overwritten* the factual truth.

And it doesn't hurt that we've all *told* the lie in addition to hearing it, rewriting our sense of the truth and even our confidence in it. After all, "liars become less confident in the truth after lying." That phrase "liars become less confident in the truth after lying," though it's something that we all know intuitively, is terrifying. But also fascinating: that you have to *tell* the lie to experience a change in belief at least suggests that "truth" is—to some degree—performative, at least for each of us individually.

Diamonds are so valuable, the story goes, because they're so rare and because absolutely everybody wants one. Here's the thing, though: as previously stated, diamonds *are not* particularly rare, and we were only *told* that we want them. Yet somehow they still retain their value—and their astronomical price tag. This is because lies (as in, the *scarcity* of diamonds) are born from a distortion of the truth. But it works the other way around too (as in the *value* of diamonds). Once critical mass has been reached for the acceptance of a "truth," it not only ceases to matter if that fact is actually a lie—it often *ceases to be one.*

You *do* want a diamond—and they *are* expensive.

Retroactive Reality

If I told you that you could believe a lie into concrete existence—not just for yourself, like a placebo, but for everyone, everywhere—would you believe me?

You're doubtful, that's fair . . . but actually, *you can.* You just can't do it alone.

There are Long Cons, and there are *really* Long Cons. Then there are cons that go on for so long, and are believed by so many generations of people, that the individual lies are gradually forgotten, while the central story is remade in our memories, as we each retell it, *as fact.*

The trick in turning a lie into truth, on a large scale, is to build slowly, layer by layer, allowing time for each lie to settle into accepted wisdom. With each successive layer, another lie is first presented (diamonds are *rare*), then believed, then accepted as obvious, and then forgotten about in any meaningful conscious way. Everybody knows diamonds are rare—you might not recall when or where you first heard that fact (you almost certainly don't), but you vaguely remember that you believe it.

For the next layer, a new lie (diamonds are *very valuable*) is once again presented, both predicated on—and inarguably reaffirmed by—the now accepted truth of the previous one. That now common knowledge is inevitably taken for granted, reordered by the human collective into a class of axiomatic assumptions about "the way things are."

Axiom: Everybody knows that diamonds are rare and very valuable.

And again, another layer: Diamonds are *necessary*. When each additional lie is presented, the cumulative strata of lies that came before it are the foundation that gives it strength. Like fossils formed in mud, each stage is built upon the concrete *memory of a belief*—at first as flimsy as a million-year-old leaf—then gradually hardened by time into stone.

Watch this trick: diamonds were valuable (thus expensive) when they were scarce. Then they ceased to be scarce. Now they're actually ubiquitous, which should make them cheap. Instead, diamonds are more valuable and *more expensive* than ever, all because of their accepted scarcity—scarcity that is only really affirmed by their exorbitant price.

Each lie becomes easier to believe as the previous ones are cemented into collective knowledge. The entire diamond industry was built this way: one lie at a time—each relying on the acceptance of the last, layer by layer, to ensure that their product—diamonds—would always be regarded as rare, expensive, and utterly necessary.

That's a hell of con. . . . And it's how you believe a lie into reality.

But, as Aldous Huxley said, "facts do not cease to exist because they are ignored." And that's a valid point—there's still the hardest fact in the world: the fact that diamonds are not rare. The fact is, the prices are artificially fixed, the supply is artificially controlled, and the idea that you need one is the result of decades of social conditioning and targeted consumer analysis. The fact is, the myth of diamonds is just short of a military-grade psyop.

Those are the facts—a few of them, anyway.

Another fact is that truth, being largely subjective, is riddled with lies—or at least opinion, perception, and bias. The truth is a matter of consensual belief, not factual evidence, which is why as soon as we develop the capacity to believe, we begin to lie. Truth and the facts may overlap from time to time. But they're not interdependent. Far more often, it's *lies* that are constructed—piece by piece—out of facts. In practice, it's almost impossible to lie without making use of facts—and the best lies utilize the most obvious facts, in the most convincing way, simply by rearranging or reframing them. To pretend that facts are the opposite of lies, rather than the component building blocks of them, simply misses the point.

The myth of diamonds is a near-perfect Long Con: it's a story, made up of lies constructed out of facts, that—whatever its original purpose—tells a deeper truth *about* the truth. Namely, that *reality is reached by consensus.* The original lie about the value of diamonds, told and believed by billions of people, has *become* real, via mass belief and long-term acceptance. The myth of diamonds has actually *manifested truth by asserting a fiction.* De Beers told their story so many times that they finally redeemed it as a truth.

We all believed it—*and just like that*—it was true. De Beers most certainly conned us, but in doing so on such an epic scale, *created a new reality, a new truth,* for the entire world. And though that truth started as a lie, it's been believed into fact: diamonds are, indeed, desperately valuable.

If I told you that you could believe a lie into concrete existence, *would you believe me now?*

A Lie About a Lie

If the truth is just a story we all agree to believe, how long can it last? De Beers likes to claim that "diamonds are forever." I assume they mean diamonds' psychological hegemony, because the gems themselves certainly are not; every diamond aboveground is slowly converting into graphite (pencil lead) at standard temperature and pressure—that's my very favorite fact about diamonds. But then if I were De Beers . . . I'm not sure I'd bank on that psychological hegemony being eternal either, at least not in the light of recent developments.

The newest iteration of the diamond Long Con involves synthetics: genuine, lab-grown diamonds. To clarify: "synthetics" are not simulants, like cubic zirconia. One only looks like a diamond—the other *is* a diamond. Synthetics are physically and chemically identical to a perfect, natural diamond. The only difference is that synthetics are grown in labs. It's basically the same difference as finding a pretty wildflower in your yard or planting a seed in a little pot and waiting for the same flower to bloom.

So . . . no big deal, right?

Well, it depends on whom you ask, and how deeply invested they are in the diamond trade—either financially or emotionally. Diamonds have always been more storytelling than substance, and the story of synthetic diamonds is starting to cause some friction. Even their existence is problematic, in that it's poking some holes in the myth.

The very foundation of the diamond Long Con (that first layer of the lie) is the idea of their extreme rarity. But that scarcity angle (fictitious as it is) gets shot to hell once you can grow them in a lab. The next iteration of that foundational idea is that each diamond is unique and *special*. This becomes even less true than it already is[*] when you can synthesize the same gem, over and over, with identical precision. Finally, diamonds are romanticized as exotic, coming from distant lands and the depths of the earth and time . . . but that gets difficult to sell (or buy) when they're coming from a lab near Palo Alto.

Which they are. The new tech diamond industry, born of lab-grown diamonds, is causing the traditional diamond industry to lose their *schist*.[†] Representatives of the traditional diamond industry say they're angry that lab-grown diamonds are "flooding the market," and thus one would assume lowering the prices. And that might be a valid complaint if it were actually happening, but it's not. They're angry about what they claim is deliberate "consumer confusion," a legal term that refers to a competitor's manipulative presentation of their own product, intended to fool the consumer without explicitly lying. They're afraid that if they don't draw a hard line between synthetic diamonds and mined diamonds (which, as of recently, they insist be called "natural diamonds"—actually a very solid marketing strategy) consumers won't be able to tell the difference or worse, they could gradually come to believe that *maybe there is no difference.*

And maybe there isn't; in all things, but particularly diamonds, it's all about the story you choose.

More than anything, the majority of the natural diamond industry is angry about the way in which lab-grown diamonds are being presented to the world: as, you know, *diamonds*. Presumably, only they

---

[*]About the majority of them, anyway. Only a handful of the tons of unearthed diamonds actually are unique or remarkable. And those can't be faked, just like natural pearls.
[†]It's funny because schist is a rock.

should have the right to the Long Con they've been working for over a century.

The reality is this: lab-grown diamonds are not especially flooding the market, at least not in the form of diamond jewelry. Lab-grown diamond jewelry has at most a 10 percent market share right now—although it's closer to 20 percent for yellow, blue, and pink diamonds, because those colors are legitimately rare and difficult to find in the ground, but relatively easy to grow in a lab. However, lab-grown diamonds are flooding *a market,* just not in the way natural-diamond advocates would have you believe.

The synthetic influx is mostly in the form of teeny, tiny pavé diamonds. They show up mixed in with "melee": big bags of very tiny diamonds that cutters produce. One could even argue that the synthetics are deliberately snuck into those bags—and a lot of people have. That's not ideal, but it's not really a new problem, either. Melee always had some degree of contamination—even before synthetics were available. Back then, the contamination was in the form of other stones, crystals, or eventually cubic zirconia. It is, and always has been, a shady way for the melee seller to charge a buyer for a full parcel, when some small percentage of the diamonds aren't really there. It only finally caused a big dustup in 2018, when a melee parcel of 9.67-carat total weight turned up containing not the typical one, or two, or even a handful of fakes (of any kind, including synthetics), but 1,092 synthetic diamonds and 9 additional unidentifiable fakes—and just *one natural diamond* out of 1,102 cut stones.[3]

So that's a lot—and it is a big deal. But that's also direct *fraud* on the part of the seller and not a marketing strategy for lab-grown diamonds.

More important, there is no deliberate consumer confusion being generated by manufacturers between natural and synthetic diamonds in jewelry. Lab-grown diamond jewelry is very clearly *marketed* as containing lab-grown diamonds. They want you to know that the stone was grown in a lab and not mined, in part because that's a major selling point for certain people—namely, their customers. And the old-guard diamond industry already *knows* all that. What's actually freaking them out is the advertising and PR strategy that presents the lab-grown gems as exactly the same as natural diamonds (which they are, technically), *but perfect.* Not to mention *cleaner, greener, and more ethical*—as you can be certain that the companies growing them aren't funding, provoking, or tacitly condoning terrorism, cartels, or civil wars.

The synthetic diamond narrative is, *at best,* selective and heavily embellished truth. And then some of it's just as man-made as the gems.

But then so was the original narrative about "real" diamonds: that they were rare, that they were somehow special or better than other gemstones, and with the invention of the diamond engagement ring, that they were somehow socially necessary. Diamonds have always been mostly marketing, but the *spin* on synthetic diamonds is causing more animosity than their actual existence. Which would make sense, if the new story contradicted or somehow undermined the old story. But that isn't the case. The mythology being spun as we speak about synthetic diamonds does nothing to undercut the original myth of diamonds. It *relies* on it, is built right on top of it—one more stratum of arbitrary belief cementing the lies that came before it.

It's quite literally *a lie about a lie.**

---

*Which I find perversely delightful.

How Long Does a Lie Last?

The diamond Long Con has basically become a Russian nesting doll of beliefs that no one can recall adopting, and now it includes man-made yet somehow "real" gems. Like their own many-sparkling facets, the diamond con has so many angles it's nearly impossible to count them, let alone keep them straight. But how much of the spin on synthetic diamonds is just straight fabrication?

Let's diagram that lie and find out.

Are synthetic diamonds actually diamonds? Well, if we define a diamond as a pure or nearly pure, extremely hard form of carbon naturally crystallized in the isometric system—a crystal formed of carbon atoms packed so tightly and under such intense pressure that they've locked into place in a three-dimensional cubic lattice—then, yes, synthetic diamonds are actually diamonds. The only difference is that they are grown in labs, relatively quickly, rather than deep in the earth. They look the same. They have the same chemical structure: they are indeed diamonds. Are those diamonds actually "cleaner"—as in clearer, more colorless, more consistent in their internal and external lack of flaws or contaminants than natural diamonds? Unfortunately, at least for De Beers and others . . . who've said for years that they'll never deal in synthetics, *yes*. Synthetic diamonds are uniform, manufactured products—not unique and inherently flawed by-products of nature.

So yeah, they're real—and they're real pretty.

Moving on to the next claim: Are lab-grown diamonds more ethical? Can you be sure that they're not funding wars, cartels, or terrorism? I don't know—and anyone who says they do is (at best) overconfident about their information. It's impossible to know with any certainty because they're not just making them in the Bay Area anymore; the labs producing them are all over the world at this point. Most of the melee comes from Asia, and one of the biggest producers of lab-grown diamonds is a company in Russia. I have no idea what goes on in Russia . . . let alone what they do with their lab-grown diamonds, or the revenue from them.

And last, are lab-grown diamonds "green"? *Hell, no.* That's just a flagrant lie. While it's true that producing them doesn't create giant town-sized craters in the earth the way traditional diamond mining does, they are *not* particularly environmentally superior. They're just doing a different kind of damage to the environment; the amount of energy required to produce them is so great that synthetics actually have a *larger carbon footprint per carat* than do natural diamonds. In fact, the FTC sent warning letters to eight U.S. lab-grown diamond companies just last year for using debatable, if not outright deceptive, terms like "eco-friendly."[4]

So that last claim about synthetic diamonds being a green alternative is just a straight-up lie—deliberately invented and test-marketed to serve a purpose. Kind of exactly like the original lie that diamonds are terribly scarce and desired by everyone. It's a little true, a lot of false, and *entirely* engineered to appeal specifically to the various conscious and unconscious desires, taboos, and impulses of the era.

The synthetic diamond industry is attempting to do the same thing to the diamond industry that the diamond industry did to the previous jewelry industry to begin with, demonstrating the continually evolving canon of truth—not to mention the *very* arbitrary nature of which lies we agree to make real. If and when the myth of the perfect, ethical, "green" diamond is known and believed widely enough, it will be nothing remarkable—just accepted reality, by constantly shifting consensus.

As we've discussed, once we believe a simple lie, it's almost impossible to correct that belief. That's just how our brains work. Regular lies are resilient, but a Long Con is even more difficult to shed. First, we don't see the lie: its scale is too large. Then we don't believe *it is* a lie: its scope is too broad. And by the time we do see it for what it is, it's only really a lie *in retrospect*—like that fake hundred-dollar bill we really spent. By the time we see the lie, we've already transformed it into truth.

So how long does a lie last? Until it's supplanted by a better story and becomes a different truth.

Gluttony

When De Beers created the myth of diamonds and began executing their Long Con, they incidentally created what we know as the diamond industry, which has had an immeasurable geopolitical impact on numerous countries—extending far beyond South Africa. That impact has been impressive but, if you look closer, somewhat corrupt. In an impoverished country with a great deal of diamonds below the surface, inaccessible to the average miner, De Beers rolls in to partner up. Botswana is one such country. As a dry, landlocked country lacking other available natural resources, Botswana has been transformed by the diamond industry from one of the poorest countries in Africa to a very successful, medium-sized economy. Industry spokesmen will tell you that more than 80 percent of diamond profits stay within Botswana and that "much of this income benefits citizens through free education, free healthcare and an expansion of local jobs in the diamond industry."[5]

But did you catch that they don't say exactly *how* 80 percent of the money stays in the country? Because most of the profit is not going into the pockets of the people of Botswana. It's reinvested in making Botswana a better and better diamond-producing machine. True, in nations like Botswana, De Beers has created whole cities, large-scale industry, and infrastructure (and the employment, education, and health care that come with it), but that development has always had a heavy tilt toward financially favoring De Beers. If and when the local governments complain or try to renegotiate terms, which they have recently, they're made to understand that all that infrastructure and employment could just go away. . . .

And it could, because the natural-diamond industry has a huge problem: a global diamond glut so substantial that the seventeen-billion-dollar diamond-mining industry has started shutting down mines all over the world to slow production and alter perception yet again, showing that they're in this Long Con for the long run. Mines have been closing all over the world for years—like the Argyle mine in Australia, famous for its pink, red, and violet diamonds. The official reason cited for the closure by Argyle's parent company, Rio Tinto, is that there are not enough of those terribly rare-colored diamonds left in the ground to make the effort worthwhile.[6] In reality, the Argyle mine was responsible for about 10 percent of the entire global diamond output last year, and almost none of it was rose-colored. The vast majority of those ten to fifteen million carats were white or brown. Closing the Argyle mine is an effort to slow production of the more common white and brown stones, and in so doing, to slow the deluge and shore up the falling market for them.

This diamond glut is an overabundance so alarming that De Beers said it had reduced rough production by 11 percent in 2019, upon finding demand for rough diamonds had diminished by 53 percent[7]—

and these are the people who spent the better part of the last century lying about the terrible natural dearth of their product. Now they're admitting to slashing production to try to control the avalanche of diamonds threatening to rain down destruction on the global market through their sheer tonnage. You see, everybody knows, nobody cares. Just like the melee.

But it raises an interesting question: If we all increasingly know this, why are natural diamonds still so expensive? Why are they worth anything at all? They're as common as carbon, even without the competition of synthetics. So why do we still believe the lie—even after we've been shown it's a lie? Because in addition to the whole recursive cycle of belief, confirmation of belief, and acceptance as truth, in the case of a Long Con, there's an added element of iterative reality in this cycle that not only changes your perception, but changes *the truth itself*, until you're not exactly believing a lie at all.

It's why some lies last forever, and others we just repeat over and over.

Don't Worry About Diamonds

Aleksandr Solzhenitsyn wrote that "everything you add to the truth subtracts from the truth," but he may have seriously discounted the fact that everything that makes up the truth has *already* been added to the truth. We create it, just as we do lies; and then we destroy them both and create them again, remaking reality perpetually in our ever-changing image.

Nothing's entirely real, none of it matters, and everything's fine. Particularly in this case.

In 2018 the Federal Trade Commission (FTC) expanded the

definition of a "diamond." That definition now includes those made in a laboratory. So, technically, we don't have to call them synthetics anymore . . . which of course is *why* traditional diamond advocates are so insistent that we call the ones that come from mines "natural diamonds." When the FTC expanded that definition, they reversed decades of rulings. And they did it almost immediately after De Beers officially announced to a stunned industry that they would be launching their own synthetic jewelry line, Lightbox. They stated that their goal for 2020 was to manufacture 500,000 carats of synthetic diamonds in white, pink, blue, and yellow as well as possibly a few other colors.

There are so many questions. . . . Why did De Beers reverse course like that? Why is the FTC punishing them? The most obvious question is *How?* That's beyond a tall order; how are they going to do all that?

Unless . . . it turns out that Element 6, one of the most advanced synthetic diamond producers in the world, is in fact a wholly owned subsidiary of De Beers. (Which you had to see coming.) Element 6 is a giant in the field, and they've been working on synthetics for years. So that whole time De Beers was protesting that they would *never*—they kinda *already were.* Now they're poised to dominate the synthetic diamond market as well. And that conveniently answers the FTC question, too, because now that expanded definition of "diamond" looks a lot less like something they did *to* De Beers and a lot more like something they did *for* De Beers.

There is no terrible battle over diamonds.

Yes, there's a massive, economically dangerous excess of natural diamonds, but there *always has been*—it's just a matter of scale. Yes, synthetics are coming—are here, actually—but there's no competition for hearts and minds. There's no competition for market share. There's no *real* competition over anything, because they're all competing with themselves . . . literally. This dustup over synthetic diamonds is little more than a dumb show; everyone's just going through the motions of that iterative process by which new facts become truth. And if it seems as if they're phoning it in a little, it's because they are. It's because *they can*.

Diamonds are truth made manifest through mass consensus and recursive reality on such a scale that it includes the whole world. Their mythology is so fully hardened into stone that *it doesn't matter that you know it's a lie—you'll still agree to believe it*. Because at this point the lie has become so foundational to everyone else's truth that diamonds can't disappear—no one will let them.

Too-Big-to-Fail Frauds

While the slickest Long Con in modern history may be the value of diamonds, the most recent can be found in banking.* The 2008 global financial meltdown perfectly captures the kind of expansive, cross-con, multioperator subversion of reality that is the basis of the Long Con. It is the epitome of grifting, not just for the many tricks of the trade it employs, but because the scale of the deliberate, coordinated undermining of your sense of truth and trust in fact surpasses mere lying. Such that when a Long Con is truely successful, it has *changed the world around you,* making the lie almost impossible to perceive, much less accept.

But that's *when* it's successful.

As Long Cons go, the global financial meltdown of 2008 is highly

---

*And not just because banking itself is another really Long Con. Not even because there *may or may not* actually be any gold in Fort Knox backing our currency. Seriously, it's a question without a definite answer.

instructive in yet another way; it contains critical lessons about truth, fact, fiction, and the relationship between them. Most crucially, embedded in its story is an illustration—not just of how a really Long Con works—but of what happens when a really Long Con finally *fails*.

What everyone remembers about the global financial meltdown is in general terms: banks went under, something about mortgage swaps triggered a crisis, and there was a massive government bailout. It all happened really fast, confusedly, on a massive scale, and pointed to a strange cause-and-effect relationship between economic threads few people had previously realized were related. People lost their jobs. People lost their homes. Everybody felt scammed—because they had been. And most of them had been willing participants, but no one likes to be reminded of that part.

When the entire Pyramid collapsed, whole economies went with it.

All the way back in chapter three, we briefly spoke about how the housing market of the early 2000s was a lot like the gold rush: a decade of sustained economic growth made everyone feel flush. Money and opportunity could be seen everywhere—which, you might recall, has the neurological effect of a moral hobbling. People, just as they did during the gold rush, were easily persuaded to gamble a little, cheat a little, and believe in get-rich-quick schemes—specifically, house flipping.

As property values rose without any signs of abating and interest rates on mortgage loans stayed weirdly low for years on end, the combination created a compelling market for both banks to lend (to literally anyone) and buyers to buy a home (or five . . .). Lots of banks signed off on lots of mortgages—to both those borrowers who could afford one and those who couldn't reasonably be expected to pay them back. Recall: that made for two kinds of mortgages, prime and subprime.

Everyone assumed property values would keep rising. Buyers believed they would get rich flipping houses, and banks believed property values couldn't go backward on a large scale, so they would not only recover losses from the inevitable defaults but also, in fact, profit from the defaulted property's inflated value. Big-money foreign investors saw high returns and (allegedly) low-risk investment in these mortgage bundles.

As you'll recall, it did not work out that way.

Load-Bearing Lies

The 2008 financial meltdown—or, at least, its precipitating deceptions—are explicitly illustrative. Here's how it all went down: first, deregulation and the repeal of Glass-Steagall in the 1990s allowed investment banks and commercial (regular) banks to intermingle as they pleased. That means your savings account was tied up in multibillion-dollar transactions on the other side of the world—without your knowledge or permission. But as long as the money kept rolling, people mostly didn't ask too many questions.

Meanwhile, the original mortgage-backed securities, developed in the 1970s as financial instruments for investment, had begun to mutate. A mortgage-backed security, or MBS, was (historically) just a big bundle of very secure mortgages, a piece of which anyone could own. People (and institutions) loved to invest in them; they were believed to be a very safe bet. And historically they had been, because property value over time tends to go up.

But that was when you could only get a mortgage if you were not at risk of defaulting—if you were, in other words, someone who could afford a mortgage and could be expected to pay it back. But only so many people are a safe bet, meaning that only so many loans can be extended. A finite number of mortgages meant a finite number of MBSs.

But as property values rose, the global demand increased for this particular product. So bankers got creative: they generated an almost endless supply of MBSs by employing the simple but deceptive practice of bundling prime and subprime loans together. They were basically watering the whiskey, which is only marginally creative. But then the bankers created an even riskier product, called a CDO (collateral debt obligation), which was a bundle of MBSs, essentially a super-bundle, comprised of many other bundles. These so-called exotic derivatives (the financial equivalent of those crushed-core samples from Guzman's fake gold mine) were very dangerous investments. If property values ever dipped, huge losses for everyone were basically baked in.

To satisfy ever-increasing investor demand for MBSs, banks also began engaging in predatory lending practices, by granting loans to people who absolutely couldn't be expected to pay them back: people with poor credit and low incomes—many of whom didn't even have steady jobs. Predatory lending practices also involved granting loans with a "teaser rate," a low interest rate that was initially manageable but would later shoot way up after an arbitrary introductory period was over, kind of like a cat jumping out of a bag you thought contained a pig.

Because this weird scam was so new, the various credit-rating agencies—whose job it was to truthfully rate a financial instrument like an MBS for safety—had no idea how to evaluate it. They looked to historical examples of normal (not salted, let alone salted and then bundled) MBSs, leaning on the collective assessment of generations past, as we are wont to do, and declared the bundles in question very safe investments.

Oops.

The combination of the looser requirements, low interest rates, and AAA ratings drove property values even higher. This led to a rapidly inflating, self-perpetuating system, otherwise known as a giant bubble: the economic version of a large-scale *Hoax*. First people got excited, then that excitement spread and got others excited, and then they so badly wanted to believe it that—through a spectacular display of motivated reasoning—they recursively found reasons to believe what they already believed. The bubble stays intact by virtue of collective belief and even as that belief detaches increasingly from any reason other than belief in and of the collective, kind of like a Pyramid. (I promised Pyramids were *everywhere*.)

In other words, everyone believes it because everyone else believes it. Until they don't.

Another really nasty instrument, a credit-default swap (CDS), was also floating around the market at the time. A CDS was basically just a bet that the bubble would *never* burst. Because that sounds like a great bet . . . AIG sold tens of billions of dollars' worth of CDSs, all to buyers willing to put money on that shockingly stupid wager. Then again: gold rush thinking. And also, you'll recall, heightened greed and exposure to sudden large amounts of wealth doesn't just morally kneecap you, it leaves you intellectually impaired as well (at least temporarily). And while we're on the subject of gold rush thinking: the bankers selling the CDSs were *so confident* in this bubble not being a bubble that they didn't even bother to keep anything close to the necessary cash on hand to pay up if they lost.

As the whole world continued to pour money in to the U.S. housing market, the MBS bundles were increasingly filled with garbage loans, deliberately salted with decent ones—like a barren mine salted with a few scattered diamonds. Wall Street only winked at this blatant *Bait and Switch,* mostly because bankers, too, had been sold the same *Big Lie*: that property values could never go down. So they insured nothing and gave loans to anyone and everyone.

Many borrowers—acting on the advice of various financial *Gurus*—took second and third mortgages to buy additional properties, houses to "flip" either for a cash profit or to hold long enough for their escalating value to be borrowed against yet again. In any case, money was borrowed to buy a property, and without being paid back, that property was borrowed against to buy additional properties, which were borrowed against. . . . Does this sound a little like *Change Raising*? Because it is.

One tiny down payment (that most people couldn't really afford to begin with) ballooned into numerous properties, each supported by the not-so-secure collateral of the previous one. All of this Change Raising accumulated into giant collateral *Pyramids,* held by banking institutions and large-scale investors all over the world, and was trusted, in part, because of the erroneous AAA ratings given to the securities by the very credit-rating agencies intended to keep them in check.

And then the bubble burst.

As people defaulted, the market was flooded with too many houses and not enough buyers, driving their value further down. Property values crashed, more people defaulted—on loans that were suddenly worth more than the properties themselves. The banks had to eat the loss, as did the investors holding the CDSs. Investors quickly stopped buying these bundles, and banks got stuck with unheard-of, unmanageable losses.

Losses so big, in fact, that by 2008, major lending institutions couldn't cover their bad bets and had to fold. Big banks declared bankruptcy. Others were forced to merge. Investors were left holding the bag on the worthless paper. At that point, panic set in: credit froze up for *everyone*; banking ground to a halt. The stock market crashed. When Lehman Brothers collapsed, it exposed not only the empty promise of those financial instruments but also, far more true and more terrible, laid bare the fact that *the money was never real to begin with*—just pieces of paper, in this case deeds, not dollars, that had no absolute value at all.

I promised that the story of the global financial meltdown was important in the end, because it's a rare object lesson in what happens when a really Long Con, a civilization-sized, load-bearing Long Con, fails. The answer, surprisingly, is not disaster or exposure or ruin: *it's nothing at all.*

Nothing happens, because a load-bearing Long Con *doesn't fail*. It can't. The con is propped up at all costs (in this particular case, over $800 billion) because, lie or not, it has become part of the bulwark of our society. Some lies become so necessary that we not only avoid confronting them but actively work to securitize them against exposure. The lie has become not merely too big, but in fact, *too real* to fail.

The truth about lies is that they're complicated and confusing and built into the entire system.

So, *can you* believe a lie into concrete existence? Yes and no.

Believing a lie doesn't make it fact. Facts are that which continue to exist, whether or not you believe in them. But over time things have a way of *becoming true*. Whether it was the unsinkable global economy or the sparkly celluloid story of diamonds, we all believed it because everyone else believed it. But did we believe it enough to make it *real*? Define "real." Diamonds really cost what they cost. Homes really were bought and sold and built; trillions of dollars were generated. And in the end it collapsed like a house of cards.

But just because it didn't last—doesn't mean it was never real.

AFTERWORD

Lies About the Truth

All your life, you live so close to truth, it becomes a permanent blur
in the corner of your eye. And when something nudges it into
outline, it is like being ambushed by a grotesque.

—TOM STOPPARD

Do you know what the biggest lie of all is? It's the lie that there is one
absolute truth: that there is one true version of events, one true answer
to any question, one true objective reality that we all experience and
recall identically. That notion is simply not true. . . .

But it is a necessary fiction; without that one, big, foundational lie
(which we all agree to believe) about the nature of truth and our physical and cognitive ability to assess it, we couldn't possibly function.
So instead we trust our eyes, our senses, our imperfect (rather creative)
memories, and our inflated senses of reason and logic to navigate an

unknown, mostly unknowable, reality—one that we collectively nego-tiate and then agree to believe in together.

The truth is that we only just barely exist in the same reality as one another. And we can't possibly know what's real or true for any-one else. And yet *coherence is a necessary fiction.* We must interact with one another and the world at large and the only way to do that is to agree to believe certain things about how we, and others, believe certain things. We agree to believe that memory may be fallible but is essentially straightforward, that objective reality exists and is expe-rientially the same for everyone, that facts are facts and anything else is a lie.

But really, "the Truth" is actually the most powerful and persua-sive deception there is. By "the Truth," I mean the myth of singular truth: the notion that facts are truth, and truth is concrete, knowable, and incompatible with other contradictory realities.

"The Truth" is the first, most powerful, and *most necessary* lie we learn to tell. Consciousness as we experience it depends on that primal lie. Without a concept of "the Truth" we would all go insane. We couldn't function (let alone interact) without the voluntary shared belief that facts are facts (we may disagree about what they are) and that things are either true or false, real or not, and that the Truth is definitely knowable. Civilization comes undone without confidence that those observations and conclusions are universal. Reality has to be objective.

Except that it's not always.

And even when reality *is* objective, none of us is actually per-ceiving that reality as it truly is; that's just the reality of perception. It wouldn't matter if we could; no one ever remembers anything the same way as anyone else. In fact, no *one* person remembers a thing the same way twice. Each time you recall an event, your memory is distorted by innumerable factors, including any previous recollections of that memory.

The human mind only remembers an event, a thought, a feeling but once. The next time you summon that memory, what you actually recall is just the *previous memory* itself. The next time you think of it, you only have the memory of the memory of the event to rely on, and each time you overwrite the previous version, however slightly. We get just one single precious experience of a memory, after which the only record we really have left to consult are copies of copies of copies—rife with transcription error.

Our individual reality is built upon faulty perception, spackled together with suggestion and expectation, plastered over with biases and then airbrushed by consensus. And then it's remade, again and again, changing a little each time with every recall. The idea that there can ever be one singular truth for everyone, let alone even for *anyone*, is the most absurd, most outrageous, *most necessary lie I know.*

The truth about lies is that they are not only constructed out of countless facts, they're the handmaidens of truth.

ACKNOWLEDGMENTS

Several years ago, I was standing in front of a restaurant late one night with some friends when out of nowhere, one said; "I want someone to write a book about famous swindles." So I did and I hope you liked it.

I don't know if this is what she had in mind. I'm not sure it's exactly what I had in mind when I started writing; but then very little over the past few years has turned out exactly as I, or anyone else, expected and I'm very grateful to all the people who have helped me along the way.

On this particular project, that includes Deborah, my agent,

ACKNOWLEDGMENTS

Elizabeth, my editor and Hannah, without whom of course there would be no book; I would just be telling interesting stories to friends.

To Laura and Stephen; said friends, who liked those stories before anyone else.

And above all, to my family, who support everything I do.

Particularly my mother.

NOTES

Part I: Lies We Tell Each Other

1. Robert Trivers, *The Folly of Fools: The Logic of Deceit and Self-Deception in Human Life* (New York: Basic Books, 2011), xiii.

1: The Oldest Trick in the Book

1. When reading the epigraph, you were probably wondering what this chapter has to do with Hitler. The answer is basically nothing. Adolf Hitler is credited with popularizing the term "big lie" in 1925 in his demented manifesto *Mein Kampf*, as he pointed out that "in the big lie there is always a certain force of credibility" as people "would not believe that others could have the impudence to distort the truth so infamously." He had a nuanced grasp of how a Big Lie works, and he was certainly a *huge liar*, but he neither invented nor identified the Big Lie. It is literally the oldest trick in the book.
2. Maria Konnikova, *The Confidence Game: Why We Fall for It Every Time* (New York: Viking, 2016), 134–36.
3. Carl Sifakis, *Hoaxes and Scams: A Compendium of Deceptions, Ruses and Swindles* (New York: Facts on File, 1993), 21.
4. Ibid.
5. Konnikova, *Confidence Game,* 134–36.
6. Ibid.
7. Ibid.
8. S. Milgram, "Behavioral Study of Obedience," *Journal of Abnormal and Social Psychology* 67 (1963): 371–78.
9. Ibid.
10. Ibid.
11. Sifakis, *Hoaxes,* 211.
12. Konnikova, *Confidence Game,* 134–36.
13. A. M. Leslie, "Theory of Mind," *International Encyclopedia of the Social and Behavioral Sciences* (Elsevier, 2001).
14. David C. Geary, *Evolution of Vulnerability* (Elsevier Academic Press, 2015).
15. Marjorie Taylor, "A Theory of Mind Perspective on Social Cognition," *Perceptual and Cognitive Development* (Elsevier, 1996).
16. Gilbert King, "The Smoothest Con Man That Ever Lived," *Smithsonian Magazine,* August 22, 2012.
17. Gabriel Cohen, "For You, Half Price," *New York Times,* November 27, 2005.
18. Sifakis, *Hoaxes,* 211.
19. Ibid.

20. Ibid.
21. Janet Christie, "Interview: Margaret Atwood on Her Novel *MaddAddam*," *The Scotsman,* September 1, 2013.
22. Todd Robbins, *The Modern Con Man: How to Get Something for Nothing* (New York: Bloomsbury, 2008).
23. Konnikova, *Confidence Game,* 134–36.
24. Philip Fernbach and Steven Sloman, "Why We Believe Obvious Untruths," *New York Times,* March 3, 2017.
25. Konnikova, *Confidence Game,* 134–36.
26. Ibid.

2. Keep Your Eye on the Ball

1. Sifakis, *Hoaxes,* 242.
2. Jeff Smith, *Alias Soapy Smith: The Life and Death of a Scoundrel* (Juneau, AL: Klondike Research, 2009).
3. Robbins, *Modern Con Man,* 85.
4. Sifakis, *Hoaxes,* 233.
5. Trivers, *Folly,* 7.
6. Ibid., 48.
7. Benjamin Libet et al., "Time of Conscious Intention to Act in Relation to Onset of Cerebral Activity (Readiness-Potential): The Unconscious Initiation of a Freely Voluntary Act," *Brain* 106, no. 3 (September 1983): 623–42.
8. David W. Green et al., *Cognitive Science: An Introduction* (Cambridge, Mass.: Blackwell, 1996).
9. Ibid.
10. Alex Stone, "The Science of Illusion," *New York Times,* June 22, 2012.
11. Gustav Kuhn et al., "Misdirection in Magic: Implications for the Relationship Between Eye Gaze and Attention," *Visual Cognition* 16, no. 2–3 (2008): 391–405.
12. Jonah Lehrer, "Magic and the Brain: Teller Reveals the Neuroscience of Illusion," *Wired,* April 20, 2009.
13. Ibid.
14. Ibid.
15. D. J. Simons and C. F. Chabris, "Gorillas in Our Midst: Sustained Inattentional Blindness for Dynamic Events," *Perception* 28, no. 9 (1999): 1059–74.
16. Ibid.
17. Daniel Simons, "But Did You See the Gorilla? The Problem with Inattentional Blindness," *Smithsonian Magazine,* September 2012.
18. Ibid.
19. Ibid.
20. Ibid.
21. Robbins, *Modern Con Man,* 136.

3. Don't Buy It

1. Robert Wilson, "The Great Diamond Hoax of 1872," *Smithsonian Magazine,* June 2004.
2. Ibid.

3. Ibid.

4. Ibid.

5. "Editorial Panorama" (filler item), quote on page 6, column 2, *Janesville Daily Gazette,* Janesville, Wisc. (Newspapers.com), May 21, 1947.

6. Ibid.

7. Ibid.

8. Eric Grundhauser, "The $6 Billion Gold Mine That Wasn't There," *Atlas Obscura,* August 21, 2015.

9. Sam Ro, "BRE-X: Inside The $6 Billion Gold Fraud That Shocked the Mining Industry," *Business Insider,* July 1, 2012.

10. "Stranger Than Fiction: The Calgary Story That Became Hollywood Gold," *Calgary Herald,* January 26, 2017.

11. Grundhauser, "$6 Billion Gold Mine."

12. "Stranger Than Fiction."

13. Grundhauser, "$6 Billion Gold Mine."

14. Dan Healing, "Former Bre-X Minerals Chief Geologist Dies in the Philippines," *Canadian Press*/AP, October 28, 2019.

15. Kathleen D. Vohs, Nicole L. Mead, and Miranda R. Goode, "Merely Activating the Concept of Money Changes Personal and Interpersonal Behavior," *Current Directions in Psychological Science* 17, no. 3 (2008): 208–12.

16. George Dvorsky, "Money Makes You Less Rational Than You Think," *Gizmodo,* November 2014.

17. Vohs, Mead, and Goode, "Merely Activating the Concept."

18. Anandi Mani et al., "Poverty Impedes Cognitive Function," *Science* (August 30, 2013): 976–80.

19. Diane Mapes, "Rich People Have No Idea What You're Thinking," NBC News, December 13, 2010.

20. Trivers, *Folly,* 21.

21. Danielle Polage, "Effects of Telling Lies on Belief in the Truth," *Europe's Journal of Psychology,* November 2017.

22. Matthew Hofer and Gary Scharnhorst, editors, *Oscar Wilde in America: The Interviews* (Urbana: University of Illinois Press), 2013.

4. Holy Shit

1. Carolyn Harris, "The Murder of Rasputin, 100 Years Later,'" *Smithsonian Magazine,* December 2016.

2. Francis Welch, *Rasputin: A Short Life* (New York: Marble Arch Press, 2014).

3. Ibid.

4. Ibid.

5. Douglas Smith, *Rasputin: Faith, Power, and the Twilight of the Romanovs* (New York: Farrar, Straus and Giroux, 2016).

6. Welch, *Rasputin.*

7. Ibid.

8. Ibid.

9. Ibid.

10. Harris, "The Murder of Rasputin."

11. Karen Abbott, "The Fox Sisters and the Rap on Spiritualism," *Smithsonian Magazine,* October 2012.
12. Ibid.
13. James Randi and Bert Randolph Sugar, *Houdini: His Life and Art* (New York: Grosset and Dunlap, 1977).
14. Ibid.
15. Lauren Effron, Andrew Paparella, and Jeca Taudte, "The Scandals That Brought Down the Bakkers, Once Among US's Most Famous Televangelists," ABC News, December 20, 2019.
16. Ibid.
17. Tom Porter, "Joel Osteen: Televangelist Whose Church Closed During Hurricane Harvey Tells Victims Not to Have 'Poor Me' Attitude," *Newsweek,* September 4, 2017.
18. Jamie Peck, "A Houston Megachurch Shut Out Flood Victims. A Twitter Storm Opened It," *The Guardian,* August 30, 2017.
19. Porter, "Joel Osteen."
20. Ibid.

5. Bitter Pill

1. Lakshmi Gandhi, "A History of 'Snake Oil Salesmen,'" *NPR Code Switch: Word Watch,* August 26, 2013.
2. Ibid.
3. C. M. Seifert, "The Continued Influence of Misinformation in Memory: What Makes a Correction Effective?" *Psychology of Learning and Motivation: Advances in Research and Theory* 41 (2002): 265–92.
4. Lydia Kang, *Quackery: A Brief History of the Worst Ways to Cure Everything* (New York: Workman, 2017).
5. Gandhi, "History."
6. Ibid.
7. Ibid.
8. Michael Specter, "The Power of Nothing," *New Yorker,* December 5, 2011.
9. Ibid.
10. Ibid.
11. Ibid.
12. Steve Silberman, "Placebos Are Getting More Effective. Drugmakers Are Desperate to Know Why," *Wired,* Aug. 24, 2009.
13. Specter, "Power."
14. Ibid.
15. Silberman, "Placebos."
16. Specter, "Power."
17. Robert Anthony Siegel, "Why I Take Fake Pills," *Smithsonian Magazine,* May 2017.
18. Silberman, "Placebos."
19. Maria Konnikova, "Trump's Lies vs. Your Brain," *Politico,* January/February 2017; Brian Resnik, "The Science Behind Why Fake News Is So Hard to Wipe Out," *Vox,* October 31, 2017.

20. Erick Trickey, "Inside the Story of America's 19th-Century Opiate Addiction," *Smithsonian Magazine,* January 4, 2018.
21. Ibid.
22. Ibid.
23. James Hamblin, "Why We Took the Cocaine out of Soda," *The Atlantic,* January 2013.
24. Ibid.
25. Ibid.
26. Van Zee A. "The Promotion and Marketing of Oxycontin: Commercial Triumph, Public Health Tragedy." *American Journal of Public Health.* 2009;99(2):221-227. doi:10.2105/AJPH.2007.131714.
27. Ibid.
28. Silberman, "Placebos."
29. Ibid.
30. Ibid.
31. Mark Dowie, "Pinto Madness," *Mother Jones,* September / October 1977.

6. It's Lovely at the Top

1. Mary Darby, "In Ponzi We Trust," *Smithsonian Magazine,* December 1998.
2. Ibid.
3. Ibid.
4. Konnikova, *Confidence Game,* 221.
5. Sifakis, *Hoaxes,* 177.
6. Konnikova, *Confidence Game,* 198.
7. Sifakis, *Hoaxes,* 177.
8. Ibid.
9. Konnikova, *Confidence Game,* 200.
10. Ibid.
11. Sifakis, *Hoaxes,* 177.
12. Konnikova, *Confidence Game,* 221-22.
13. Ibid., 215.
14. Ibid.
15. Ibid., 221.
16. Ibid., 215.
17. Sifakis, *Hoaxes,* 177.
18. Ibid.
19. Konnikova, *Confidence Game,* 221.
20. Ibid., 223.
21. Sifakis, *Hoaxes,* 177.
22. Ibid.
23. Diana B. Henriques, "From Prison, Madoff Says Banks 'Had to Know' of Fraud," *New York Times,* February 15, 2011.
24. Ibid.
25. Ibid.
26. Ibid.

27. "Skin Care Products Maker Nu Skin Settles Class Action Suit." Reuters, February 26, 2016.
28. Frank Partnoy, "Is Herbalife a Pyramid Scheme?" *The Atlantic,* June 19, 2014.
29. Ibid.
30. Ibid.
31. Ibid.
32. Ibid.
33. Ibid.
34. Ibid.
35. Ibid.
36. John M. Taylor, *The Case (for and) Against Multi-Level Marketing* (Consumer Awareness Institute, Center for Inquiry, 2012), chapter 7.
37. Dan McCrum, "Bitcoin's Place in the Long History of Pyramid Schemes," *Financial Times,* November 10, 2015.
38. Ibid.
39. Ibid.
40. Tom Metcalf, "Wealthy Bankers Are Hoarding $10 Billion of Bitcoin in Bunkers," Bloomberg, May 9, 2018.
41. Ibid.

7. Fake News

1. Sifakis, *Hoaxes,* 25.
2. Ibid.
3. Ibid.
4. Ibid., 172–74.
5. Ibid.
6. A. Brad Schwartz, "The Infamous 'War of the Worlds' Radio Broadcast Was a Magnificent Fluke," *Smithsonian Magazine,* May 6, 2015.
7. Ibid.
8. Ibid.
9. Sifakis, *Hoaxes,* 172.
10. Ibid.
11. Ibid., 173–74.
12. Ibid., 174.
13. Ibid.
14. Ibid., 110.
15. Ibid.
16. Ibid.
17. Baizhu Chen, "Tear Down This Wall—The Chinese Tariff Wall," *Forbes,* July 12, 2012.
18. Sifakis, *Hoaxes,* 110.
19. Ibid.
20. H. L. Mencken, "A Neglected Anniversary," *ETC: A Review of General Semantics* 58, no. 4 (2001): 420–24.
21. Ibid.

22. Ibid.
23. Mencken, Henry L., "Melancholy Reflections," *Chicago Tribune,* May 23, 1926.
24. Ibid.
25. Libby Nelson, "What a 1917 Prank About the History of the Bathtub Can Tell Us About Modern Hoaxes," *Vox,* April 1, 2016.
26. Ibid.
27. Ibid.
28. Lynn Hasher, David Goldstein, and Thomas Toppino, "Frequency and the Conference of Referential Validity," *Journal of Verbal Learning and Verbal Behavior,* 16 (1977): 107–12.
29. Seifert, "Continued Influence."
30. David Schiffman, "No, Mermaids Do Not Exist," *Slate,* May 30, 2013.
31. Andrew David Thaler, "The Politics of Fake Documentaries," *Slate,* August 31, 2016.
32. Aaron Blake, "A New Study Suggests Fake News Might Have Won Donald Trump the 2016 Election," *Washington Post,* April 3, 2018.
33. Ibid.
34. Ibid.
35. Katie Langin, "Fake News Spreads Faster Than True News on Twitter—Thanks to People, Not Bots," *Science,* March 8, 2018.
36. Ibid.
37. Ibid.
38. Ibid.
39. Ibid.
40. Ibid.
41. Schwartz, "The Infamous 'War of the Worlds' Radio Broadcast."
42. Ibid.
43. Ibid.
44. Ibid.
45. Sifakis, *Hoaxes,* 173–74.

8. How to Make a Buck

1. Robert Hughes, "Brilliant, but Not for Real," *Time,* June 24, 2001.
2. Redmon Bacon, "The Ten Most Notorious Art Forgers of All Time," *Sleek,* March 28, 2017.
3. Sifakis, *Hoaxes,* 182.
4. Ibid.
5. Bacon, "Ten Most Notorious Art Forgers."
6. Sifakis, *Hoaxes,* 175.
7. Ibid.
8. Ibid.
9. Ibid.
10. Marko Perko, *Did You Know That . . . ? "Revised and Expanded" Edition: Surprising-but-True Facts About History, Science, Inventions, Geography, Origins, Art, Music, and More* (Open Road Distribution; Digital Original Edition, August 22, 2017).

11. Ibid.

12. Sifakis, *Hoaxes,* 183.

13. King, "Smoothest Con Man."

14. Sifakis, *Hoaxes,* 183.

15. Mark Jones, Paul Craddock, and Nicholas Barker, *Fake? The Art of Deception* (Berkeley: University of California Press, 1990), 185.

16. Hughes, Robert, "Brilliant, But Not for Real," *Time,* June 24, 2001.

17. Ibid.

18. Sifakis, *Hoaxes,* 166–67.

19. Ibid.

20. Jones, Craddock, and Barker, *Fake,* 185.

21. Sifakis, *Hoaxes,* 166–67.

22. Sifakis, *Hoaxes,* 235.

23. Rick Paulas, "The Weird and Fraudulent World of Catholic Relics," *Vice,* March 4, 2015.

24. Ibid.

25. Ibid.

26. Frank Viviano, "Why Shroud of Turin's Secrets Continue to Elude Science," *National Geographic,* April 17, 2015.

27. "How Did the Turin Shroud Get Its Image?" *BBC News Magazine,* June 19, 2015.

9. Wait for It . . .

1. Tom Stoppard, *Rosencrantz and Guildenstern Are Dead* (New York: Samuel French, 1967), 30.

2. Raden, Aja, *Stoned;: Jewelry, Obsession, and How Desire Shapes the World,* Ecco, 2015, 40.

3. "Melee Parcel Contains Just One Natural Stone," *Rapaport News,* August 16, 2018.

4. Barbara Lewis, "Mine Versus Lab: How Green Is Your Diamond?" Reuters, May 2, 2019.

5. Anthony DeMarco, "New Film Details How Botswana Benefits from Diamonds," *Forbes,* February 6, 2020.

6. Elizabeth Paton, "The World Has a Diamond Glut. Why Is That a Problem?" *New York Times,* August 16, 2019.

7. Ibid.

BIBLIOGRAPHY

Ariely, Dan. *The (Honest) Truth About Dishonesty: How We Lie to Everyone—Especially Ourselves*. New York: HarperPerennial, 2012.

Cialdini, Robert B. *Influence: The Psychology of Persuasion*. New York: Collins Business Essentials, 2007.

Crockett, Zachary, Rohin Dhar, and Alex Mayyasi. *Everything Is Bullshit*. Priceonomics, 2014.

Green, David W., et al. *Cognitive Science: An Introduction*. Cambridge, Mass.: Blackwell, 1996.

Kang, Lydia. *Quackery: A Brief History of the Worst Ways to Cure Everything*. New York: Workman, 2017.

Konnikova, Maria. *The Confidence Game: Why We Fall for It Every Time*. New York: Viking, 2016.

Lehrer, Jonah. *How We Decide.* Boston: Houghton Mifflin Harcourt, 2009.

Maurer, David W. *The Big Con: The Story of the Confidence Man.* New York: Anchor Books, 1999.

Nash, Jay Robert. *Hustlers and Con Men: An Anecdotal History of the Confidence Man and His Games.* New York: M. Evans, 1976.

Pinker, Steven. *How the Mind Works.* New York: W. W. Norton, 2009.

Raden, Aja. *Stoned: Jewelry, Obsession, and How Desire Shapes the World.* New York: Ecco, 2015.

Robbins, Todd. *The Modern Con Man: How to Get Something for Nothing.* New York: Bloomsbury, 2008.

Sifakis, Carl. *Hoaxes and Scams: A Compendium of Deceptions, Ruses, and Swindles.* New York: Facts on File, 1993.

Smith, Douglas. *Rasputin: Faith, Power, and the Twilight of the Romanovs.* New York: Farrar, Straus and Giroux, 2016.

Trivers, Robert. *The Folly of Fools: The Logic of Deceit and Self-Deception in Human Life.* New York: Basic Books, 2011.

Weir, William. *History's Greatest Lies: The Startling Truth Behind World Events Our History Books Got Wrong.* Beverly, Mass.: Fair Winds Press, 2009.

Welch, Francis. *Rasputin: A Short Life.* New York: Marble Arch Press, 2014.

INDEX